Lighting Fixtures of the Depression Era

BOOK I

Jo Ann Thomas

COLLECTOR BOOKS
A Division of Schroeder Publishing Co., Inc.

Cover design: Beth Summers
Book design: Holly Long

Collector Books
P.O. Box 3009
Paducah, KY 42002-3009
www.collectorbooks.com

Contents

Introduction

The 1920s decade was a fabulous, flamboyant time of innovation and creativity in the use of color, designs, and materials.

This decade saw sweeping changes over the entire country due greatly to the increased availability and dependability of electricity. New manufacturing processes were initiated and old ones improved upon. Architects found many new uses for the abundant electrical power, to accent the exteriors of buildings and to better illuminate and beautify the interiors. Not to be left behind, the residential builders quickly eliminated that poor single light bulb dangling from the ceilings of rooms by installing new ceiling fixtures and wall sconces, many of which were making their debut in this decade.

I could easily write many pages because of my love of and enthusiasm for old lighting, be it ceiling fixtures, wall sconces, or floor and table lamps. I feel that those of you who bought this book didn't buy it to read my ramblings. So I am going to make mention of a few points that I feel will be interesting as well as helpful to you in selecting your Depression era lighting. Where applicable I have added some notes with additional information.

There is a tendency today to lump together many of the styles of light fixtures, wall sconces, and lamps and call them all Art Deco. This is very misleading and confusing as there are many distinct styles: Art Deco, Early American, which is different from Country, Moderne, and Victorian, as well as Egyptian, Oriental, Moorish, and Spanish, just to name a few. The classic styles of Colonial, English/Tudor, and Country remain as popular as ever while the beautiful crystal chandeliers and wall sconces are always in vogue.

Each style deserves to be recognized for its own individuality and beauty for each style is a work of art.

I cannot stress enough the importance of reading the description shown beside the pictures of the fixtures, wall sconces, and lamps, as well as the introduction pages which introduce a specific line of fixtures and wall sconces. *Please*, it is *vitally important to read these descriptions!* Most of the information that you will need and want to know is written into descriptions: the style, kind of metal used, the color or patina, if any, used on the metal parts, number of lights, 1, 2, 3, 5, etc., the dimensions, the kind of glass the shades are made of, what types and colors in the decoration if any, and the guide to prices.

Following is some additional information regarding the kind of glass the shades are made of and the specific uses for which they are intended and why. Some glass gives a soft, warm, overall light, others direct the light to a specific area for reading, sewing, or working at a desk, while others illuminate a larger area such as a dining room or kitchen.

Satin glass was used frequently during this period and aptly named as it has a sensuous, satiny feel and sheds a subdued, warm, flattering light. This glass is also quite lovely when made in colors of pastel pinks, greens, mauves, and different shades of gold or amber.

Cut glass, a term we are all familiar with, means the decoration is cut into the glass leaving an incised pattern on the glass. This is used on both frosted and clear glass with the frosted glass allowing a more subdued light while the clear glass allows the light to diffuse out over a large area.

Ivory glass, very popular for this time period, is a soft, creamy color which complements hand painting or decalcomania decorating, and gives a warm, shaded light to the area where it is used. "Decalcomania" refers to the decoration used which is a special type of decal-like decoration which can be subjected to high heat in firing on the shade. Beautiful detailing results from this type of decoration.

Iridescence is a shimmering rainbow of color that plays across the surface of the glass like the shifting colors you see on soap bubbles.

Etching glass can be done by acid, wheel, or needled to put an incised decoration on the glass. This is used on clear and frosted glass as well as on colored glass.

Feathered etching covers the entire surface area of the glass with tiny lines that make the glass seem to be full of tiny cracks, hence the sometimes used name "crackle" glass. It is a very pretty effect when the lights are lit.

The term "opal" glass is a glass used extensively in commercial shades as well as in kitchen and bathroom shades. When light is applied this glass appears to have some fire in it like an opal. This glass provides good overall illumination for areas such as kitchens and bathrooms as well as large rooms and hallways without emitting a glaring light.

The metal part of a fixture is called a frame, the part of the wall sconce that affixes to the wall is called a back plate. The descriptions I spoke of earlier tell what kind of metal the frame or back plate is made of, i.e., brass, bronze, cast metal, etc. The kind of metal used has a bearing on the price of the fixture, wall sconce, or lamp with bronze being the most expensive of the three. Sometimes a color finish is put on the metal such as Ivory Pastelle, Butler Silver, Bank Bronze, or Antique Gold, to name a few. Some of the lines had painted fixtures and wall sconces in colors to complement bedrooms, bathrooms, kitchens, and sun porches. Regardless of the metal used the metal work of the frames and back plates is very decorative, some appearing very lacy, others as though someone has hit them with a hammer leaving minute dents all over the surface. Many of the frames especially have a cut work pattern much like the cut work on linens called Battenburg. The fixture on pages 82 and 83 in the Meletio Electrical Supply Co. section is a fine example of the lacy metal work. In the Radiant Lighting Styles Co. section on pages 38 and 39, you can see excellent examples of the cut work in the metal frames.

Porcelain was also used for fixtures and wall sconces especially for kitchens and bathrooms. These came in plain white, white with colored bands on them, and in colors such as red, green, pink, blue, and even orange. The shades matched the porcelain parts of the fixtures and wall sconces.

Fixtures and wall sconces were made for various specific areas of one's home — porches and sun porches, kitchens and breakfast rooms, dining rooms, bedrooms and bathrooms, even "odd rooms." The fixtures and wall sconces made for the porch were usually made of iron, brass, or copper, and many used frosted or amber crackle glass for the shades.

I hope I have been helpful to you so you too will love these old fixtures, wall sconces, and lamps as I do. They will enhance any room or area and give that room or area an ambience of beauty and comfort in addition to the light at a touch of your fingertip. This book has been a labor of love for me. I hope you enjoy reading it as much as I have enjoyed writing it.

Good luck in your quest for Depression era lighting. May you find just exactly the special fixture, wall sconce, or lamp that you are seeking.

Jo Ann Thomas

Radiant Lighting Fixture Co., Inc.

RADIANT LIGHTING STYLES OF AUTHENTIC DESIGNS

THE merchandise in this book is the culmination of years of experience of Radiant designers and producers. It is complete in every respect and lighting equipment can be found for every room in the home.

The reputation for original designs, made of the best materials, careful workmanship and superior finish, has placed Radiant in the fore part of the industry, so that its product is well known in every state of the Union.

Now for the first time Radiant Lighting Equipment can be bought at prices which enable even the most modest purse to avail itself of quality and design heretofore found only in Radiants of far higher cost.

You need not wait for fixtures when placing your order for Radiants. This merchandise is all carried in stock and within twenty-four hours after order is received your lighting equipment will be on its way to you.

Radiants are packed in individual cartons constructed so as to prevent damage in transit. They are completely wired and are made to enable speedy installation in a minimum space of time.

•

RADIANT LIGHTING FIXTURE CO., INC.
176-178 MOTT STREET
NEW YORK CITY

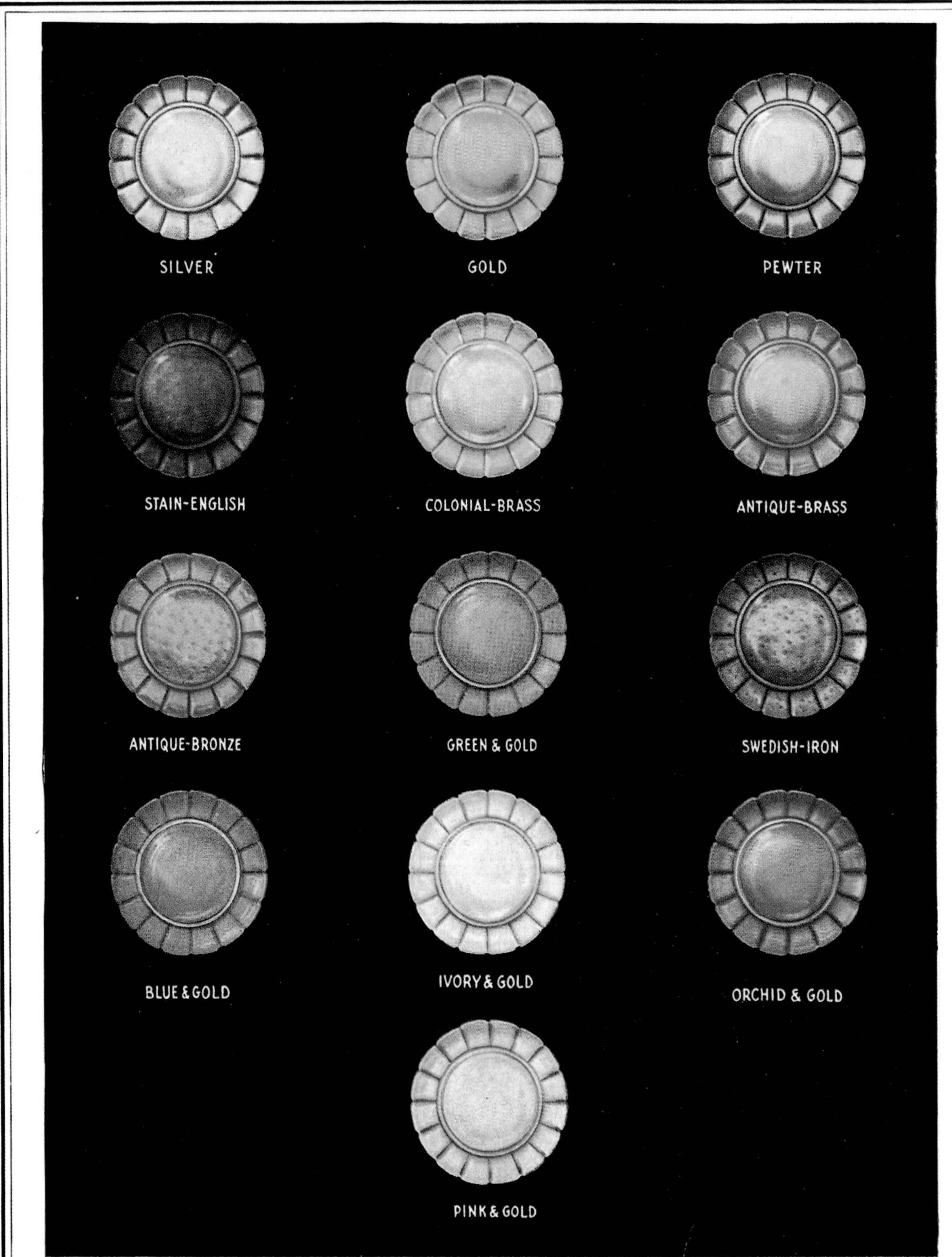

FINISHES

WE have inserted this plate to illustrate the various finishes in which Radiants are made. The colors shown are as near the actual finishes as is possible for the printer's art to reproduce, although the beauty of Radiant finishes cannot very well be brought out even by the modern printer's skill. We have shown under each fixture the finish in which it is made. A sufficient variation is given to meet the requirements of the most discriminating color scheme. No finishes will be furnished other than shown.

JEFFERSON RADIANTS

No. L-103

AS good lighting contributes so much to the health and comfort of the individual, it seems obvious to assume that when considering lighting equipment you are planning a most important element of your home.

Lighting styles shown in this line are Colonial in design. They will add dignity to the most pretentious surroundings.

Materials used are heavy gauge brass, for which a variation of beautiful metal finishes have been devised. The finishes are shown under each item illustrated in this book.

Glass shades used are the very finest quality, decorated with beautiful hand cut design. Crystals used are the very best wood polished variety.

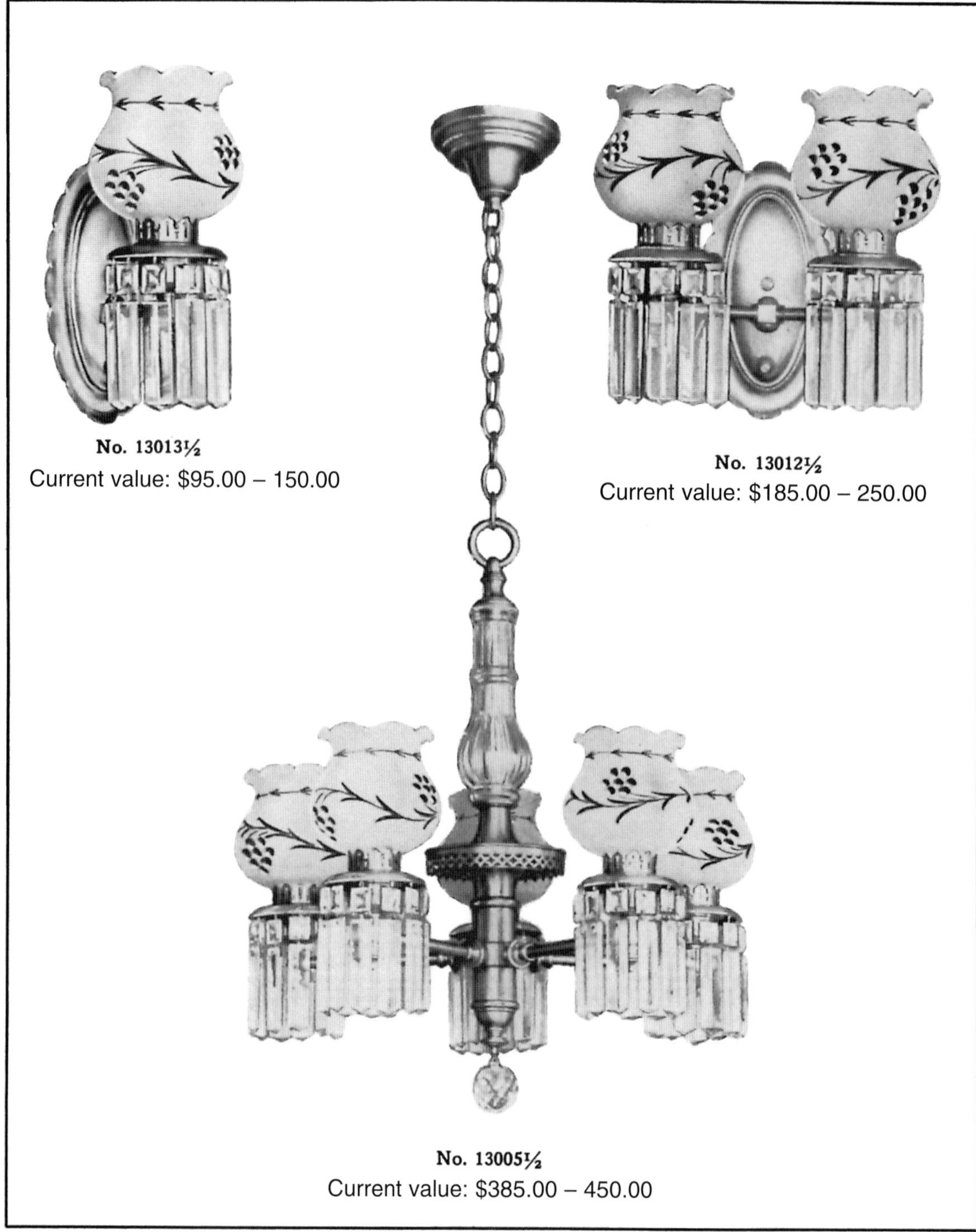

No. 13013½
Current value: $95.00 – 150.00

No. 13012½
Current value: $185.00 – 250.00

No. 13005½
Current value: $385.00 – 450.00

No. 13013½
Back, 4x7½" Extension, 5½"
Wired Pin Switch
Price, **$8.55**

Hand Cut Glass
Wood Polished Crystals

No. 13005½
Length, 42" Width, 18"
Wired Keyless
Price, **$43.50**

No. 13012½
Back, 4x7½" Width, 10"
Wired Pin Switch
Price, **$14.25**

Finish—Antique Brass or Pewter or Colonial Brass

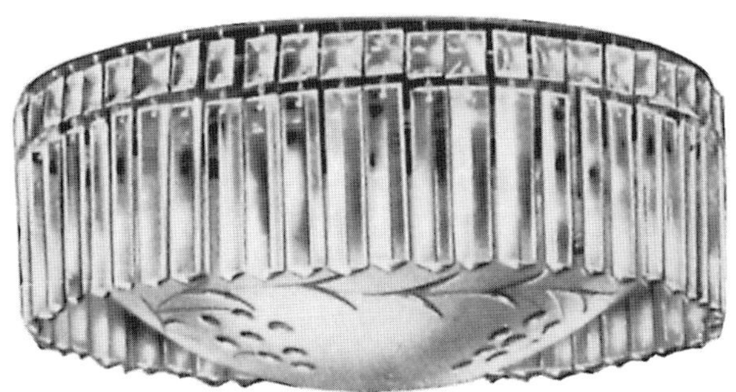

No. 10038½—3 Lt.

Current value: $350.00 – 450.00

No. 13009

Current value: $10.00 – 15.00

No. 13002—1 Lt.

Current value:
$35.00 – 65.00

No. 10032½—1 Lt.

Current value: $325.00 – 375.00

No. 13009
Length, 5" Width, 7"
Wired Keyless
Price, **$3.75**

Hand Cut Glass
Wood Polished Crystals

No. 10038½
Length, 8½" Width, 14"
Wired Keyless
Price, **$39.00**

No. 13002
Length, 11" Width, 6½"
Wired Keyless
Price, **$8.25**

No. 10032½
Length, 9" Width, 10"
Wired Keyless
Price, **$21.75**

Finish—Antique Brass or Pewter or Colonial Brass

GEORGIAN RADIANTS

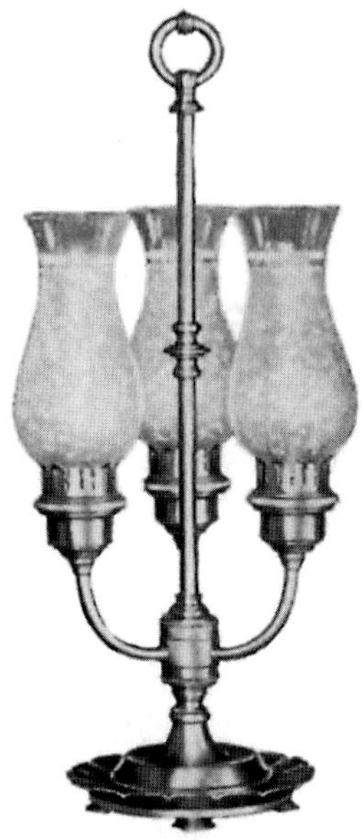

No. L-106

IN planning the lighting fixtures for your home, it is deserving of a good amount of consideration. Surely the importance of good lighting is in evidence. The beauty of your furnishings are to a great extent dependent on well selected lighting equipment.

Georgian Radiants, influential of the English, are characteristic of the old baronial mansions. The robustness of this splendid merchandise will add charm to any home.

These fixtures are made of Brass throughout, and finished in the well known Radiant quality. Glass shades, as illustrated, are crystal satin white with design, cut by high class artisans.

No. 13051½
Current value: $75.00 – 100.00

No. 13058½
Current value: $115.00 – 140.00

No. 13060½—5 Lt.
Current value: $300.00 – 350.00

No. 13051½
Back, 11x4" Extension, 7½"
Wired Pin Switch
Price, **$8.25**

Hand Cut Glass

No. 13058½
Back, 11x4" Width, 11"
Wired Pin Switch
Price, **$12.00**

No. 13060½
Length, 42" Width, 20"
Wired Keyless
Price, **$39.75**

Finish—Antique Brass or Pewter or Colonial Brass

No. 10083—3 Lt.
Current value: $175.00 – 200.00

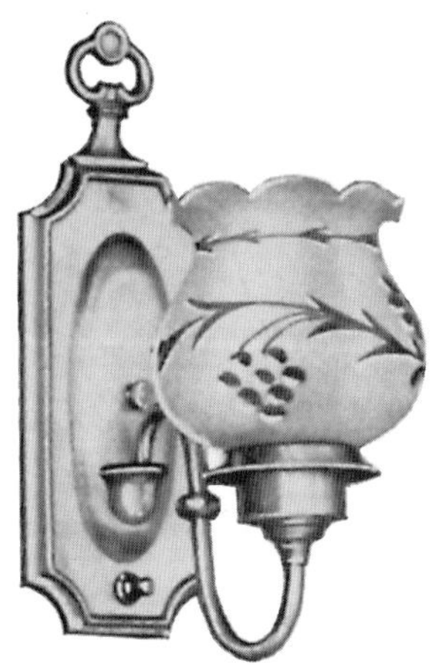

No. 13061½
Current value: $75.00 – 100.00

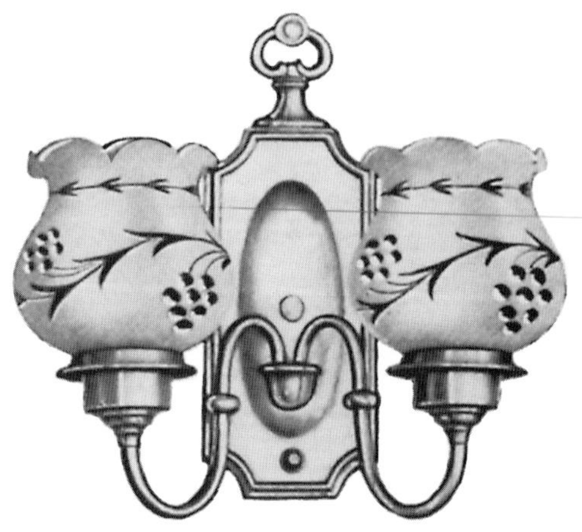

No. 13062½
Current value: $125.00 – 150.00

No. 13061½
Back, 3½x9¾ Extension, 6½"
Wired Pin Switch
Price, **$7.95**

Hand Cut Glass

No. 13062½
Back, 3½x9¾" Width, 11"
Wired Pin Switch
Price, **$11.70**

No. 10083
Length, 5½" Width 15"
Wired Keyless
Price, **$24.00**

Finish—Antique Brass or Pewter or Colonial Brass

No. 750—3 Lt.
Current value: $200.00 – 235.00

No. 13054—1 Lt.
Current value: $125.00 – 140.00

No. 13053—1 Lt.
Current value: $200.00 – 225.00

No. 13053
Length, 36" Width, 9"
Wired Keyless
Price, **$20.25**

Hand Cut Glass

No. 13054
Length, 10" Width, 9"
Wired Keyless
Price, **$10.50**

No. 750
Length, 7" Width, 12"
Wired Keyless
Price, **$17.25**

Finish—Antique Brass or Pewter or Colonial Brass

EARLY AMERICAN RADIANTS

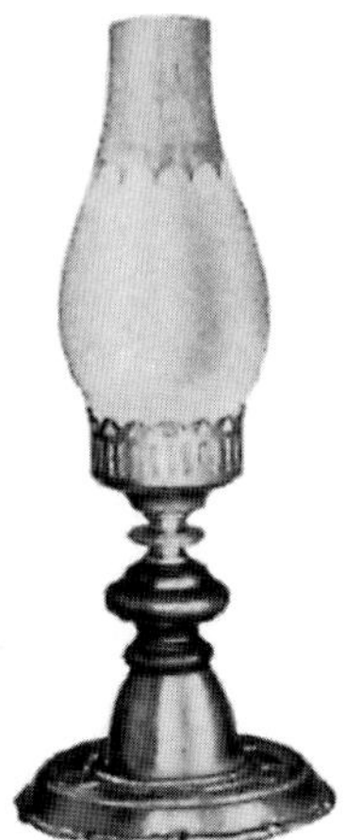

No. L-115

THE architects of our land favor, to a great extent, the Early American influence. This is not surprising, as it embodies the democratic spirit which is the foundation of our national greatness.

Probably unknown to them, our forefathers devised a simple, rugged, artistic influence which will be everlasting in our land.

The Radiants shown are a true reproduction of this beauty, and will add to the proper surroundings a lasting charm.

Early American Radiants are finished in Swedish Iron with Antique Brass trim and turned wood body. This makes a very handsome combination.

The Colonial chimneys used are crystal satin white.

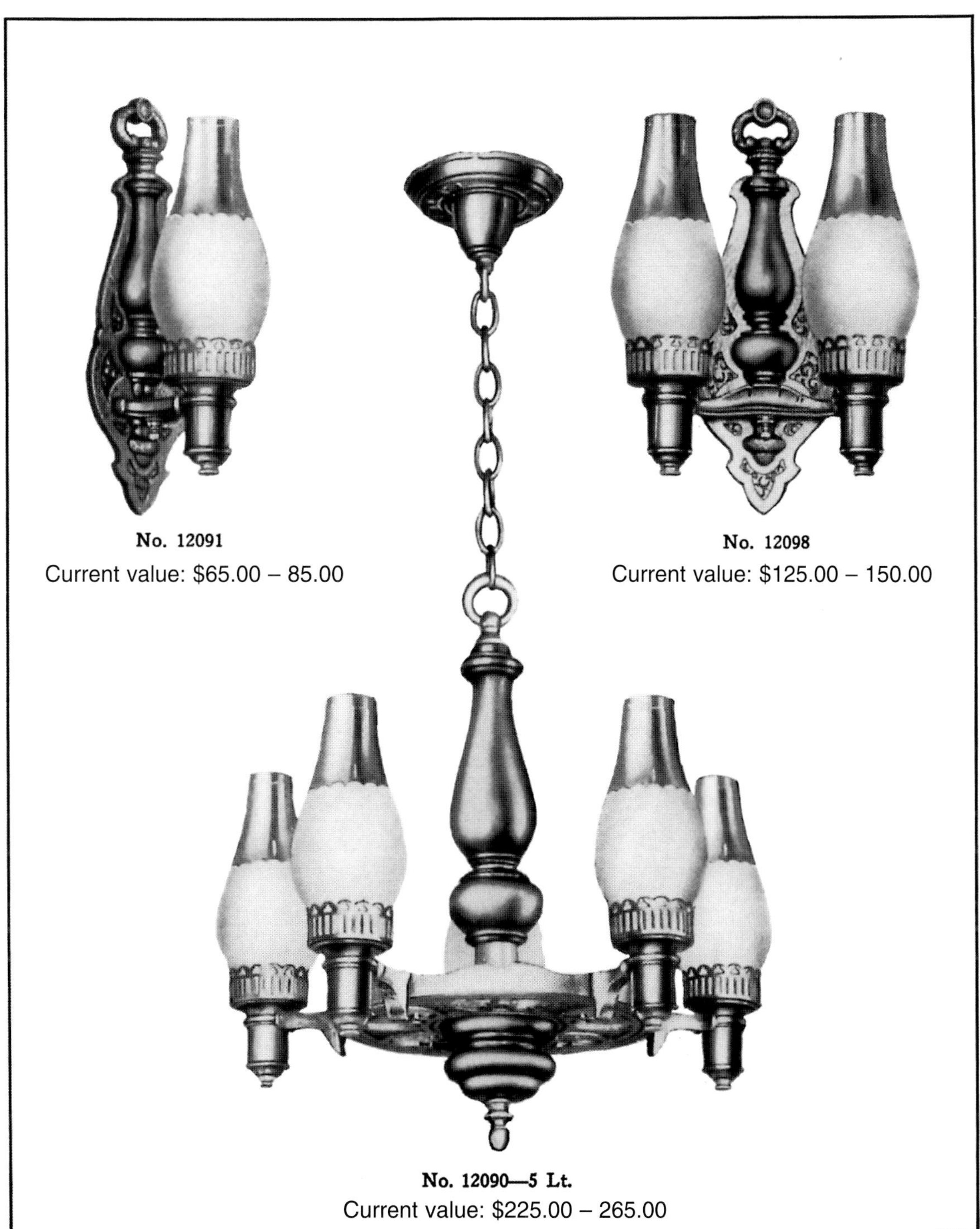

No. 12091
Current value: $65.00 – 85.00

No. 12098
Current value: $125.00 – 150.00

No. 12090—5 Lt.
Current value: $225.00 – 265.00

No. 12091
Back, 4½x12" Extension 5"
Wired Pin Switch
Price, **$6.75**

Crystal Satin Glass

No. 12098
Back, 4½x12" Width, 10"
Wired Pin Switch
Price, **$9.00**

No. 12090
Length, 42" Width, 18"
Wired Keyless
Price, **$27.00**

Finish—Swedish Iron with Antique Brass and Wood

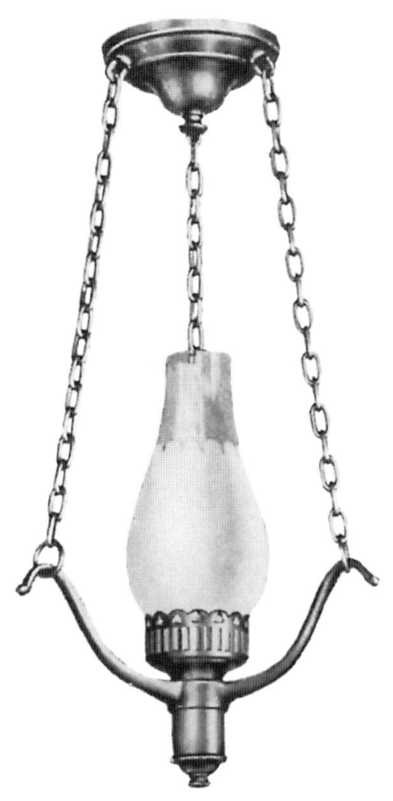

No. 12099
Current value: $100.00 – 125.00

No. 12097
Current value: $135.00 – 150.00

No. 12097
Length, 36" Width, 7"
Wired Keyless
Finish—Swedish Iron with Antique Brass and Wood
Price, **$13.50**

No. 12099
Length, 19" Width, 9"
Wired Keyless
Finish—Swedish Iron and Antique Brass
Price, **$9.00**

Crystal Satin Glass

RADIANT LAMPS

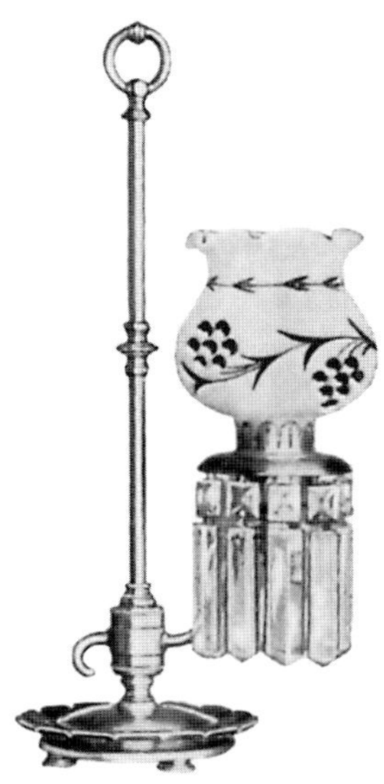

No. L-101

IN order to enable the purchaser of Radiant lighting equipment to secure complete harmony for the home, both in finish and design, a line of well selected lamps has been designed which ties in perfectly with our Colonial, Early American, English and Ironart Radiants.

The lamps illustrated, therefore, are not merely lamps, but purposeful lamps, each one conceived and constructed to fill a definite need, made to truly grace the home.

Radiant lamps are furnished in the same high grade finishes used throughout all Radiant merchandise.

No. L-110—2 Lt.
Oval Shade
Current value: $200.00 – 235.00

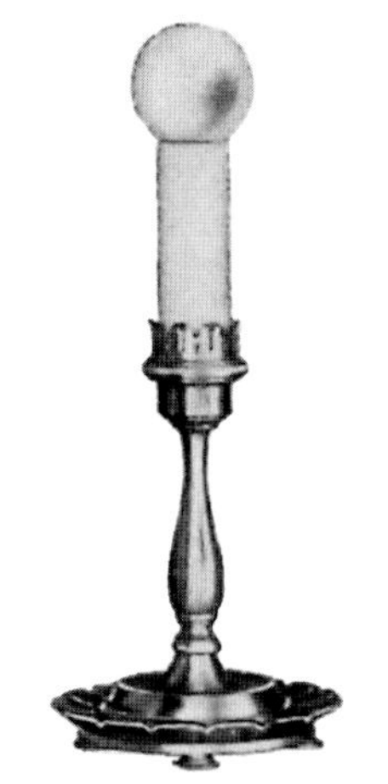

No. L-112
Current value: $25.00 – 35.00

No. L-115
Current value: $25.00 – 40.00

No. L-111—3 Lt.
Round Shade
Current value: $235.00 – 265.00

No. L-110
Height, 19" Diameter of Oval Shade, 7½x14"
Finish—Antique Brass with Decorated Hand-toned Parchment Shade to Match Finish of Lamp
Wired with Switch
Price, **$22.50**

No. L-111
Height, 19½"
Diameter of Round Shade, 8x14"
Finish—Antique Brass with Hand-toned Parchment Shade to Match Finish of Lamp
Wired with Switch
Price, **$25.50**

No. L-115
Height, 13½" Diameter, 6"
Finish—Swedish Iron with Antique Brass and Wood
Wired with Switch
Price, **$6.75**

No. L-112
Height, 13½" Diameter, 6"
Finish—Antique Brass or Pewter or Colonial Brass
Wired with Switch
Price, **$8.25**

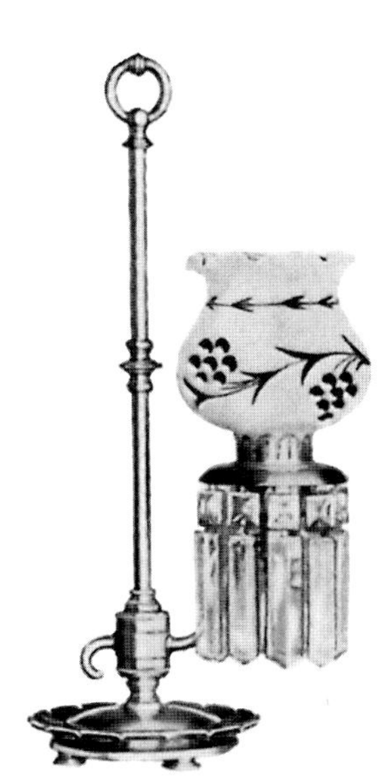

No. L-101
Current value: $115.00 – 135.00

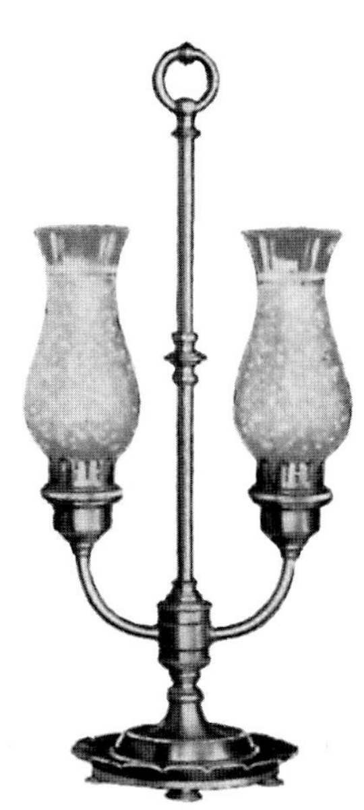

No. L-104—2 Lt.
Current value: $125.00 – 150.00

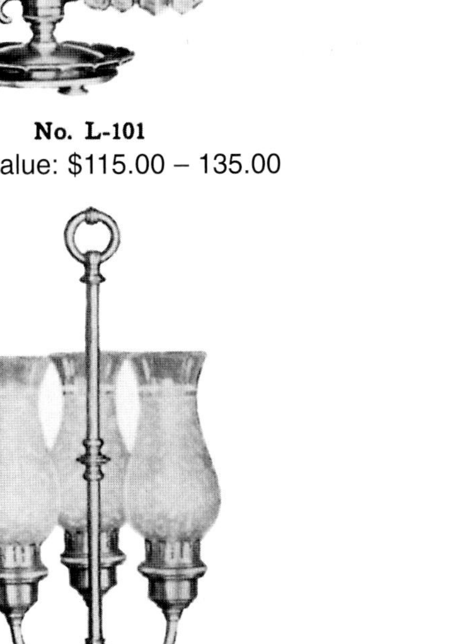

No. L-106—3 Lt.
Current value: $130.00 – 175.00

No. L-103—2 Lt.
Current value: $150.00 – 185.00

No. L-101
Height, 16½" Diameter, 8½"
Wired with Switch
Wood Polished Crystals
Hand Cut Crystal Satin Glass
Price, **$14.25**

No. L-104
Height, 17" Diameter, 8"
Wired with Switch
Crystal Satin Frosted Glass
Price, **$16.50**

No. L-106
Height, 17½" Diameter, 7½"
Wired with Switch
Crystal Satin Frosted Glass
Price, **$20.25**

No. L-103
Height, 16½" Diameter, 10½"
Wired with Switch
Wood Polished Crystals
Hand Cut Crystal Satin Glass
Price, **$21.00**

Finish—Antique Brass or Pewter or Colonial Brass

IRONART RADIANTS

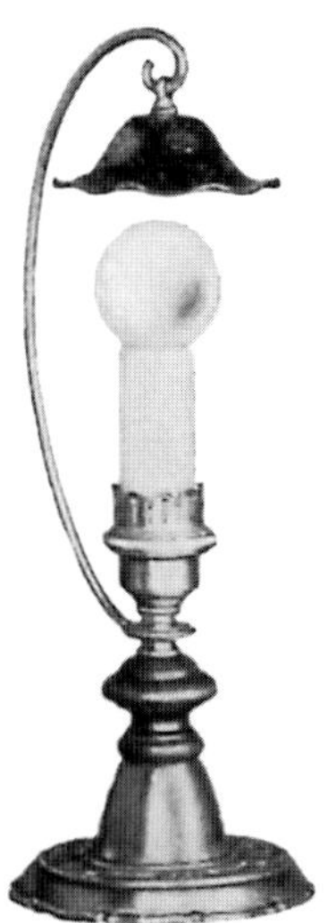

No. L-114

THE distinguishing characteristics of the products turned out by the village smith, or, in cases of the nobility by the armorers attached to the retinue, have offered their inspiration to lighting designers even as they have had their appeal to many home owners.

England and Spain were particularly noted for the skill of their iron workers, who traveled all over the known world, and, of course, left the influence of their styles behind them.

Ironart Radiants have been designed after long painstaking study of the product of these humble craftsmen. The Swedish Iron finish has the richness and brilliance of the more precious metals. Contrasted with white satin crackled glass, it makes a beautiful combination.

These fixtures are also furnished in a rich natural Bronze with amber crackled glass.

No. 1741½
Current value: $150.00 – 190.00

No. 1748½
Current value: $200.00 – 265.00

No. 1750½—5 Lt.
Current value: $295.00 – 385.00

No. 1741½
Back, 4x11½" Extension, 6"
Wired Pin Switch
Price, **$3.75**

Amber Crackled Glass

No. 1748½
Back, 4x11½" Width, 10½"
Wired Pin Switch
Price, **$5.70**

No. 1750½
Length, 42" Width, 17½"
Wired Keyless
Price, **$18.00**

Finish—Swedish Iron or Antique Bronze

No. 1741
Current value: $65.00 – 100.00

No. 1748
Current value: $125.00 – 150.00

No. 1750—5 Lt.
Current value: $200.00 – 300.00

No. 1741
Back, 4x11½" Extension, 4½"
Wired Pin Switch
Price, $3.15

No. 1748
Back, 4x11½" Width, 9"
Wired Pin Switch
Price, $4.50

No. 1750
Length, 42" Width, 15"
Wired Keyless
Price, $14.25

Finish—Swedish Iron or Antique Bronze

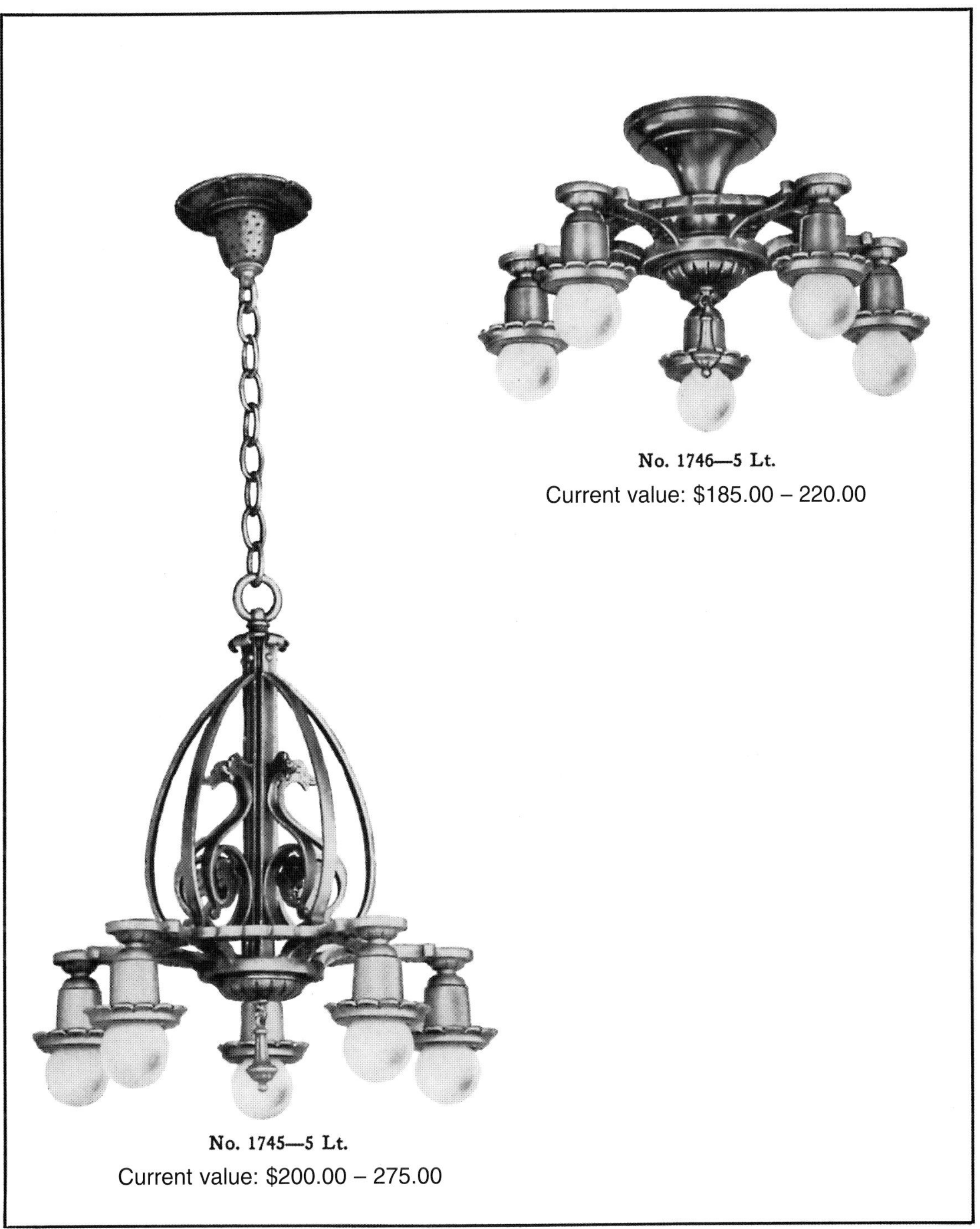

No. 1746—5 Lt.
Current value: $185.00 – 220.00

No. 1745—5 Lt.
Current value: $200.00 – 275.00

No. 1745
Length, 36" Width, 17"
Wired Keyless
Price, **$15.00**

No. 1746
Length, 9½" Width, 17"
Wired Keyless
Price, **$13.50**

Finish—Swedish Iron or Antique Bronze

No. 701—1 Lt.
Current value: $75.00 – 125.00

No. 1809
Current value: $20.00 – 30.00

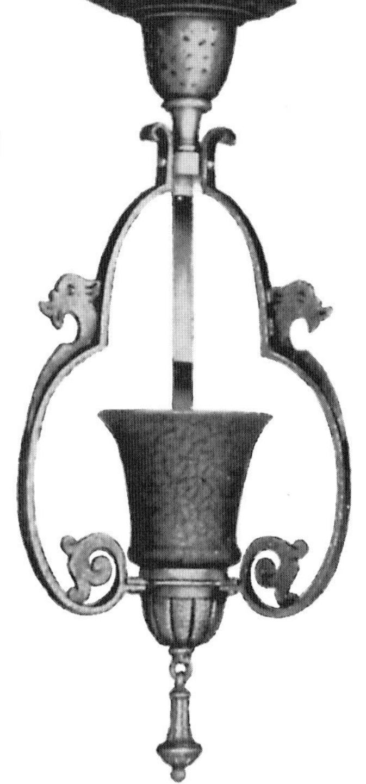

No. 1747½—1 Lt.
Current value: $165.00 – 195.00

No. 701
Length, 10" Width, 5½"
Wired Keyless
Amber Crackled Glass
Price, **$6.75**

No. 1747½
Length, 18" Width, 8"
Wired Keyless
Amber Crackled Glass
Price, **$7.50**

No. 1809
Length, 6" Width, 7"
Wired Keyless
Price, **$2.10**

Finish—Swedish Iron or Antique Bronze

No. 705—2 Lt.
Current value: $165.00 – 195.00

No. 679
Current value: $20.00 – 35.00

No. 706—1 Lt.
Current value: $195.00 – 200.00

No. 706
Length, 36" Width, 12"
Wired Keyless
Amber Crackled Glass
Price, **$16.50**

No. 705
Length, 10" Width, 14"
Wired Keyless
Amber Crackled Glass
Price, **$12.00**

No. 679
Length, 5" Width, 7"
Wired Keyless
Price, **$2.10**

Finish—Swedish Iron or Antique Bronze

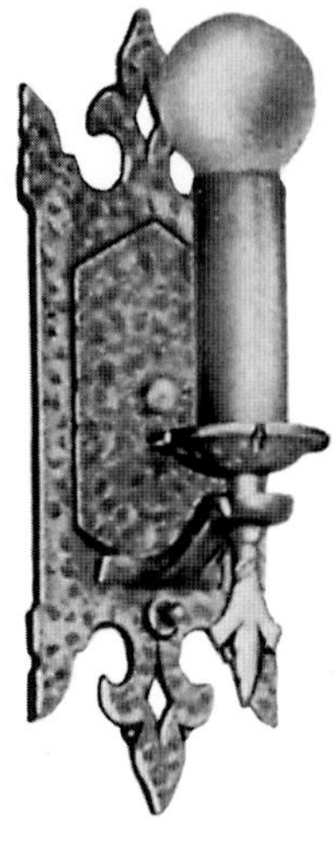

No. 671
Current value: $100.00 – 115.00

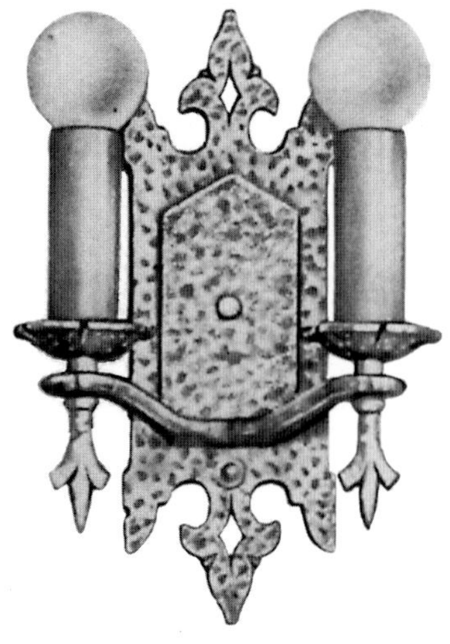

No. 678
Current value: $135.00 – 185.00

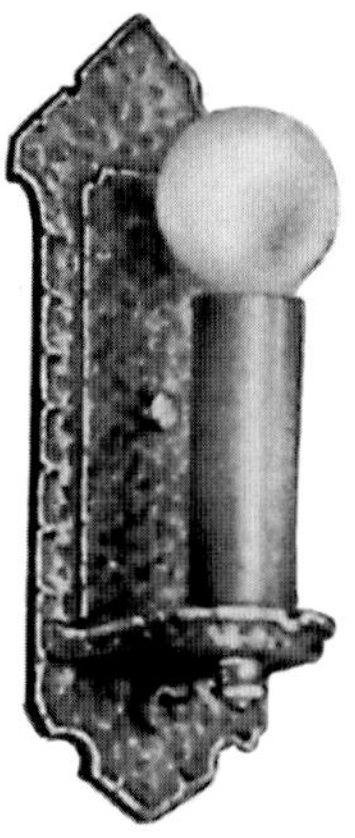

No. 672
Current value: $55.00 – 85.00

No. 671
Back, 12x4" Extension, 4½"
Wired Pin Switch
Price, **$4.05**

No. 678
Back, 12x4" Width, 8¼"
Wired Pin Switch
Price, **$5.25**

No. 672
Back, 10x4" Extension, 3½"
Wired Pin Switch
Price, **$4.05**

Finish—Swedish Iron or Antique Bronze

No. 765—1 Lt.
Current value: $200.00 – 225.00

No. 764—1 Lt.
Current value: $175.00 – 200.00

No. 763—1 Lt.
Current value: $135.00 – 150.00

No. 764
Length, 12" Width, 8½"
Wired Keyless
Finish—Ivory and Gold, Amber Glass or Green and Gold, Green Glass or Rose and Gold, Rose Glass
Price, $6.00

No. 765
Length, 13" Width, 11"
Wired Keyless
Finish—Ivory and Gold, Amber Glass or Green and Gold, Green Glass or Rose and Gold, Rose Glass
Price, $7.50

No. 763
Length, 9" Width 7"
Wired Keyless
Finish—Antique Brass or Ivory and Gold, Amber Glass
Price, $4.80

TUDOR RADIANTS

CHARACTERISTIC of the English Tudor, this line is a true reproduction of a beautiful style, the thistle, the oak leaf, ruggedness of line, sturdiness of construction and simplicity of finish. You will find all these in the Tudor Radiants combined in an artistic composition rarely found.

The workmanship and execution is of the high quality always associated with our Radiants. The finishes, Antique Bronze and color, or Swedish Iron and color, are particularly happy choices, as there is not a room in the home into which either will not blend. You will find the price as gratifying as the fitment itself.

No. 1701
Current value: $55.00 – 75.00

No. 1708
Current value: $100.00 – 140.00

Current value: $195.00 – 250.00

No. 1710

No. 1701
Back, 10x4½" Extension, 3"
Wired Pin Switch
Price, **$4.50**

No. 1708
Back, 10x4½" Width, 8½"
Wired Pin Switch
Price, **$6.00**

No. 1710—5 Lt.
Length, 42" Width, 19"
Wired Keyless
Price, **$24.00**

Finish—Antique Bronze and Color or Swedish Iron and Color

DESIGN PAT'D.

No. 1706
Current value: $185.00 – 215.00

No. 1705
Current value: $200.00 – 250.00

No. 1706—5 Lt.
Length, 16" Width, 20"
Wired Keyless
Price, **$19.20**

No. 1705—5 Lt.
Length, 36" Width, 20"
Wired Keyless
Price, **$24.00**

Finish—Antique Bronze and Color or Swedish Iron and Color

DESIGN PAT'D.

No. 1701½
Current value: $100.00 – 125.00

No. 1708½
Current value: $175.00 – 200.00

No. 1710½
Current value: $300.00 – 385.00

No. 1701½
Back, 10x4½" Extension, 5"
Wired Pin Switch
Amber Globe
Price, **$6.30**

No. 1710½—5 Lt.
Length, 42" Width, 20"
Wired Keyless
Amber Globes
Price, **$33.00**

No. 1708½
Back, 10x4½" Width, 10½"
Wired Pin Switch
Amber Globes
Price, **$9.60**

Finish—Antique Bronze and Color or Swedish Iron and Color

DESIGN PAT'D.

No. 1702
Current value: $350.00 – 400.00

No. 1702—5 Lt.
Length, 42″ Width, 19″
Wired Keyless
Mica Shade
Price, **$30.00**

Finish—Antique Bronze and Color or Swedish Iron and Color

DESIGN PAT'D.

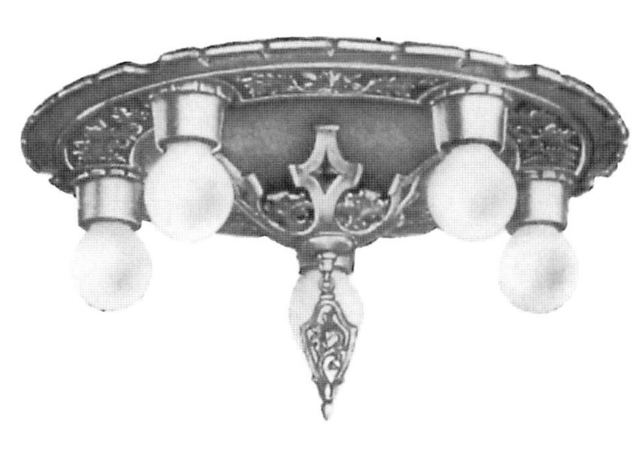

No. 1704
Current value: $170.00 – 200.00

No. 1704—5 Lt.
Length, 9" Width, 17"
Wired Keyless
Price, **$11.25**

Finish—Antique Bronze and Color or Swedish Iron and Color

DESIGN PAT'D.

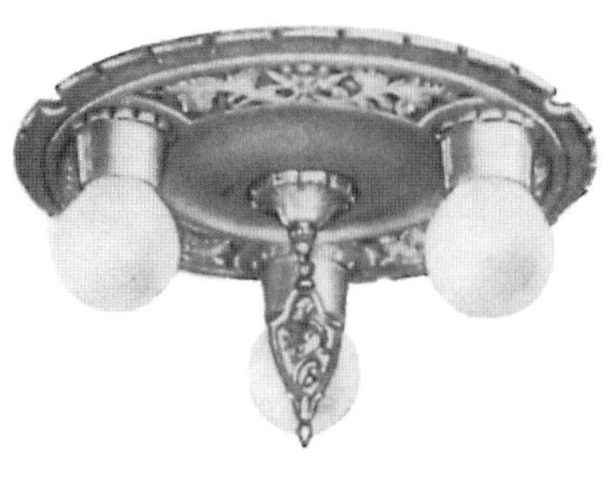

No. 1703
Current value: $115.00 – 135.00

No. 1709
Current value: $20.00 – 30.00

No. 1703—3 Lt.
Length, 6" Width, 12"
Wired Keyless
Price, **$5.25**

No. 1709
Length, 6" Width, 7"
Wired Keyless
Price, **$2.05**

Finish—Antique Bronze and Color or Swedish Iron and Color or Old Ivory

DESIGN PAT'D.

MODERN RADIANTS

THE Radiants shown are glowing examples of the steps taken to meet design changes of the modern age in which we live.

In producing these new ideas, however, Radiant designers have been careful not to sacrifice proportion and beauty for novelty. These Radiants have been designed to harmonize with the surroundings of the average American home.

Modern Radiants are furnished in Gold or Pewter finishes, a happy choice for these fitments. Glass shades are a beautiful Ivory, which give a particularly artistic mellow glow.

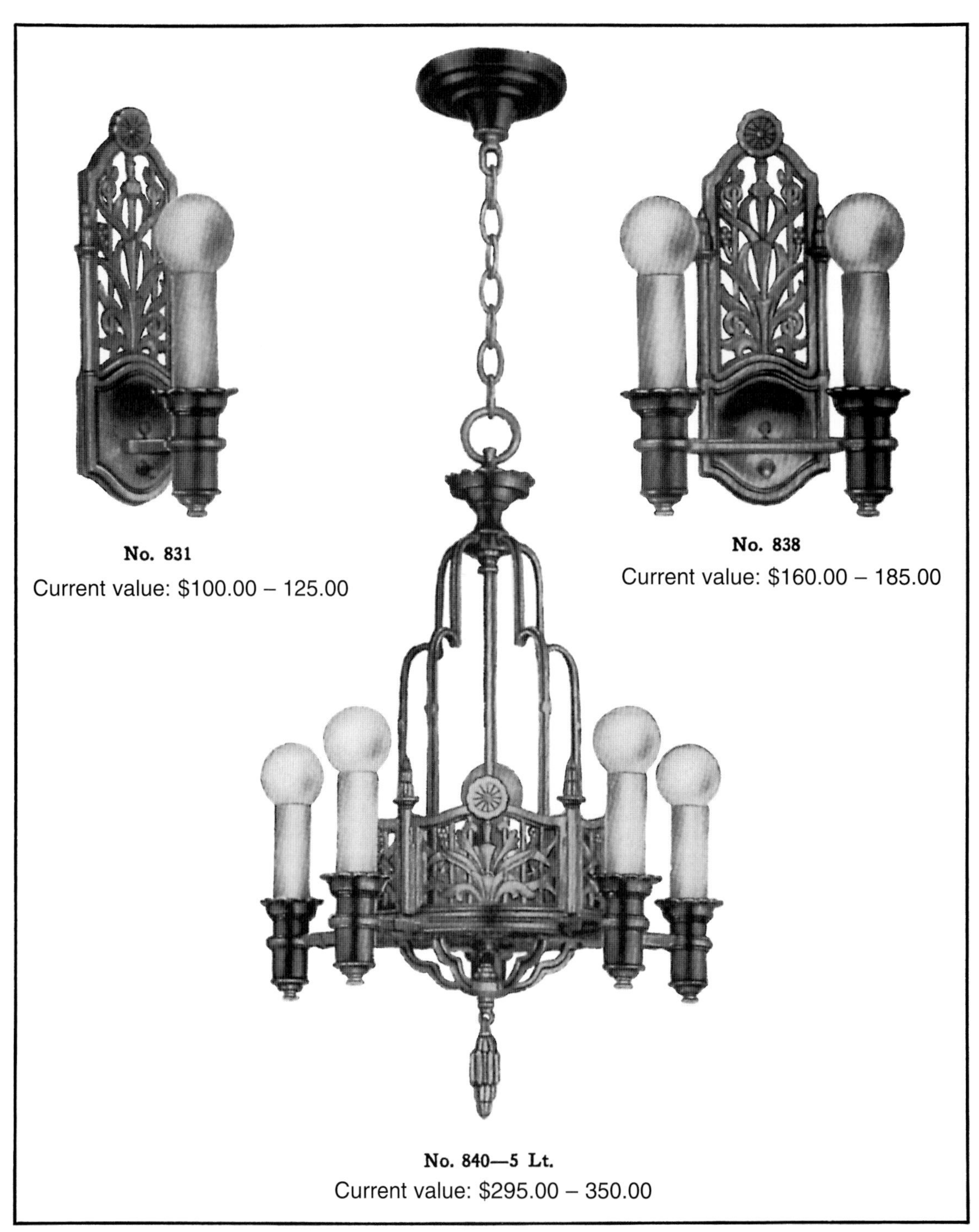

No. 831
Current value: $100.00 – 125.00

No. 838
Current value: $160.00 – 185.00

No. 840—5 Lt.
Current value: $295.00 – 350.00

No. 831
Back, 4x11½" Extension, 4½"
Wired Pin Switch
Price, **$4.35**

No. 838
Back, 4x11½" Width, 8½"
Wired Pin Switch
Price, **$6.00**

No. 840
Length, 42" Width, 17"
Wired Keyless
Price, **$28.50**

Finish—Gold or Pewter and Gold

No. 836—5 Lt.
Current value: $250.00 – 300.00

No. 833—3 Lt.
Current value: $100.00 – 135.00

No. 833
Length, 36" Width, 9"
Wired Keyless
Price, **$12.00**

No. 836
Length, 14" Width, 18"
Wired Keyless
Price, **$22.50**

Finish—Gold or Pewter and Gold

No. 396—5 Lt.
Current value: $400.00 – 650.00

Plan

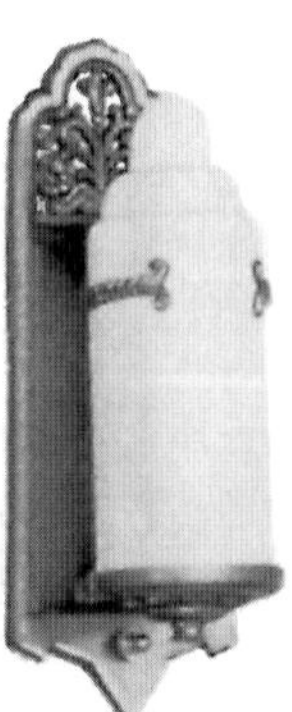

No. 391
Current value: $150.00 – 185.00

No. 396
Length, 18" **Width, 15"**
Wired Keyless
Price, $37.50

Ivory Glass

No. 391
Back, 12x4½" **Extension, 4½"**
Wired Pin Switch
Price, $8.25

Finish—Gold or Pewter

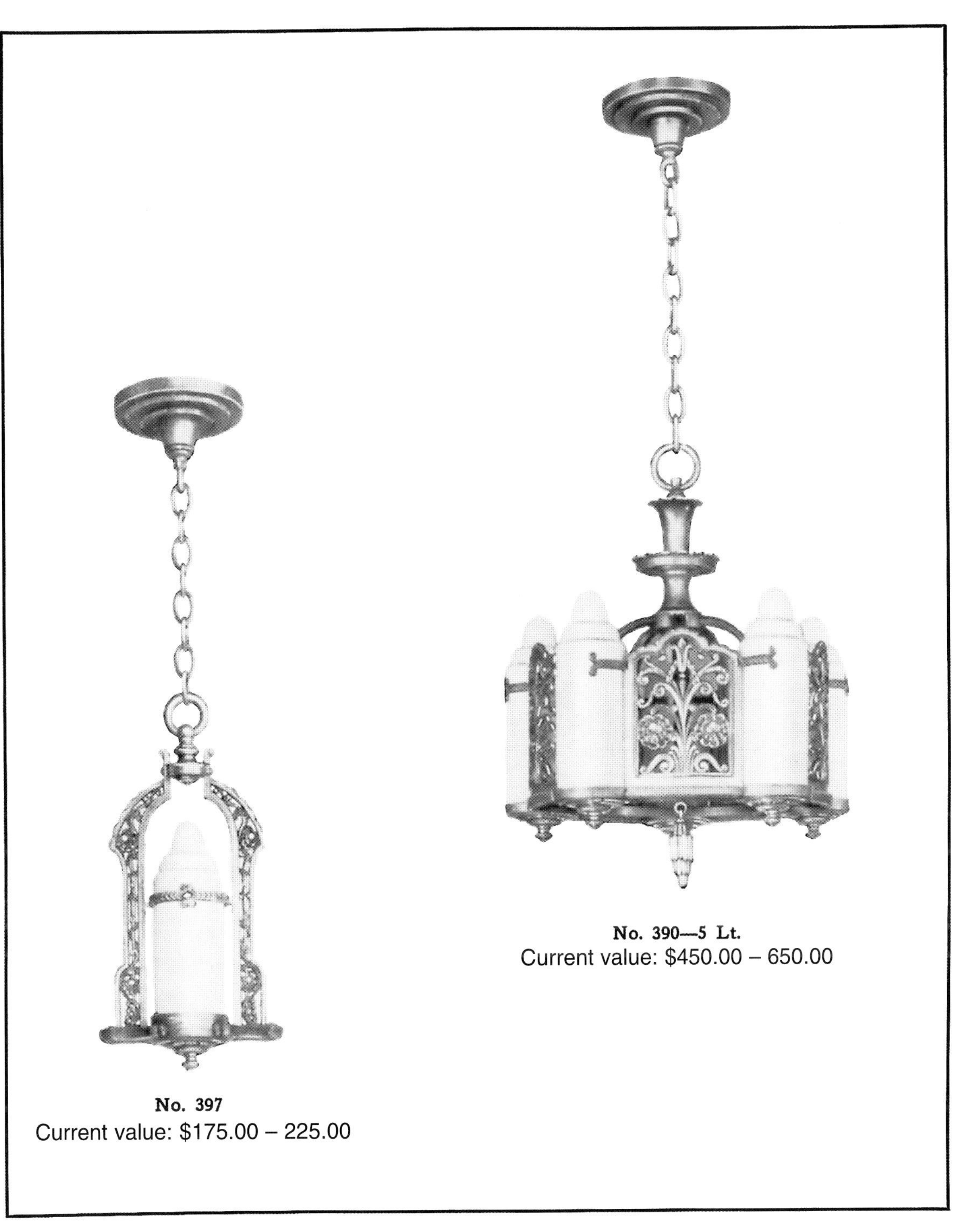

No. 390—5 Lt.
Current value: $450.00 – 650.00

No. 397
Current value: $175.00 – 225.00

No. 397
Length, 36" Width, 8"
Wired Keyless
Price, **$16.50**

Ivory Glass

No. 390
Length, 42" Width 15"
Wired Keyless
Price, **$39.00**

Finish— Gold or Pewter

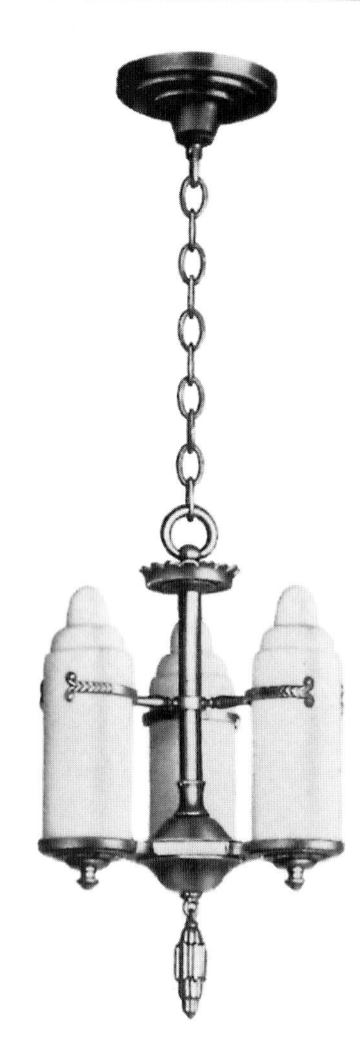

No. 393—3 Lt.
Current value: $225.00 – 285.00

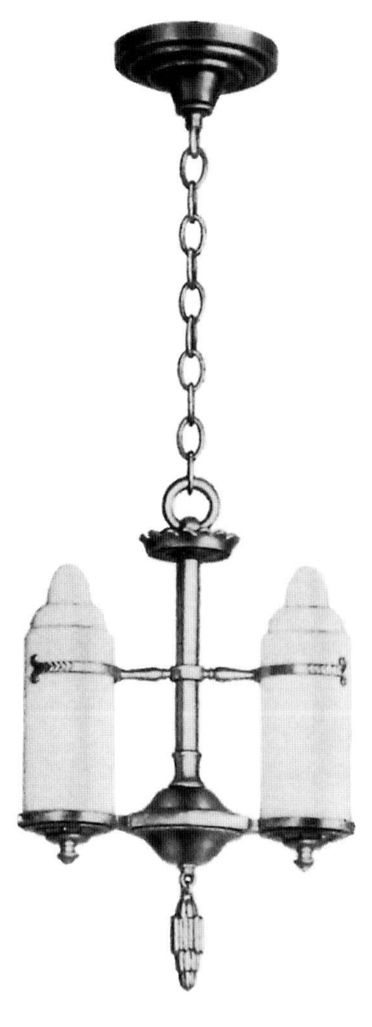

No. 392
Current value: $195.00 – 225.00

No. 393
Length, 36" Width, 10"
Wired Keyless
Price, **$25.50**

Ivory Glass

No. 392
Length, 36" Width, 10"
Wired Keyless
Price, **$19.50**

Finish—Gold or Pewter

No. 765—Length, 13". Width, 11". Wired Keyless
Finish—Ivory and Gold, Amber Glass or Green and Gold, Green Glass or Rose and Gold, Rose Glass
Price, **$7.50**

No. 766—Length, 9". Width, 10". Wired Keyless
Finish—Ivory and Gold, Amber Glass or Green and Gold, Green Glass
Price, **$15.00**

No. 745—Length, 6". Width, 9½". Wired Keyless
Finish—Ivory or Gold or Green with Ivory Decorated Glass
Price, **$9.00**

No. 749—Length, 6". Width, 11½" Wired Keyless
Finish—Ivory or Gold or Green with Ivory Decorated Glass
Price, **$11.25**

No. 767—Length, 9". Width, 8". Wired Keyless
Finish—Ivory and Gold, Amber Glass or Green and Gold, Green Glass
Price, **$12.00**

No. 764—Length, 12". Width, 8½". Wired Keyless
Finish—Ivory and Gold, Amber Glass or Green and Gold, Green Glass or Rose and Gold, Rose Glass
Price, **$6.00**

RADIANT INCIDENTALS

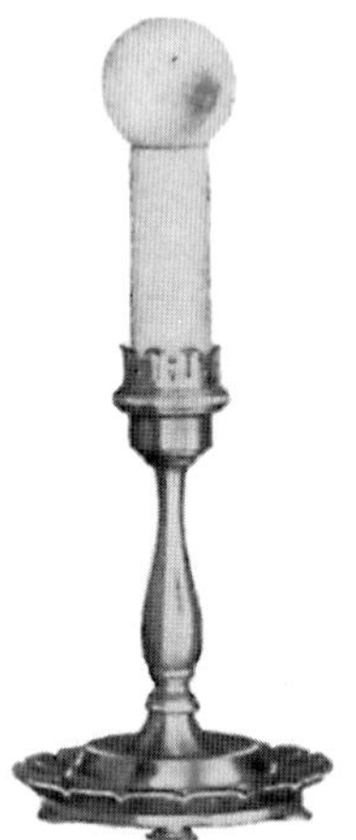

No. L-112

IN the bedrooms the general trend is to use items of dainty design and delicate colorings, reflecting the feminine side of the family.

The sun room usually calls for soft warm colors with suggestion of the gardens, and, of course, totally informal. It is the playroom of the entire family.

The breakfast room is generally gay and colorful.

Radiant Incidentals have been designed to meet these requirements, with a large variety of color combinations given to harmonize with almost any decorative scheme.

Materials are of the same high grade quality used in all Radiant fitments. Glassware is furnished in color combinations to properly harmonize with design and color of fixture.

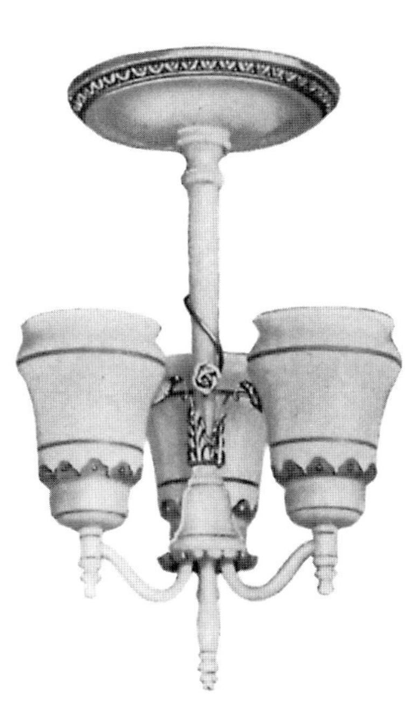

No. 376½—3 Lt.
Current value: $175.00 – 195.00

No. 376—3 Lt.
Current value: $135.00 – 150.00

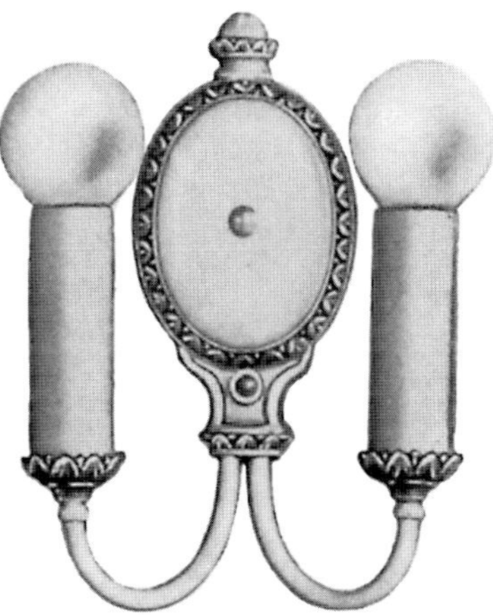

No. 378
Current value: $95.00 – 115.00

No. 376½
Length, 14½" Width, 9"
Wired Keyless
Price, **$20.25**

No. 376
Length, 14½" Width, 8"
Wired Keyless
Price, **$15.00**

No. 378
Back, 7x3½" Width, 7"
Wired Pin Switch
Price, **$6.75**

Finish—Green and Gold or Ivory and Gold or Orchid and Gold or Pink and Gold or Blue and Gold

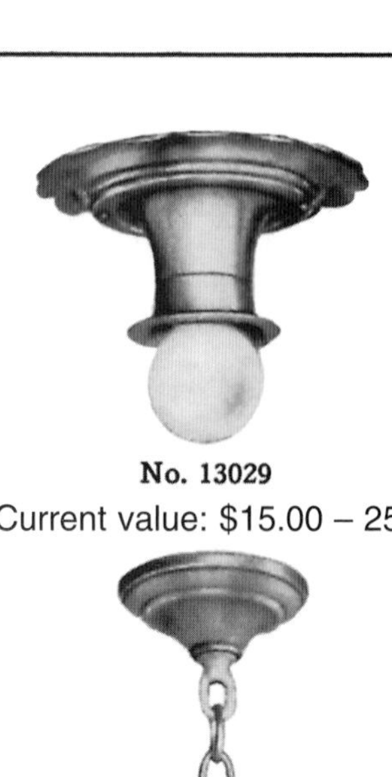

No. 13029
Current value: $15.00 – 25.00

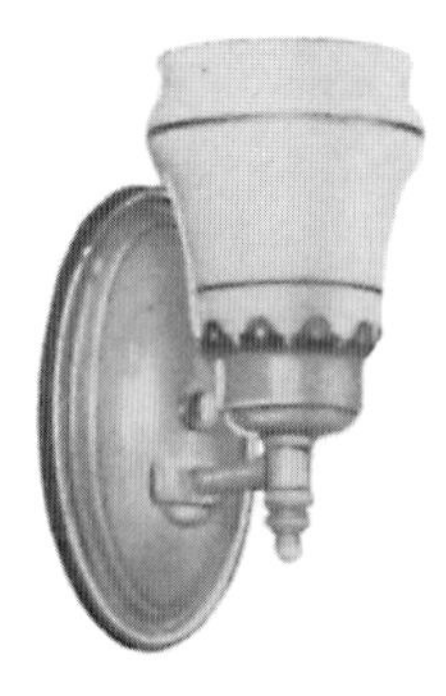

No. 381
Current value: $75.00 – 100.00

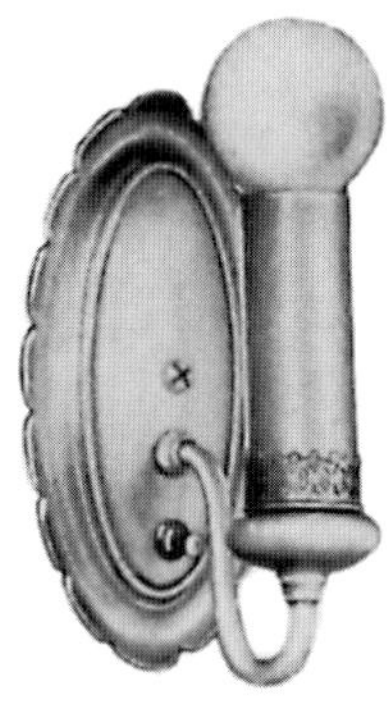

No. 740
Current value: $40.00 – 65.00

No. 380
Current value: $150.00 – 185.00

No. 381
Back, 3¼x6" Extension, 5"
Wired Pin Switch
Finish—Ivory and Gold or Green and Gold, Ivory Glass
Price, **$6.00**

No. 740
Back, 7½x4" Extension, 5"
Wired Pin Switch
Finish—Ivory or Green
Price, **$3.75**

No. 380
Length, 36" Width, 12"
Wired Keyless
Finish—Ivory and Gold or Green and Gold, Ivory Glass
Price, **$21.00**

No. 13029
Length, 5" Width, 6¾"
Wired Keyless
Finish—Antique Brass or Pewter or Colonial Brass or Ivory and Gold or Green and Gold
Price, **$2.70**

No. 745—9½"
No. 749—11½"
Current value
745:
$150.00 – 175.00
749:
$175.00 – 195.00

No. 707
Current value: $165.00 – 195.00

No. 10088
Current value: $200.00 – 275.00

No. 707
Length, 36" Width, 9"
Wired Keyless
Finish—Green and Gold or Ivory and Gold
Price, **$10.50**

No. 10088
Length, 36" Width, 11"
Wired Keyless
Finish—Antique Brass or Ivory and Gold, Vellemesque Shade
Price, **$19.50**

No. 745
Length, 6" Width, 9½"
Wired Keyless
Price, **$9.00**

No. 749
Length, 6" Width, 11½"
Wired Keyless
Price, **$11.25**

Finish—Ivory or Gold or Green. Ivory Decorated Glass

ODD ROOM RADIANTS

ODD ROOM RADIANTS represents a line of well thought out fixtures for use in bedroom, sun porch, breakfast room, hall, etc. The simplicity of design, reflecting the modern trend, lends itself readily to the delicate color combinations demanded in the present vogue.

The material used is cast Radone, a metal perfected by Radiant, which is noteworthy for its ability to show detail sharply and take lasting finishes.

Odd Room Radiants are finished in Plated Gold with a wide range of color combination to meet the requirements of the newer color schemes employed in present day homes.

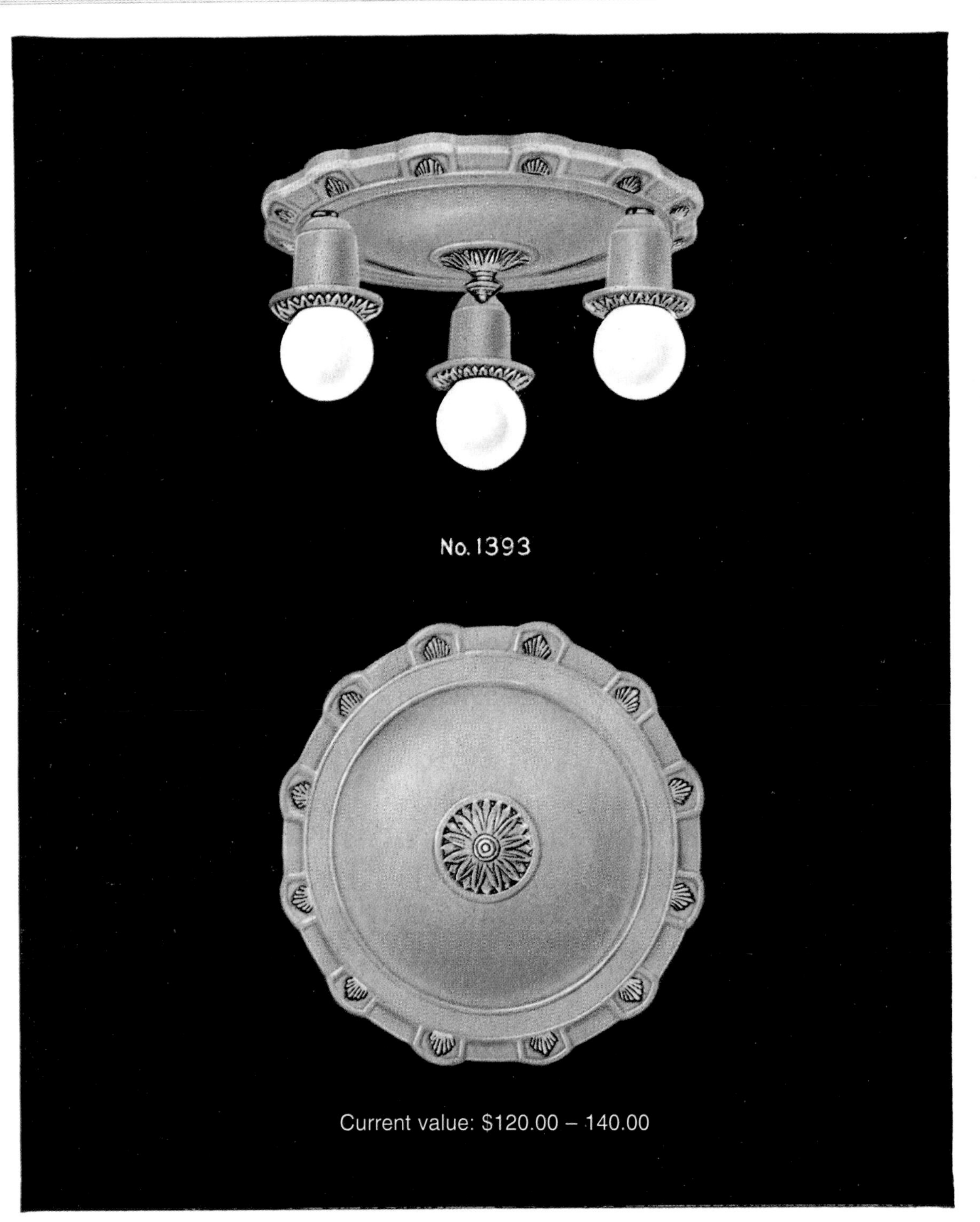

No. 1393
Length 6½″ Width 12″
Wired Keyless

Price, **$6.00**

Finish—Green and Gold or Ivory and Gold or Orchid and Gold or Gold or Blue and Gold or Rose and Gold

DESIGN PAT'D.

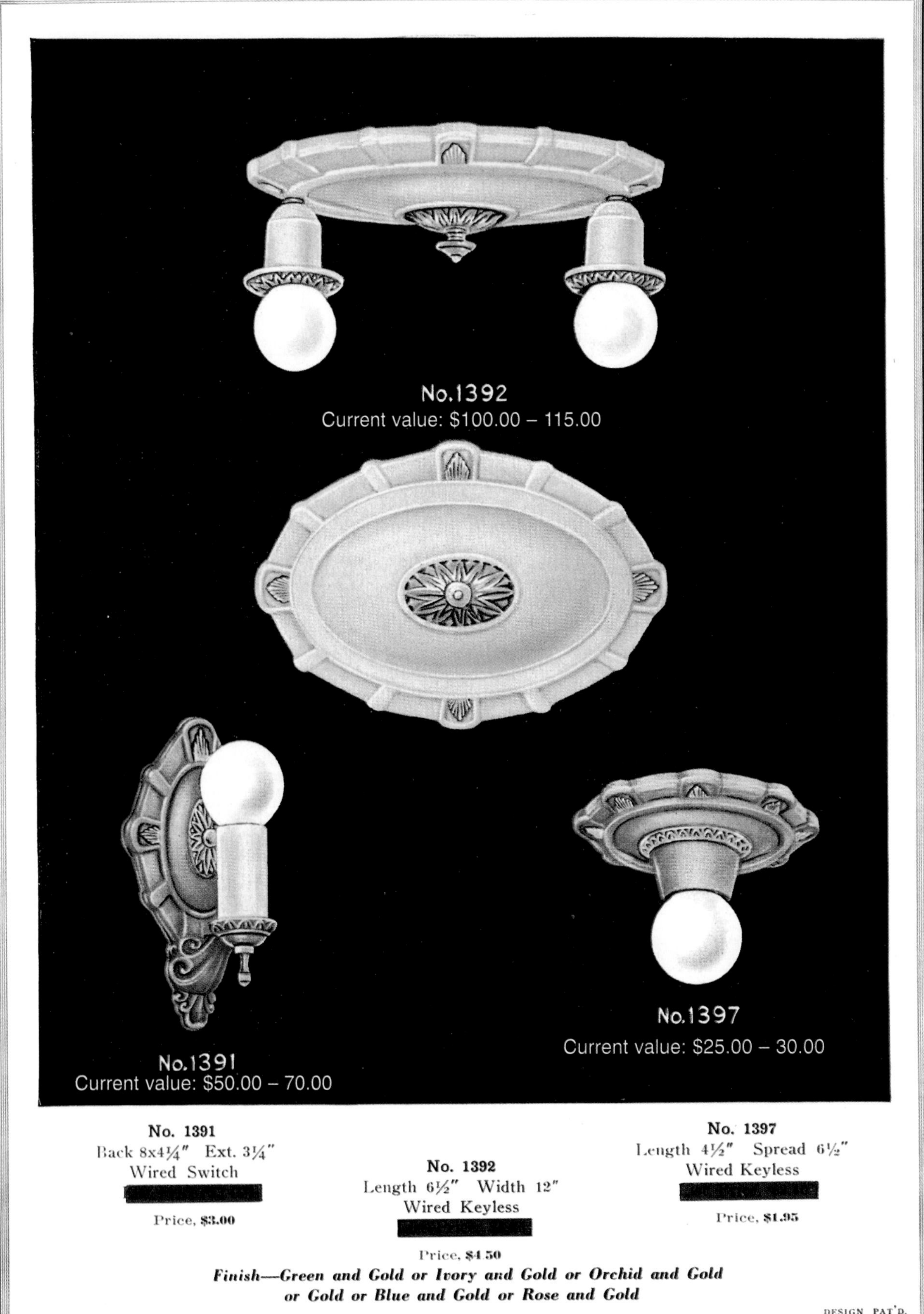

No. 1391
Back 8x4¼″ Ext. 3¼″
Wired Switch

Price, $3.00

No. 1392
Length 6½″ Width 12″
Wired Keyless

Price, $4.50

No. 1397
Length 4½″ Spread 6½″
Wired Keyless

Price, $1.95

Finish—Green and Gold or Ivory and Gold or Orchid and Gold or Gold or Blue and Gold or Rose and Gold

DESIGN PAT'D.

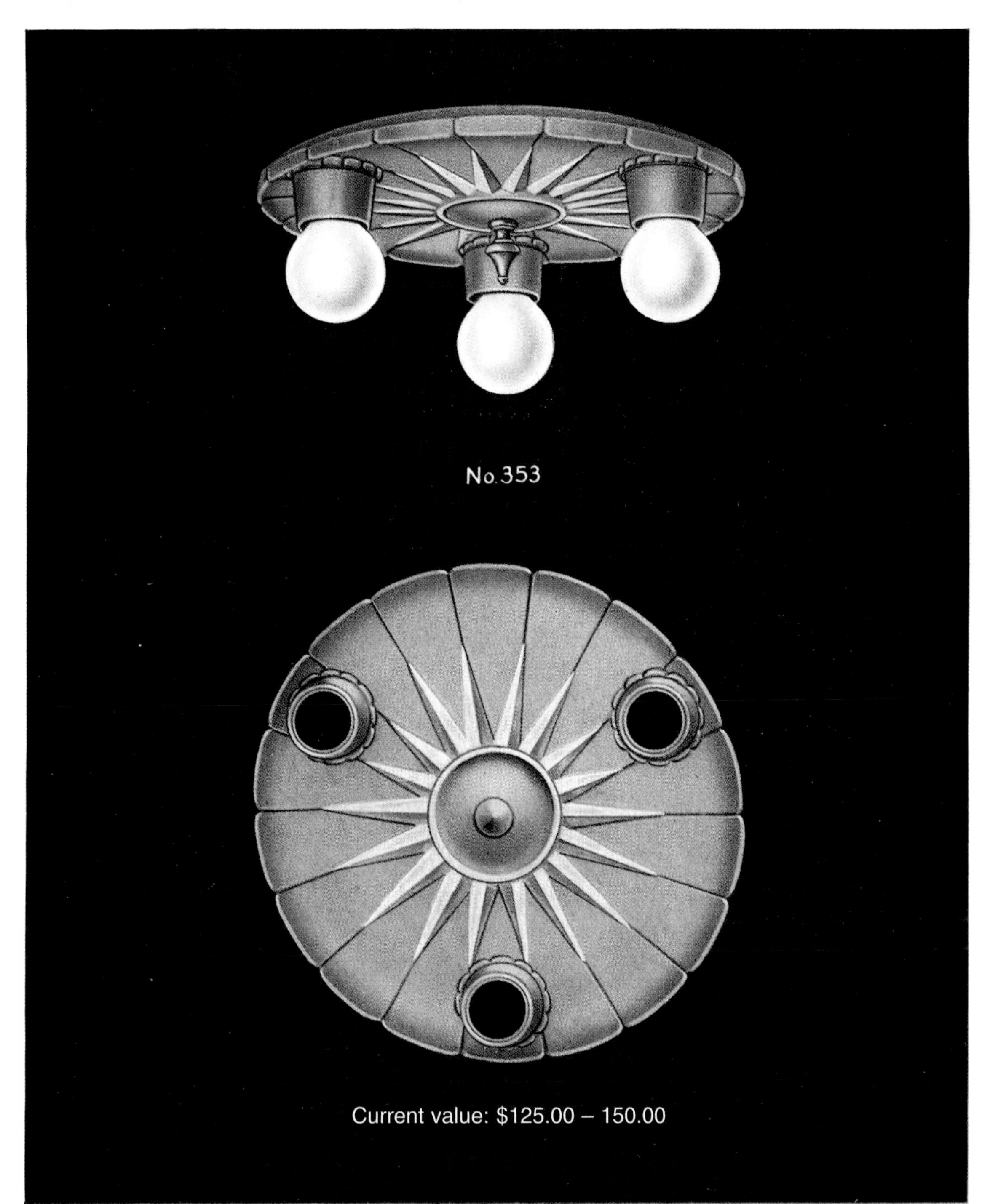

No. 353

Length, 4½"   Width, 12"
Wired Keyless
Price, **$4.50**

Finish—Green and Gold or Ivory and Gold or Orchid and Gold or Gold or Blue and Gold or Pink and Gold

DESIGN PAT'D.

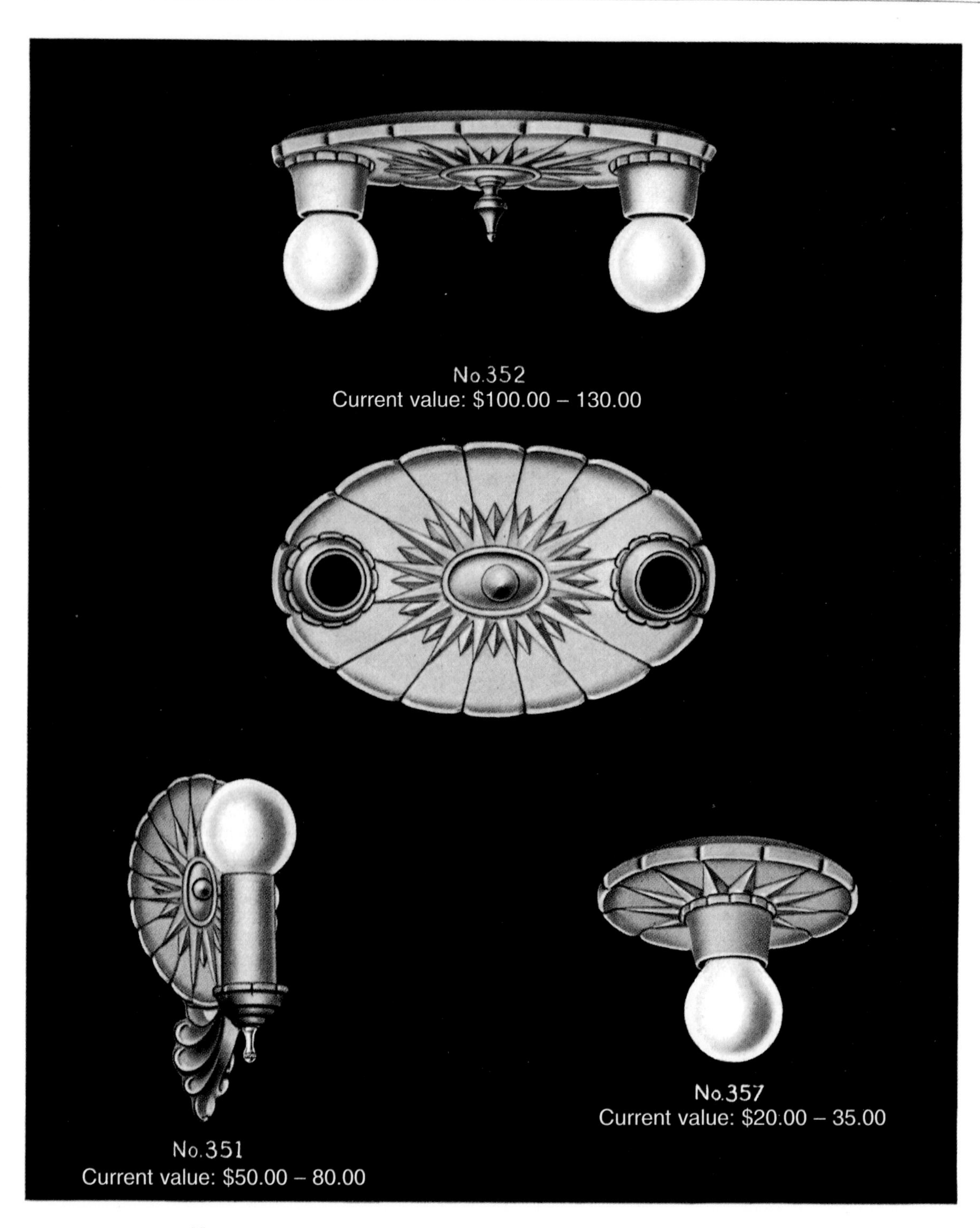

No. 351
Back, 8x4¼″ Extension, 3¼″
Wired Switch
Price, **$3.00**

No. 352
Length, 4½″ Width, 11″
Wired Keyless
Price, **$3.45**

No. 357
Length, 4½″ Spread, 6½″
Wired Keyless
Price, **$1.95**

Finish—Green and Gold or Ivory and Gold or Orchid and Gold or Gold or Blue and Gold or Pink and Gold

DESIGN PAT'D.

No. 770—Keyless
No. 770-P—Pull-Switch

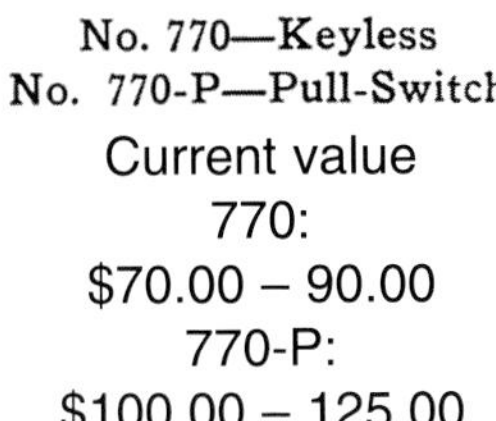

Current value
770:
$70.00 – 90.00
770-P:
$100.00 – 125.00

No. 768—Plain Glass
No. 768-D—Dec. Glass

Current value
768:
$115.00 – 130.00
768-D:
$175.00 – 200.00

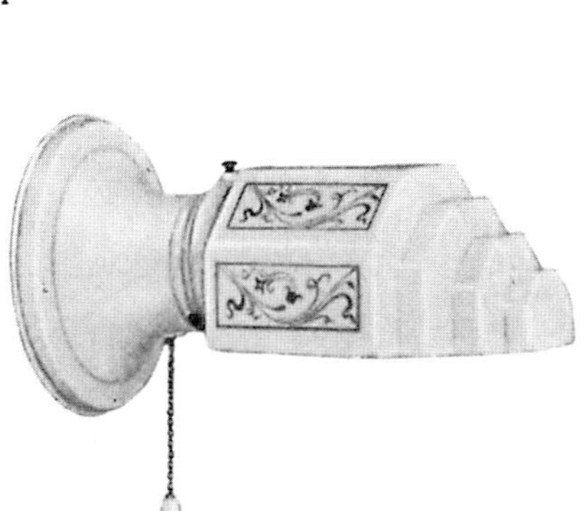

No. 769—Plain Glass
No. 769-D—Dec. Glass

Current value
769:
$60.00 – 75.00
769-D:
$125.00 – 150.00

No. 769—Price, **$2.40**
Finish—White Enamel or Green or Ivory with Opal Glass
Back, 4½" Extension, 9"
Wired Pull Switch

No. 769-D—Price, **$3.00**
Finish—White Enamel with Black Decoration on Glass or Ivory with Tan Decoration on Glass or Green with Green Decoration on Glass

No. 770—Price, **$2.85**

No. 770-P—Price, **$3.30**
Length, 11" Width, 8"
Finish—White Enamel with Black Decoration on Glass or Green with Green Decoration on Glass

No. 768—Price, **$4.50**
Finish—White Enamel or Green or Ivory with Opal Glass
Length, 9" Width, 7"
Wired Keyless

No. 768-D—Price, **$5.70**
Finish—White Enamel with Black Decoration on Glass or Ivory with Tan Decoration on Glass or Green with Green Decoration on Glass

OUTDOOR RADIANTS

No. 762

THE entrance to the home being of primary importance, designers and architects give it more attention proportionately than any other part of the structure.

The lighting of the doorway plays no small part in this general scheme. It must harmonize with the architecture, be in correct proportion to the surroundings, and, at the same time, light up the steps and pathway adequately and pleasantly.

Outdoor Radiants cover these requirements perfectly. Of good proportion and pleasing authentic design, they contain features that permit their use with the average American dwelling.

Materials and workmanship are of the high grade Radiant quality, made to withstand the weather and last a lifetime. The crackled glass is of such character that while the light is soft and pleasant, there is no loss in useful illumination.

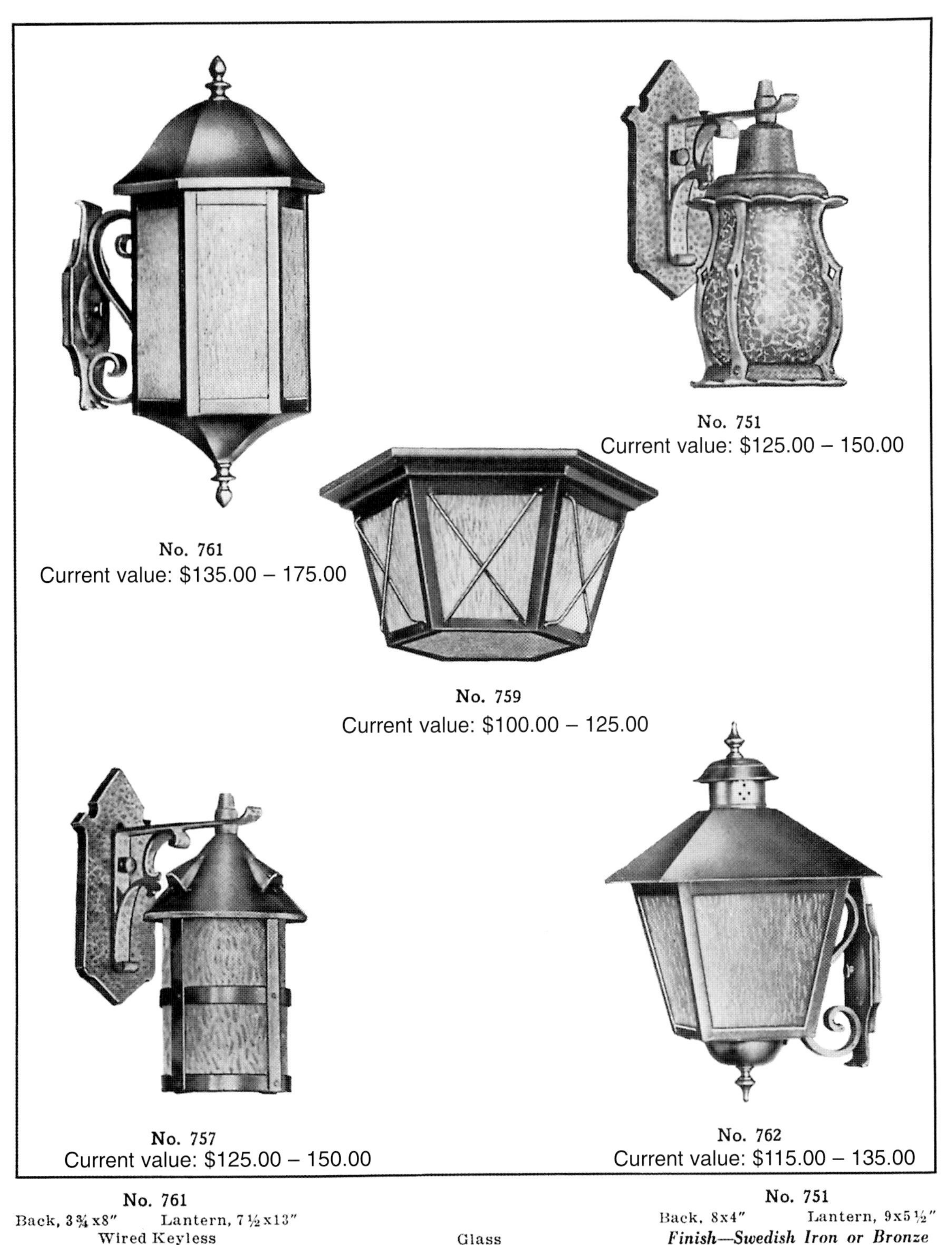

No. 761
Current value: $135.00 – 175.00

No. 751
Current value: $125.00 – 150.00

No. 759
Current value: $100.00 – 125.00

No. 757
Current value: $125.00 – 150.00

No. 762
Current value: $115.00 – 135.00

No. 761
Back, 3¾x8" Lantern, 7½x13"
Wired Keyless
Finish—Antique Copper or Verde
Price, **$19.50**

No. 757
Back, 8x4" Lantern, 8½x5½"
Wired Keyless
Finish—Antique Copper or Verde
Price, **$9.00**

Glass
Amber Crackled

No. 759
Length, 5½" Width, 11½"
Wired Keyless
Finish—Antique Copper or Verde
Price, **$9.75**

No. 751
Back, 8x4" Lantern, 9x5½"
Finish—Swedish Iron or Bronze
Price, **$7.50**

No. 762
Back, 3¾x8" Lantern, 9½x13"
Wired Keyless
Finish—Antique Copper or Verde
Price, **$17.25**

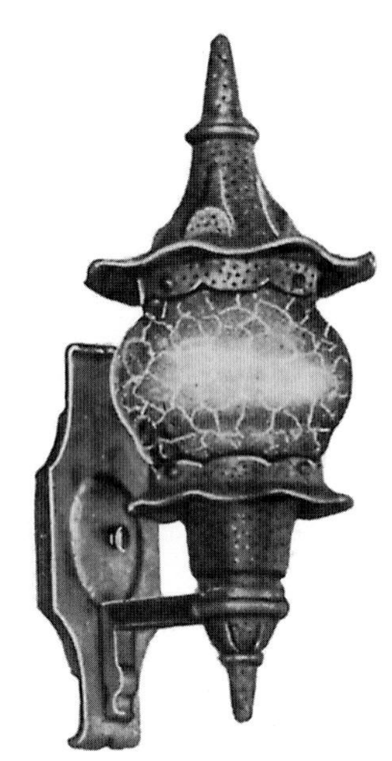

No. 755
Current value: $135.00 – 175.00

No. 760
Current value: $85.00 – 125.00

No. 754
Current value: $125.00 – 165.00

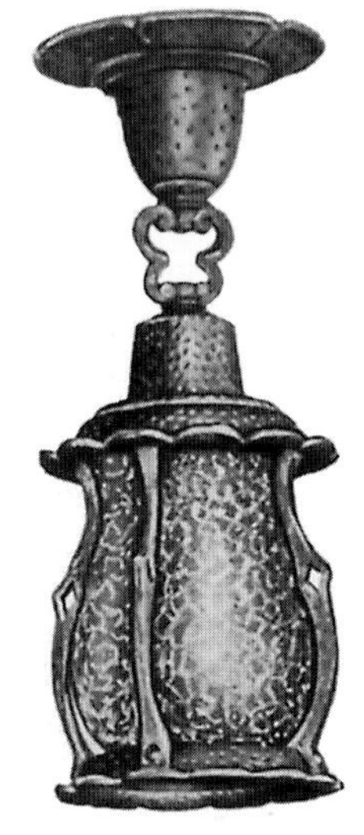

No. 752
Current value: $115.00 – 145.00

No. 756
Current value: $125.00 – 165.00

No. 755
Back, 8x4" Lantern, 14x6½"
Wired Keyless
Finish Swedish Iron or Bronze
Price, **$8.25**

No. 752
Length, 13" Width, 5½"
Wired Keyless
Finish—Swedish Iron or Bronze
Price, **$7.50**

Glass
Amber-Crackled

No. 760
Length, 11" Width, 7"
Wired Keyless
Finish—Antique Copper or Verde
Price, **$9.00**

No. 754
Length, 14" Width, 6½"
Wired Keyless
Finish—Swedish Iron or Bronze
Price, **$7.50**

No. 756
Back, 8x4" Lantern, 12x6½"
Wired Keyless
Finish—Swedish Iron or Bronze
Price, **$7.50**

No. 700
Current value: $135.00 – 165.00

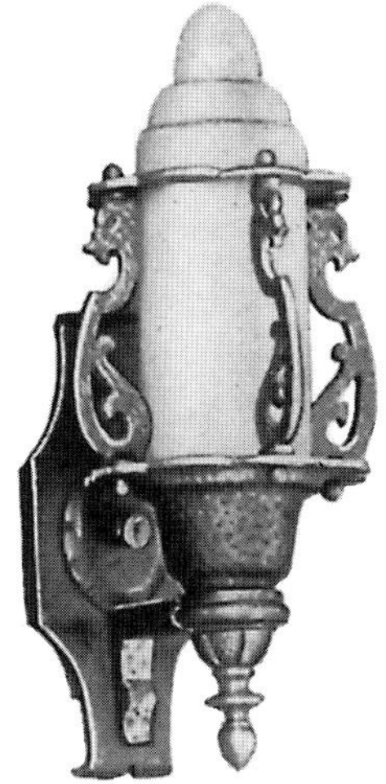

No. 753
Current value: $150.00 – 175.00

No. 701
Current value: $85.00 – 125.00

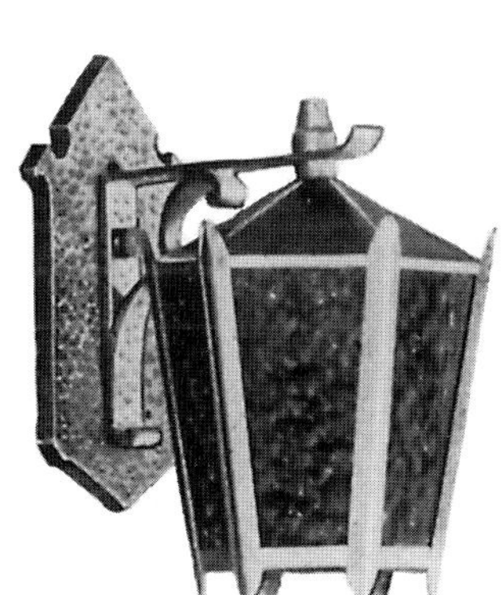

No. 758
Current value: $125.00 – 150.00

No. 702
Current value: $140.00 – 175.00

No. 700
Back, 8x4½" Lantern, 12x6"
Wired Keyless
Finish—Natural Copper or Verde
Price, **$12.00**

No. 758
Back, 8x4" Lantern, 7½x6"
Wired Keyless
Finish—Antique Copper or Verde
Price, **$8.25**

Glass
Amber Crackled

No. 701
Length, 10" Width, 5½"
Wired Keyless
Finish—Natural Copper or Verde
Price, **$6.75**

No. 753
Back, 3¾x8" Lantern, 12x6"
Wired Keyless
Finish—Swedish Iron or Bronze
Price, **$9.00**

No. 702
Length, 14" Width, 5"
Wired Keyless
Finish—Natural Copper or Verde
Price, **$9.00**

Meletio Electrical Supply Co.

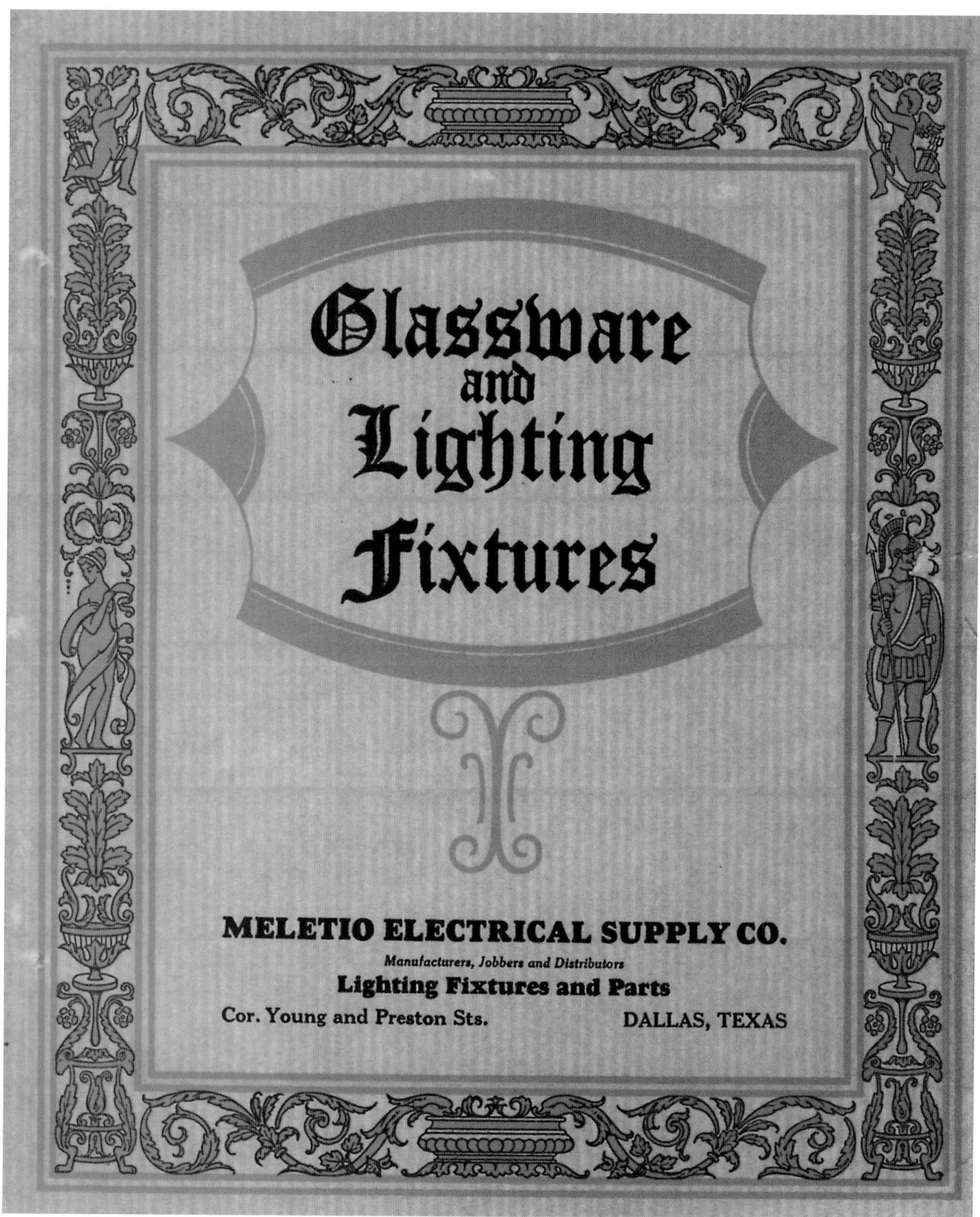

FOREWORD

IN COMPILING a catalog of Lighting Equipment it is essential that the designs selected be representative of the prevailing styles being installed in modern homes throughout the country. On the following pages we have endeavored to show such a representative group of designs, taking care to select only those lines of Lighting Equipment that are attractive in design and appearance, as well as in price. The demand for better Lighting Equipment is continually growing, and it is to meet this demand that we are offering the equipment shown in this book.

OUR GUARANTEE

We guarantee every fixture in this catalog to be exactly as shown and described. This applies to materials and workmanship as well as to appearance. If you are not satisfied with the quality or price of any fixture purchased from us, simply return the fixture to us and we will refund your money.

RETURN OF GOODS

Please do not return any goods without first getting our permission to do so. This will greatly facilitate our giving you prompt and full adjustment. We are always glad to adjust any claims and to make good any defective equipment.

PACKING

Our packing is done by expert packers and we cannot assume responsibility for any damage or breakage of goods in transit. We will, however, do our utmost to help you obtain adjustment and replacement. Every package should be opened and inspected immediately upon delivery.

THE NILE GROUP

No.	Finish	Each Wired
8402	Chromium Gold	$ 9.80
8403	Chromium Gold	15.95
8405	Chromium Gold	23.50
8406	Chromium Gold	6.40
8412	Chromium Gold	9.50
8413	Chromium Gold	15.60
8415	Chromium Gold	22.90
8402	Orchid & Ivory or Green & Iv.	10.80
8403	Orchid & Ivory or Green & Iv.	17.40
8406	Orchid & Ivory or Green & Iv.	6.90
8412	Orchid & Ivory or Green & Iv.	9.90
8413	Orchid & Ivory or Green & Iv.	17.10

The shades for the Nile Group are made of satin glass in frost, soft gold, and pastel pinks, green, and mauve.

Current value: $650.00 – 800.00

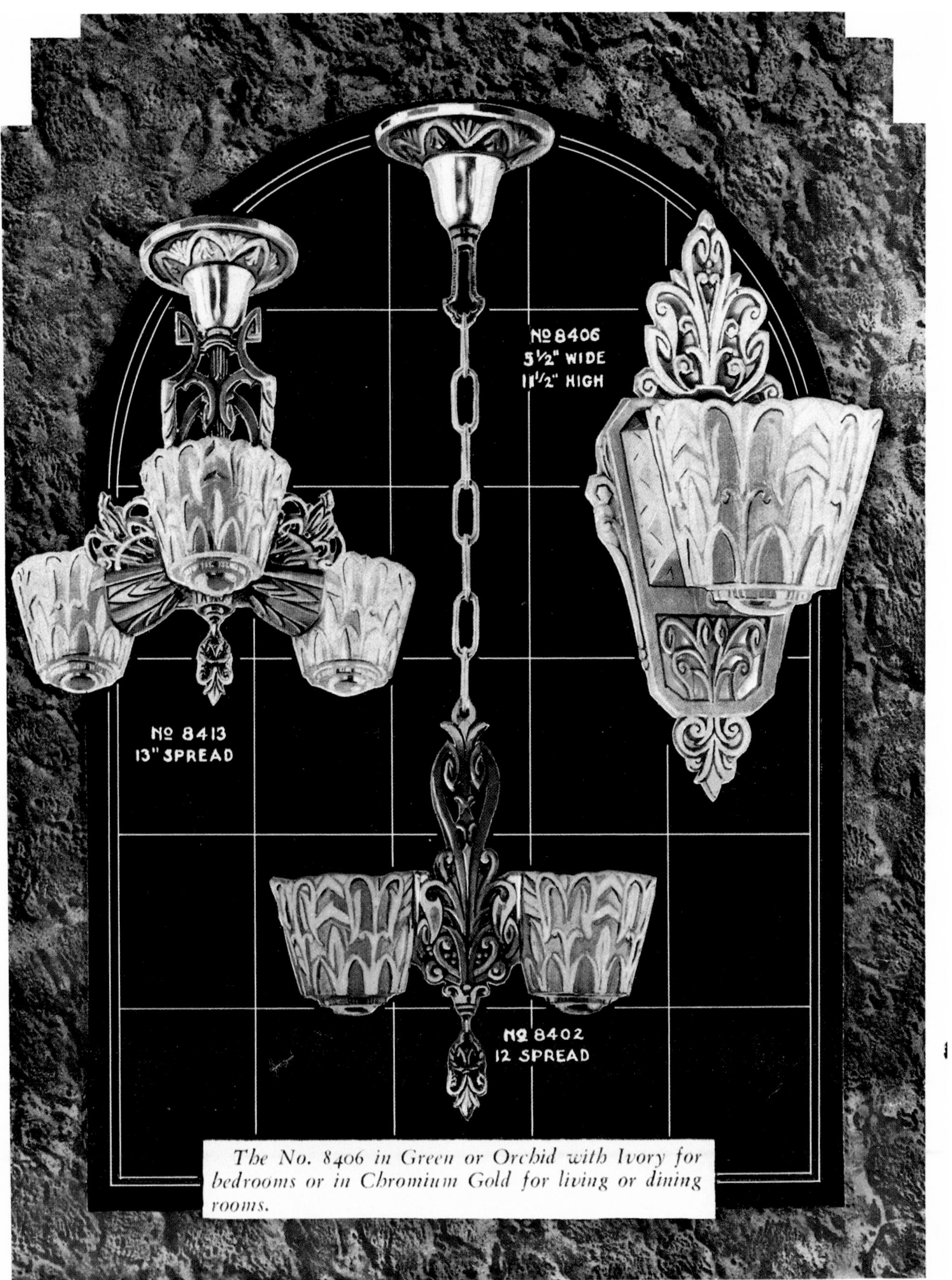

The No. 8406 in Green or Orchid with Ivory for bedrooms or in Chromium Gold for living or dining rooms.

Current value
#8402: $285.00 – 325.00
#8413: $400.00 – 550.00
#8406: $200.00 – 265.00

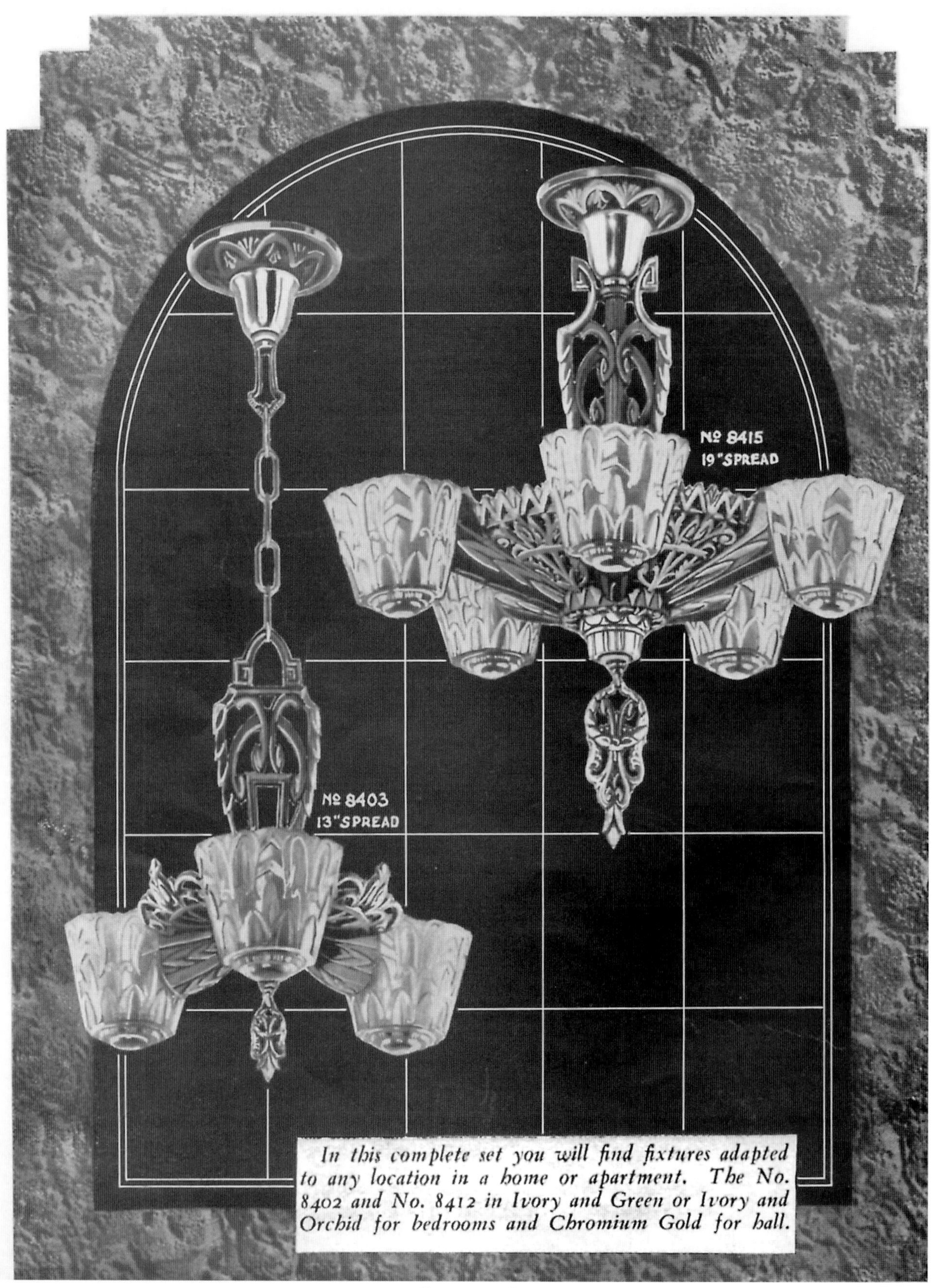

Current value
#8403: $425.00 – 575.00
#8415: $600.00 – 700.00

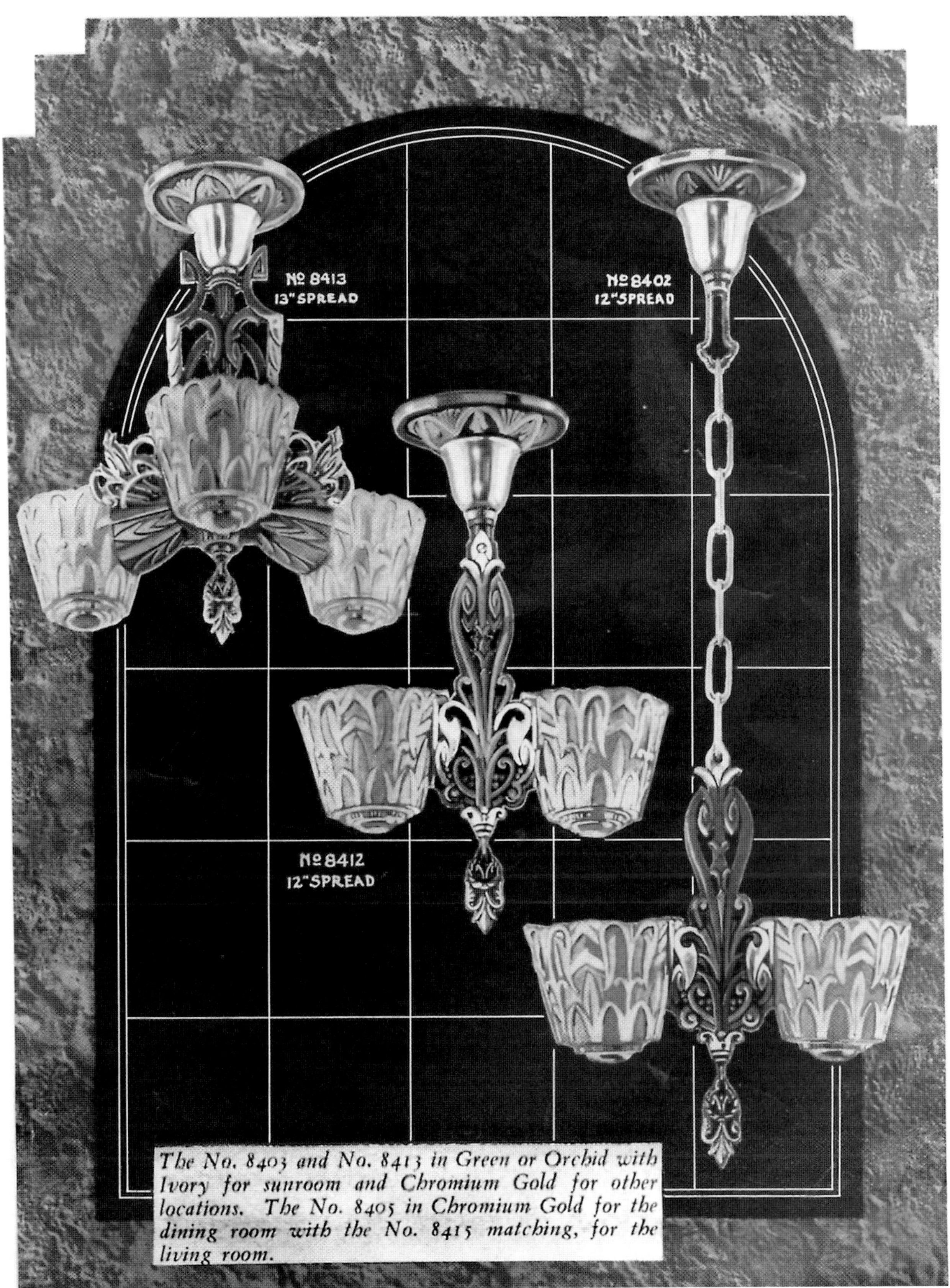

Current value
#8413: $385.00 – 500.00
#8412: $250.00 – 300.00
#8402: $285.00 – 325.00

The No. 4200 Line

The massiveness of design and the warm tones in the finish of this group of fixtures are reminiscent of Oriental splendor. This is especially true of the Cellini Gold finish, illustrated on the following page, in which the predominating color is an Oriental shade of gold enlivened with occasional touches of color.

We also make this group in Antique Bronze and Gold which is also very attractive and harmonizes especially well with certain decorative schemes.

Quality of materials used and skill in workmanship and finish are of our usual high standard.

PRICES ON No. 4200 LINE

No.	Lights	Standard Package		Wired
4215	5E	1 to Carton	KEYLESS	$22.95
4225	5E	1 to Carton	KEYLESS	22.95
4255	5E	1 to Carton	KEYLESS	21.80
4291	1E	2 to Carton, 24 to Case	KEYLESS W/PIN SWITCH	5.20
4292	2E	1 to Carton, 12 to Case	KEYLESS W/PIN SWITCH	6.42
4233	3E	1 to Carton, 6 to Case	KEYLESS	10.80
4270	1E	25 to Carton, 100 to Case	KEYLESS W/CROSS BAR	1.26
4275	1E	20 to Carton, 80 to Case	KEYLESS W/CROSS BAR	1.38
4280	1E	3 to Carton, 24 to Case	KEYLESS W/CROSS BAR	3.56

FINISHES

CELLINI GOLD or
ANTIQUE BRONZE and GOLD

THE 4200 LINE

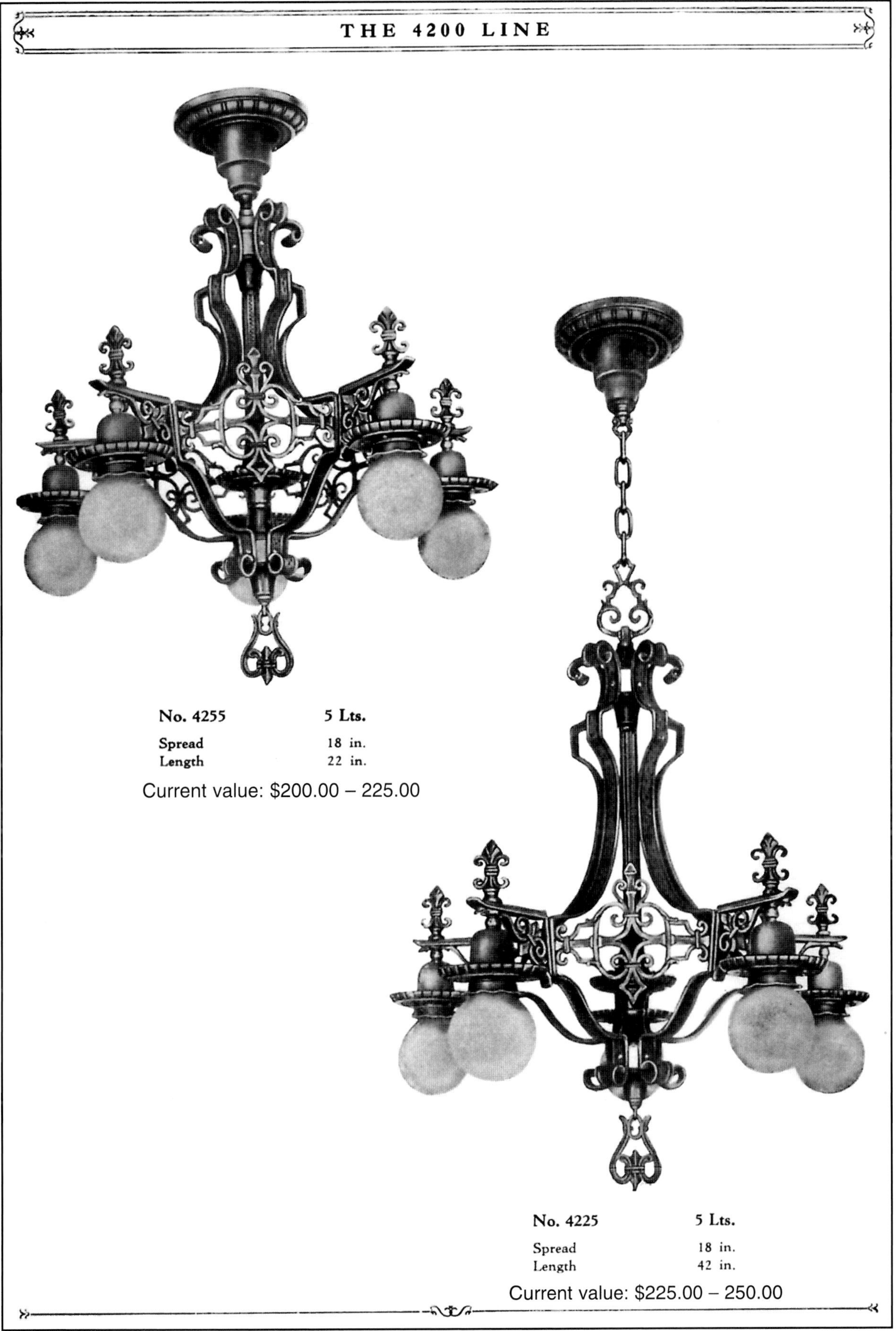

No. 4255 **5 Lts.**

Spread 18 in.
Length 22 in.

Current value: $200.00 – 225.00

No. 4225 **5 Lts.**

Spread 18 in.
Length 42 in.

Current value: $225.00 – 250.00

THE 4200 LINE

No. 4291	**1 Lt.**	**No. 4215**	**5 Lts.**	**No. 4292**	**2 Lts.**
Extension	3½ in.	Spread	18 in.	Spread	6½ in.
		Length	42 in.	Extension	3½ in.

The above illustration represents our Cellini Gold Finish.

The No. 8300 Line

Our new line of lighting fixtures illustrated on the following pages is distinctive in its massiveness of design and its unusually attractive finish.

This finish, known as Acier Gold, is a new shade of gold somewhat similar to the color generally known as Roman Gold. Here and there, throughout the design, the gleam of polished pewter is permitted to show through the surrounding gold and both shields and bands are enlivened by touches of color that effectively set-off the entire decorative scheme. The illustration on the following page scarcely does justice to this new finish.

Fixtures come wired complete except for lamps. They are shipped packed in individual cartons.

PRICES ON No. 8300 LINE

No.	Lights	Standard Package		Wired
8315	5E	1 to Carton	KEYLESS	$25.70
8325	5E	1 to Carton	KEYLESS	25.70
8355	5E	1 to Carton	KEYLESS	24.30
8391	1E	2 to Carton, 24 to Case	KEYLESS WITH PIN SW.	5.20
8392	2E	1 to Carton, 12 to Case	KEYLESS WITH PIN SW.	6.75
8335	1E	1 to Carton, 6 to Case	KEYLESS	7.15
8333	3E	1 to Carton, 6 to Case	KEYLESS	12.00
8375	1E	3 to Carton, 24 to Case	KEYLESS WITH C/B	1.65

FINISH

ACIER GOLD

THE 8300 LINE

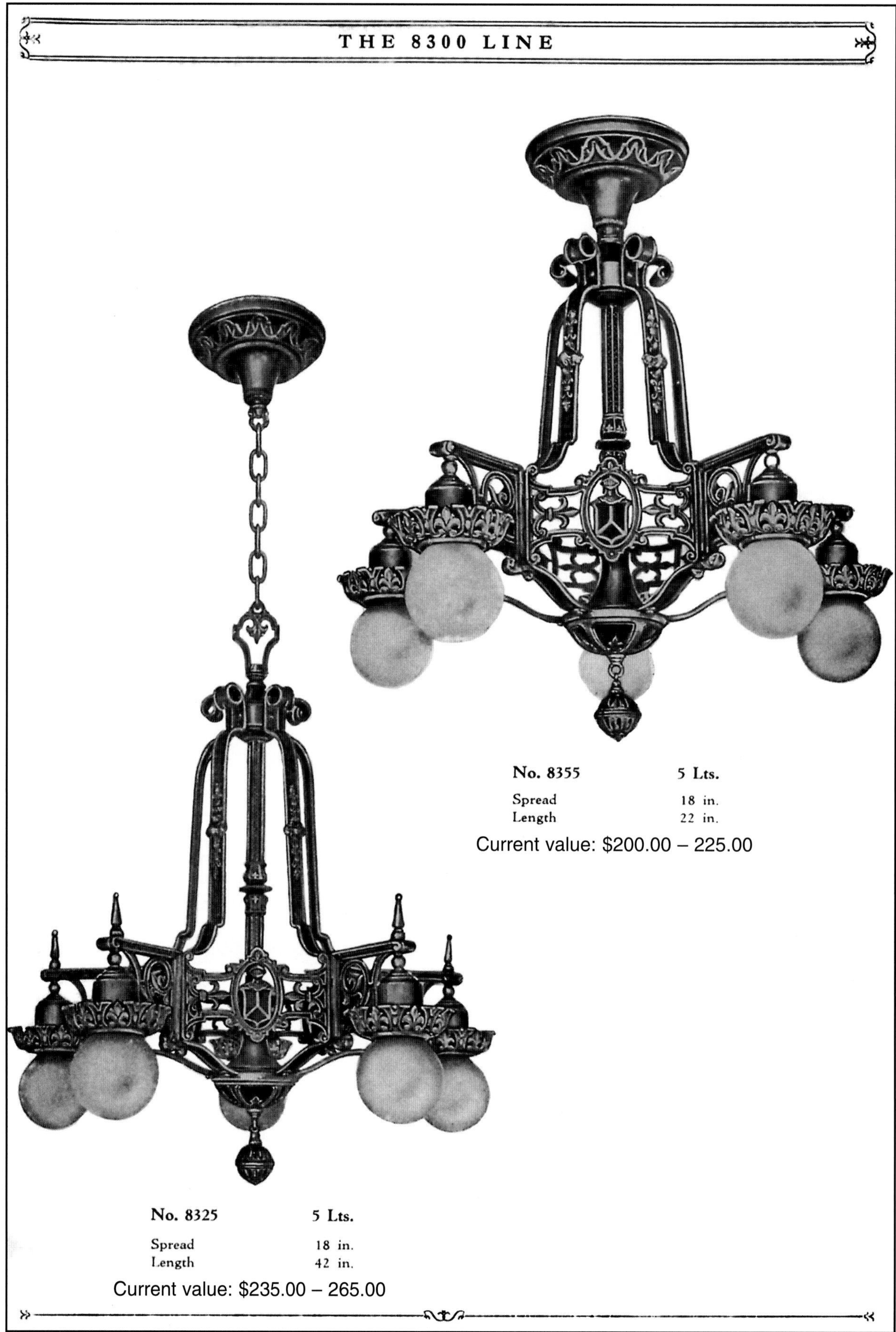

No. 8355 **5 Lts.**

Spread 18 in.
Length 22 in.

Current value: $200.00 – 225.00

No. 8325 **5 Lts.**

Spread 18 in.
Length 42 in.

Current value: $235.00 – 265.00

THE 8300 LINE

No. 8375 **1 Lt.**
Diameter at Top 6½ in.
Current value: $20.00 – 30.00

No. 8333 **3 Lts.**
Harp 7 in. wide; 15 in. long
Length 42 in.
Current value: $145.00 – 175.00

No. 8335 **1 Lt.**
Harp 6 in. wide; 12½ in. long
Length 42 in.
Current value: $100.00 – 125.00

THE 8300 LINE

No. 8391	1 Lt.	No. 8315	5 Lts.	No. 8392	2 Lts.
Extension	3½ in.	Spread	18 in.	Extension	3½ in.
		Length	42 in.	Spread	6½ in.

The above illustration shows our Acier Gold Finish

THE 8600 LINE

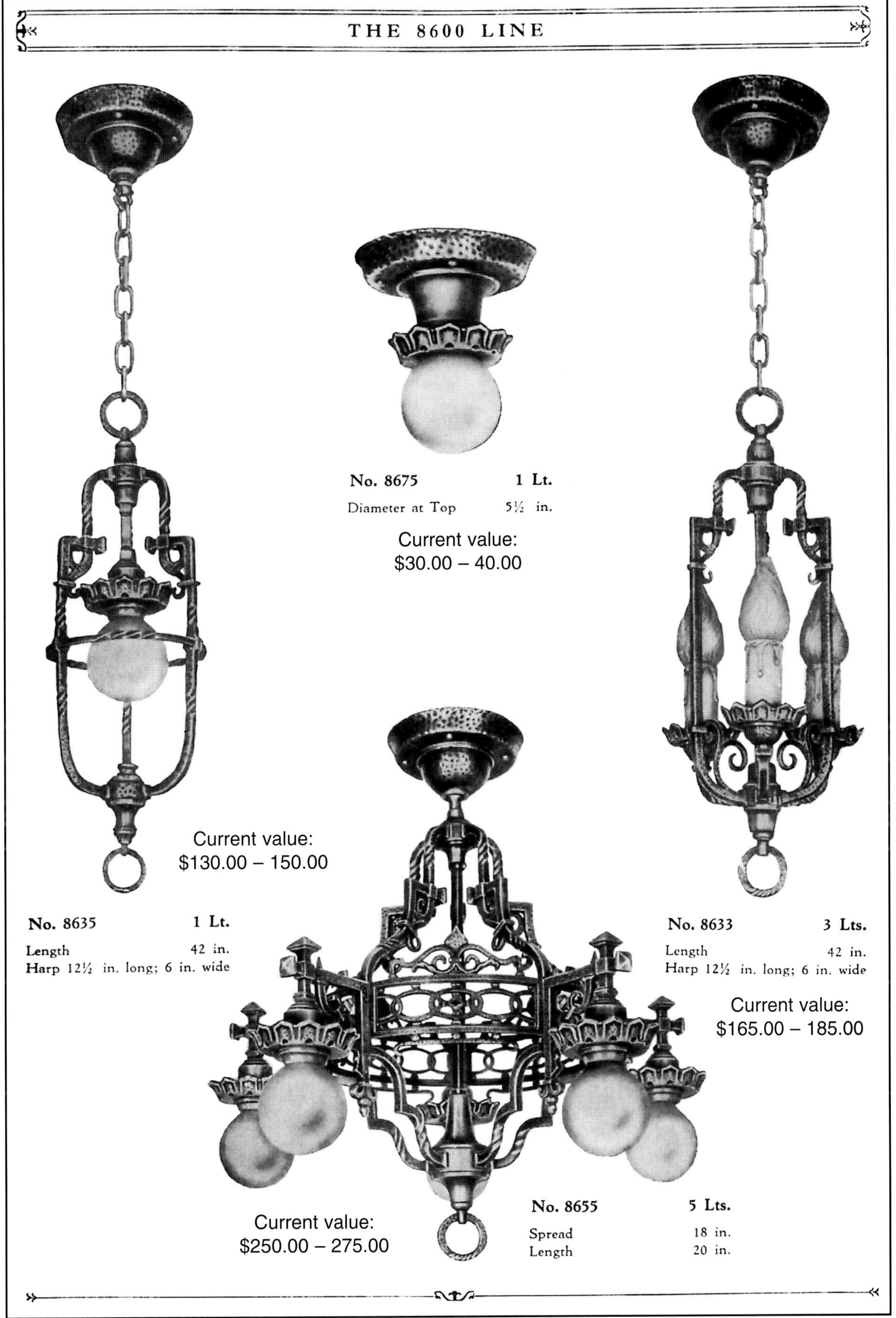

No. 8675 **1 Lt.**
Diameter at Top 5½ in.

Current value:
$30.00 – 40.00

No. 8635 **1 Lt.**
Length 42 in.
Harp 12½ in. long; 6 in. wide

Current value:
$130.00 – 150.00

No. 8633 **3 Lts.**
Length 42 in.
Harp 12½ in. long; 6 in. wide

Current value:
$165.00 – 185.00

No. 8655 **5 Lts.**
Spread 18 in.
Length 20 in.

Current value:
$250.00 – 275.00

The No. 8600 Line

REMINISCENT of Ancient England, the rugged finish and massive construction of the Artcraft 8600 Line impart a typically Tudor touch that harmonizes particularly well with the simpler decorative themes.

The hammered wrought brass contributes materially to the beauty of this group of fixtures.

PRICES ON NO. 8600 LINE

No.	Lights	Standard Package			Wired
8615	5E	1 to Case	KEYLESS		$38.40
8625	5E	1 to Case	"		38.40
8655	5E	1 to Case	"		38.40
*8623	3E	1 to Case	"		21.42
†8653	3E	1 to Case	"		21.42
8691	1E	2 to Carton, 24 to Case	"	W/PIN SWITCH	6.30
8699	2E	1 to Carton, 12 to Case	"	" "	8.10
8692	2E	1 to Carton, 12 to Case	"	" "	8.10
8635	1E	1 to Carton, 6 to Case	"		10.20
8633	3E	1 to Carton, 6 to Case	"		15.00
8675	1E	3 to Carton, 24 to Case	"	W/CROSS BAR	1.80
8680	1E	1 to Carton, 12 to Case	"	" "	6.00

*No. 8623—3 Lights, is similar in style to No. 8625.
†No. 8653—3 Lights, is similar in style to No. 8655.

FINISH

TUDOR

THE 8600 LINE

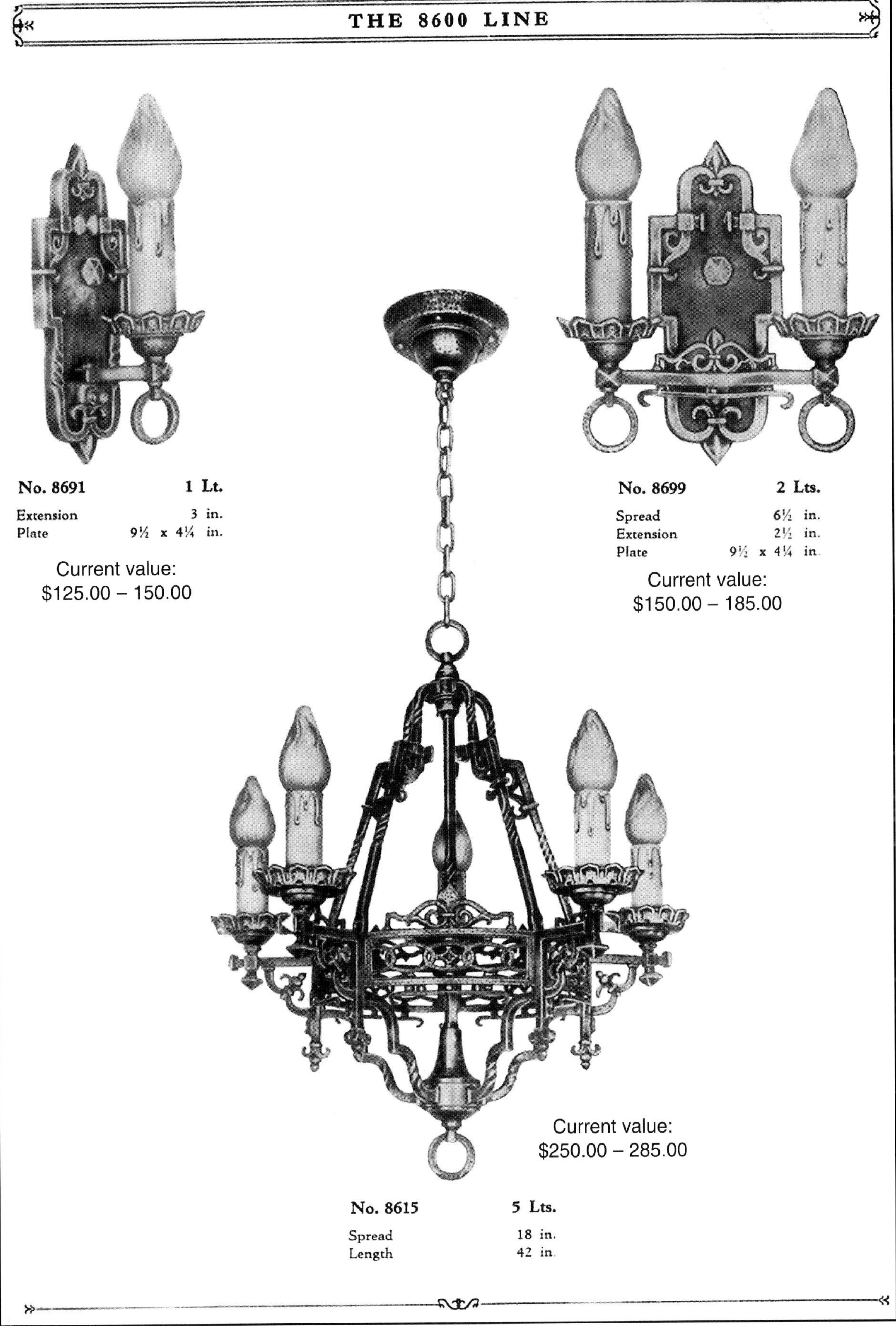

No. 8691 **1 Lt.**

Extension 3 in.
Plate 9½ x 4¼ in.

Current value:
$125.00 – 150.00

No. 8699 **2 Lts.**

Spread 6½ in.
Extension 2½ in.
Plate 9½ x 4¼ in.

Current value:
$150.00 – 185.00

Current value:
$250.00 – 285.00

No. 8615 **5 Lts.**

Spread 18 in.
Length 42 in.

THE 8600 LINE

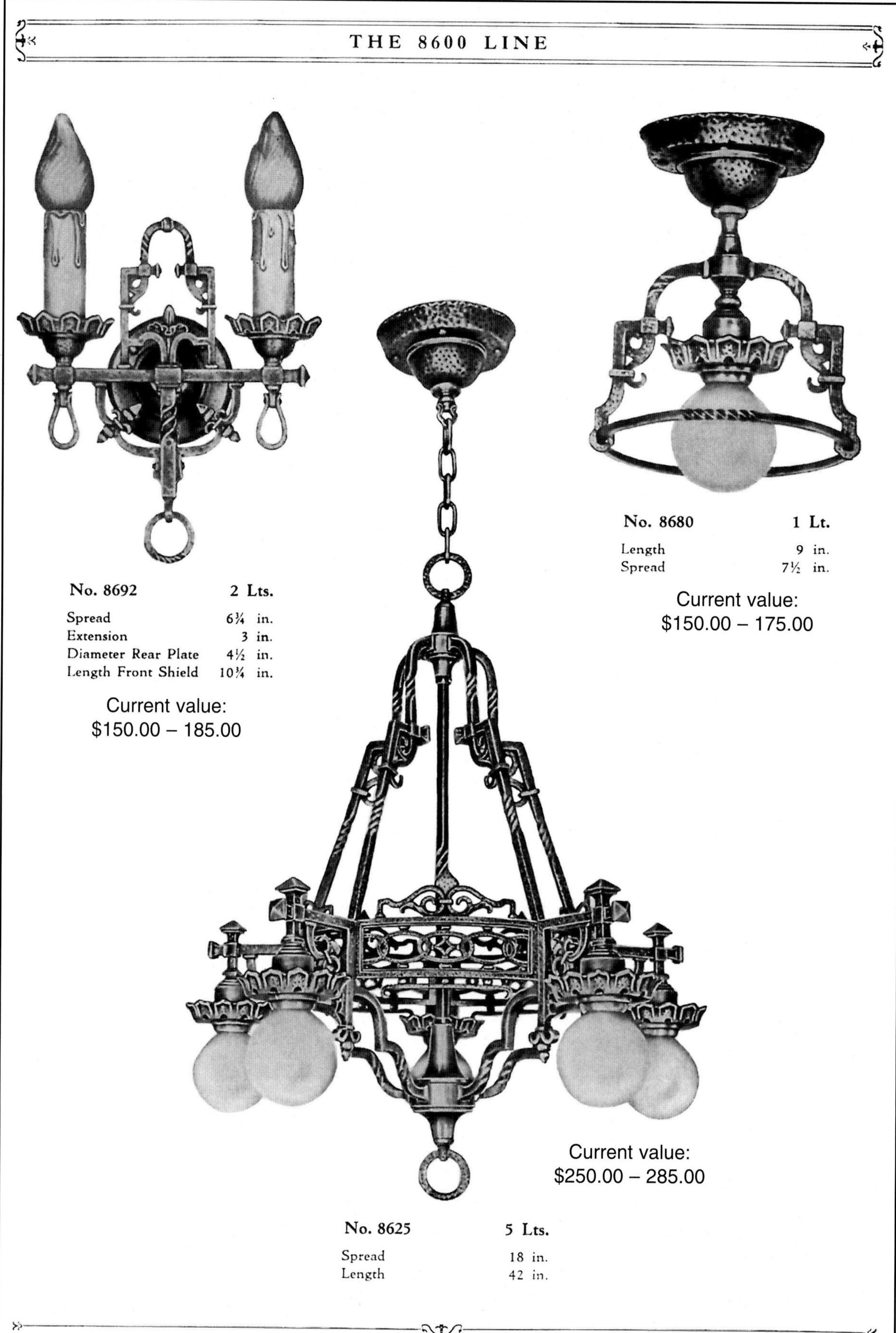

No. 8692 **2 Lts.**

Spread	6¾ in.
Extension	3 in.
Diameter Rear Plate	4½ in.
Length Front Shield	10¾ in.

Current value:
$150.00 – 185.00

No. 8680 **1 Lt.**

Length	9 in.
Spread	7½ in.

Current value:
$150.00 – 175.00

Current value:
$250.00 – 285.00

No. 8625 **5 Lts.**

Spread	18 in.
Length	42 in.

The No. 8700 Line

THIS group of fixtures, one of our recent creations, is sufficiently distinguished in design and finish to enhance the beauty of the modern home.

On the following page we illustrate in color the finish, Fierro Gold, in which this line is made. The illustration can, in only a modest way, convey the beauty of this new finish.

PRICES ON No. 8700 LINE

No.	Lights	Standard Package		Wired
8715	5E	1 to Carton	KEYLESS	$30.00
8725	5E	1 to Carton	KEYLESS	30.00
8755	5E	1 to Carton	KEYLESS	26.25
8791	1E	2 to Carton, 24 to Case	KEYLESS WITH PIN SW.	5.70
8799	2E	1 to Carton, 12 to Case	KEYLESS WITH PIN SW.	7.50
8733	3E	1 to Carton, 6 to Case	KEYLESS	14.00
8775	1E	3 to Carton, 24 to Case	KEYLESS W/CROSS BAR	1.65

FINISH

FIERRO GOLD

THE 8700 LINE

No. 8755 **5 Lts.**

Spread 18 in.
Length 16 in.

Current value:
$225.00 – 250.00

No. 8725 **5 Lts.**

Spread 18 in.
Length 42 in.

Current value:
$250.00 – 275.00

THE 8700 LINE

No. 8791	1 Lt.	No. 8715	5 Lts.	No. 8799	2 Lts.
Extension	3 in.	Spread	18 in.	Extension	3 in.
		Length	42 in.	Spread	6½ in.

The above illustration shows our Fierro Gold Finish

MELETIO ELECTRICAL SUPPLY COMPANY, DALLAS, TEXAS

No. 2735 *Six-Light*
5 outside — 1 in center
Spread 22″ Length 42″
Trimmed with crystal pencil prisms

No. 2745 *Six-Light*
5 outside — 1 in center
Spread 22″ Length 42″
Trimmed with crystal pencil prisms

Fixtures above have five exterior lights which are controlled by a switch at the base of the chandelier, allowing the use of the center light as an individual unit when so desired.

FINISH: **BRONZLUME**

No.	Price Wired Complete
2735	$19.90
2745	19.90

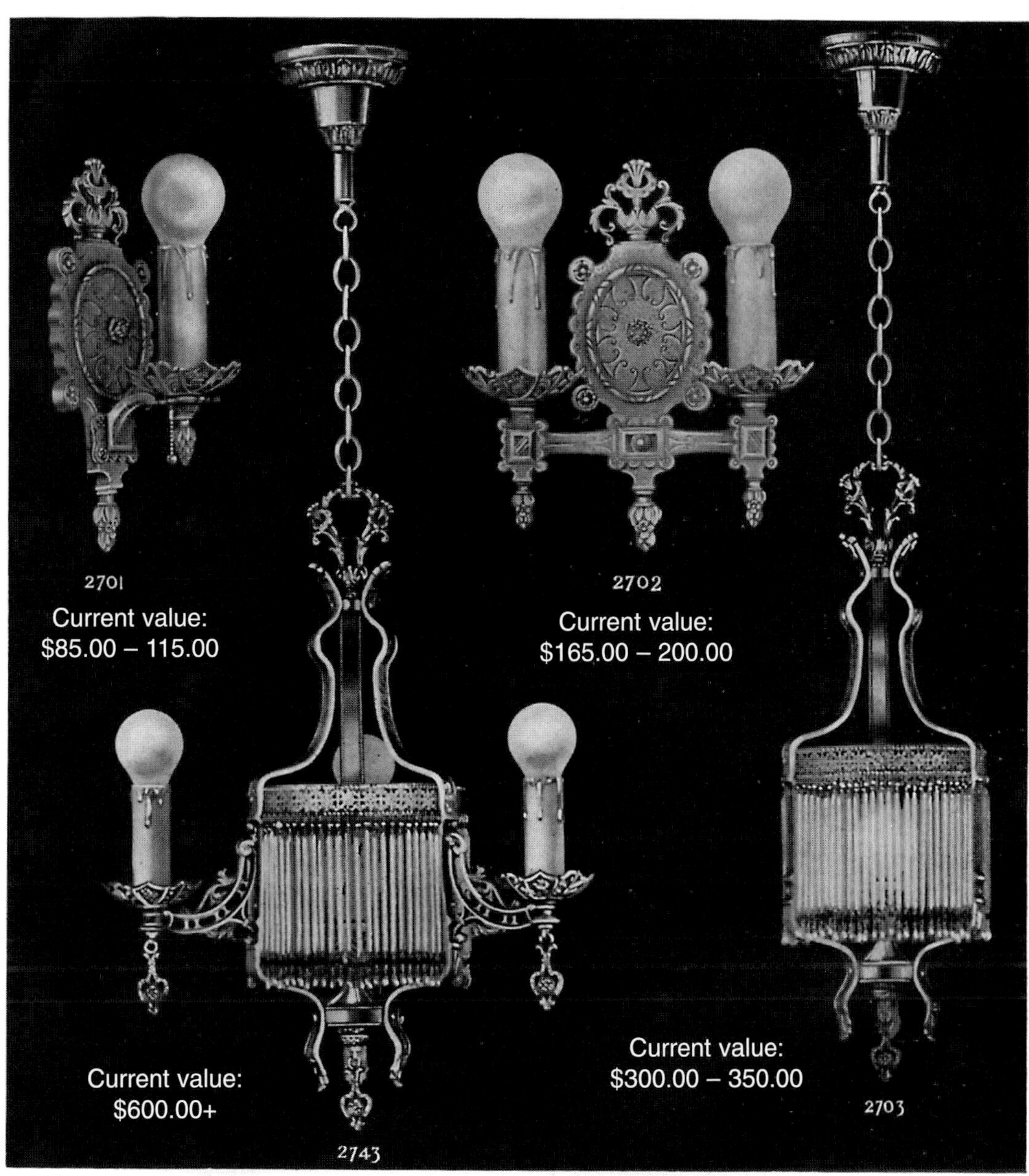

No. 2701 *One-Light*
Wall Plate 11¼"x4¼"
Extends 5"

No. 2702 *Two-Light*
Wall Plate 11¼"x4¼"
Extends 4" Spread 9"

No. 2703 *One-Light*
Diameter 10" Length 42"
Trimmed with crystal pencil prisms

*No. 2743 *Four-Light*
No. 2733 Four-Light Drop
3 outside — 1 inside
Spread 21" Length 42"
Trimmed with crystal pencil prisms

*Fixture No. 2743 has three exterior lights controlled by a switch at the base of the chandelier, allowing use of center light as an individual unit when so desired.

No.	Price Wired Complete
2701	$ 5.50
2702	7.50
2703	11.50

FINISH: **BRONZLUME**

No.	Price Wired Complete
2733	$17.00
2743	17.00

MELETIO ELECTRICAL SUPPLY COMPANY, DALLAS, TEXAS

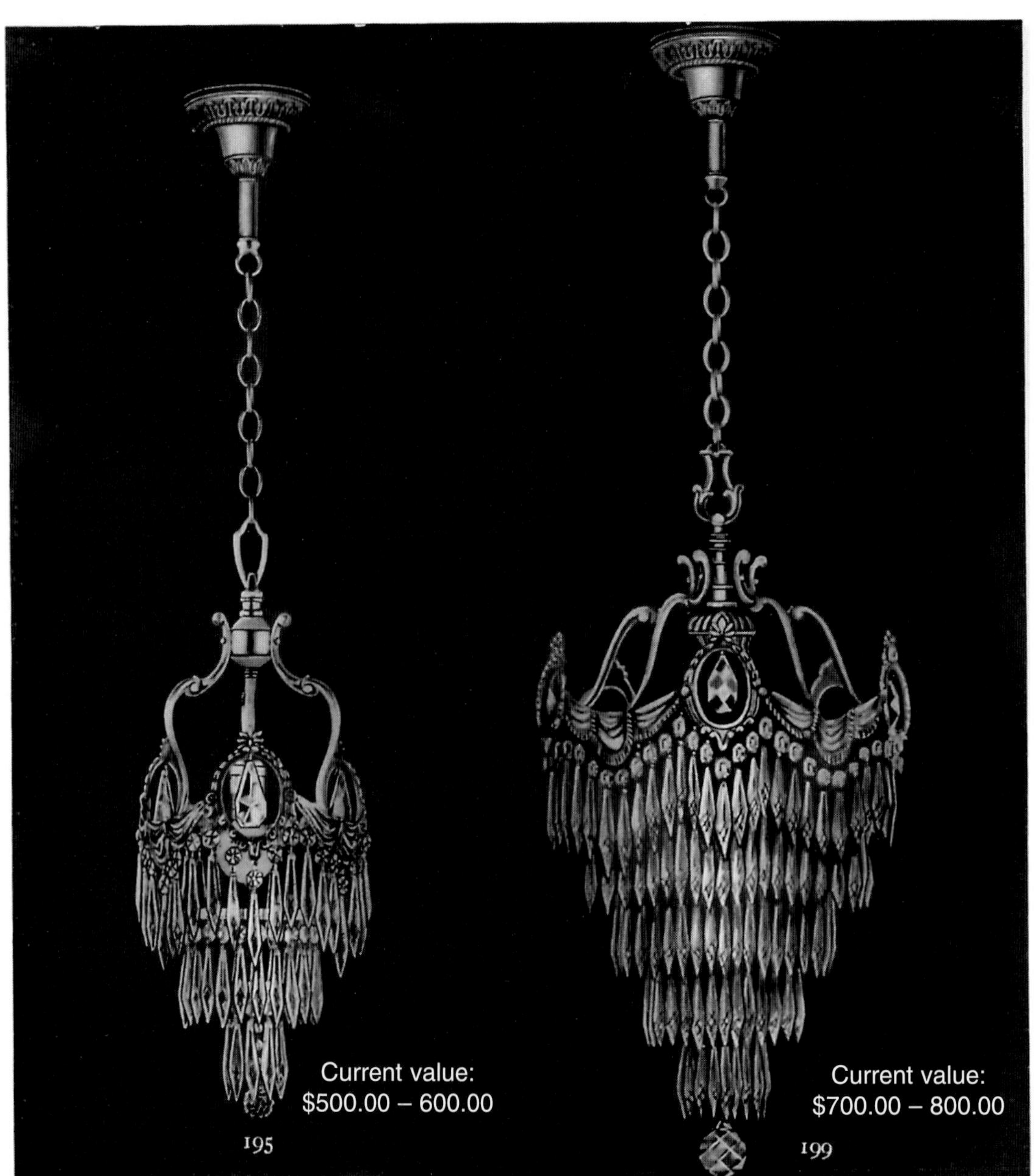

No. 195 *One-Light*
CAST BRASS
Length 42″
Width 8″
Three Rows, Trimmed with 62-3″ Crystal U Drops and Three Amber Pendalogues

No. 199 *Three-Light*
CAST BRASS
Length 42″
Width 14″
Five Rows, Trimmed with 180-3″ Crystal U Drops and Five Amber Pendalogues

FINISH: **SILVER AND BLACK**

No.	Price Wired Complete
195	$27.00
199	38.00

No. 8918—3 Lights

Extreme spread........16 inches
Length ....22 inches
Finish: Silver

Wired Complete.............$55.50

Current value: $650.00 – 775.00

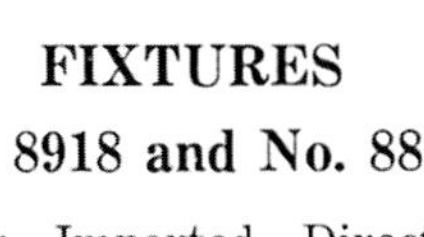

FIXTURES
No. 8918 and No. 8874

Are Being Imported Directly from Europe. Both Fixtures are all Glass and are Equipped with Genuine W o o d-Polished Crystals. Cut Glass Designs in Hoods and Canopies.

No. 8874—3 Lights

Extreme Spread......18 inches
Length ....22 inches
Finish: Silver

Wired Complete...........$58.50

Current value: $725.00 – 775.00

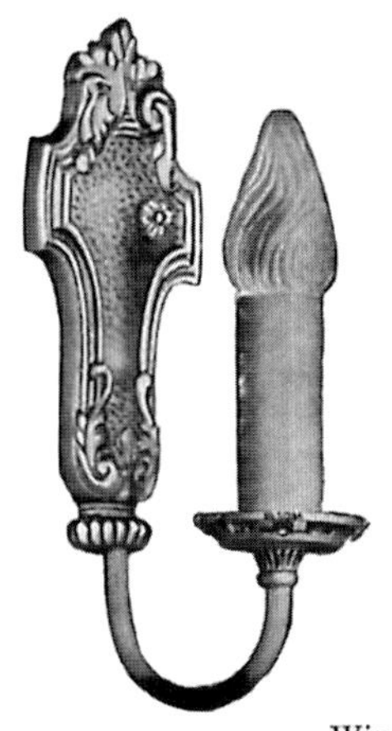

Wired Complete

No. 328—1 Lt. Bracket....**$6.30**
No. 329—2 Lt. Bracket.... **9.75**

Each candle cup has 7 crystals as on No. 8918, No. 8874 and No. 2610. Equipped with canopy switch.

Finish: Silver

Current value
1 light bracket: $165.00 – 195.00
2 light bracket: $225.00 – 250.00

No. 2610 is a High Grade Crystal Chandelier, Finished in a Durable Silver. Comes Wired Complete in Individual Container.

Current value
14" spread: $625.00 – 700.00
12" spread: $600.00 – 675.00
Finish – Silver

No. 2610—3 Lights

Wired Complete

No. 2610/14, spread 14 inches........**$27.00**
No. 2616/12, spread 12 inches........ **24.00**

Finish: Silver

No. 2201 *One-Light*

Wall Plate 11¾"x4¼" Extends 5"

Metal backplate in Maroon

No. 2202 *Two-Light*

Spread 9" Extends 4½"

Wall Plate 11¾"x4¾"

Metal backplate in Maroon

No. 2245 *Five-Light*

Spread 19" Length 42"

FINISH: **BRONZLUME**

No.	Price Wired Complete
2201	$ 4.50
2202	6.50
2245	13.90

No. 2243 *Three-Light*
No. 2233 Three-Light Drop
Spread 19″
Length 42″

No. 2235 *Five-Light*
Spread 19″
Length 42″

FINISH: **BRONZLUME**

No.	Price Wired Complete
2233	$12.50
2243	12.50
2235	13.90

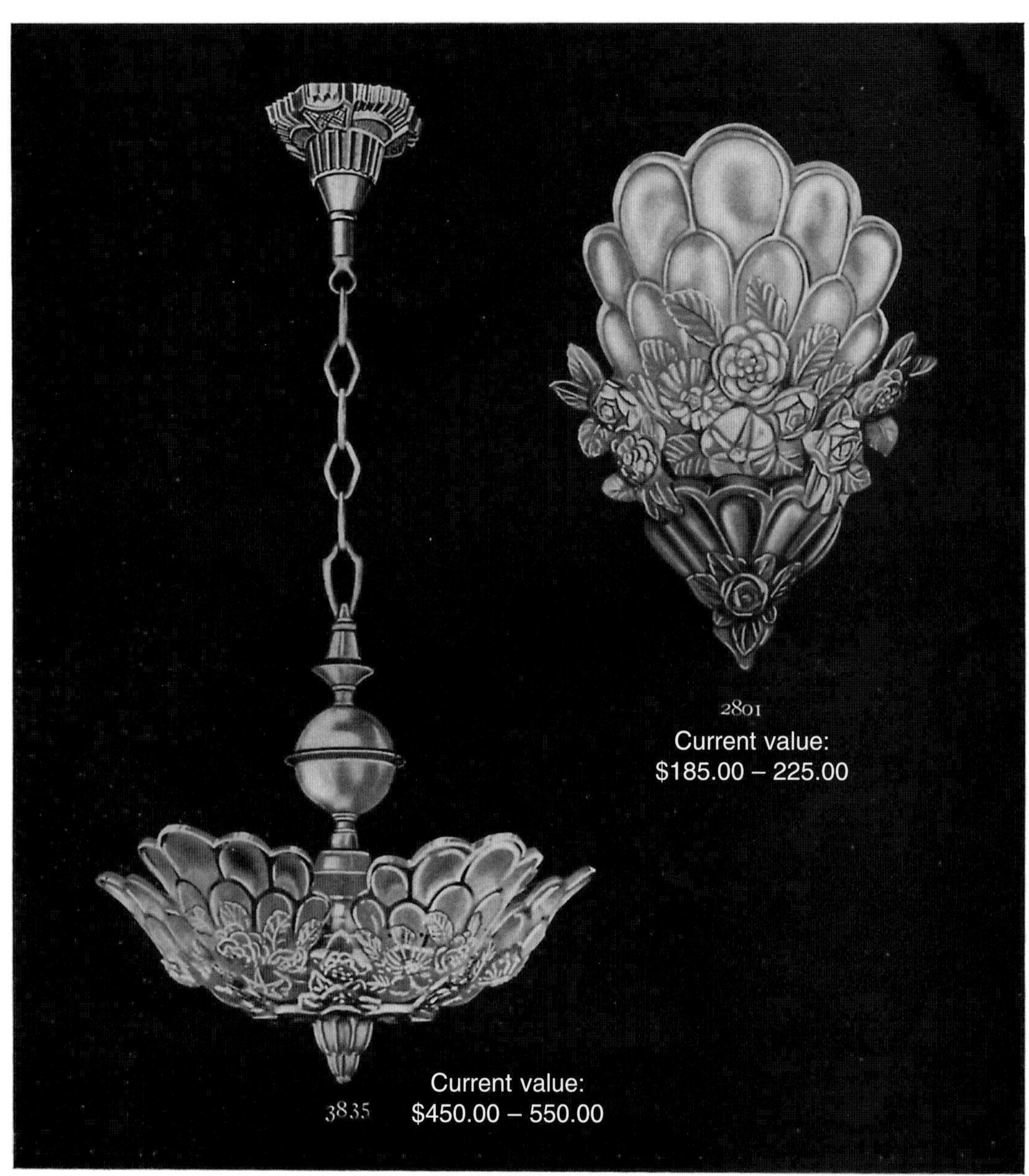

No. 3835 *Five-Light*

Diameter 18″ Length 42″

No. 2801 *One-Light*

Wall Plate 5¾″x9¼″ Extends 5½″

FINISH: **ANTIQUE GOLD PLATED**

"Hand wrought glass panels in French Crystal or Honey Color as desired."

No.	Price Wired Complete
3835	$38.00
2801	12.00

NO. 91

An appropriate piece for breakfast room or sun room. Hanger is finished in gold polychrome or IVORY-TINT. 10-inch ball is tinted, with parrot of brilliant colors.

Specify finish when ordering.

Price Wired..**$7.50**

NO. 92

A new design for bed room or sun room. Finish: IVORY-TINT. Equipped with 4-inch shades of attractive design. Extra shades furnished at $1.00 each, list.

Price Wired... ....**$7.50**

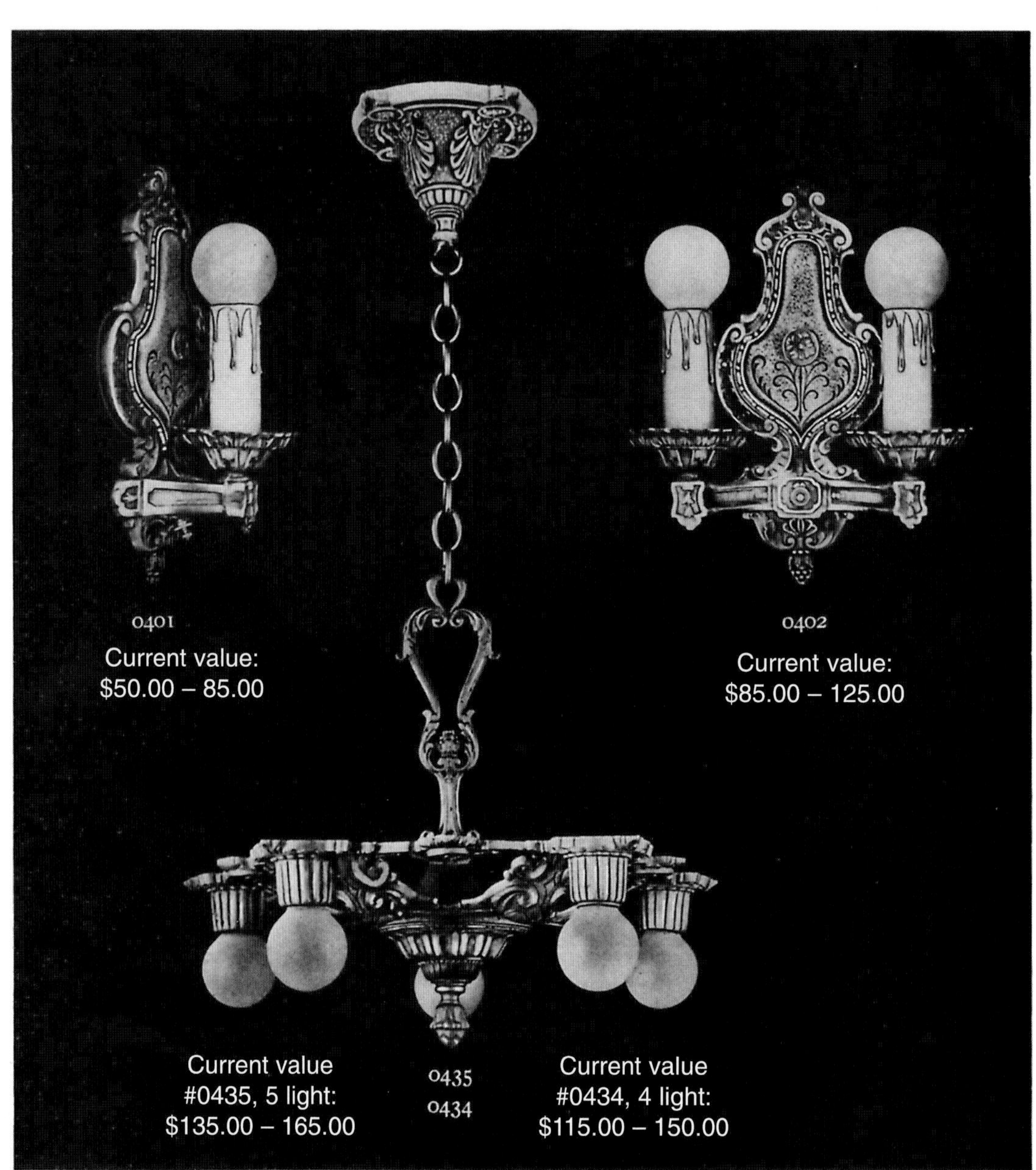

No. 0401 *One-Light*
Wall Plate 11½"x5"
Extends 4½"

No. 0435 *Five-Light*
No. 0434 Four-Light
Length 42" Spread 17"

No. 0402 *Two-Light*
Wall Plate 11½"x5"
Extends 4¼"

BRONZLUME — FLORALUME

"Two Beautiful Finishes."

"Our complete stock assures prompt delivery of your requirements."

No.	Price Wired Complete
0401	$3.80
0402	4.80
0435	9.70
0434	9.00

No. 0403 *One-Light*
Length 42″
8″x6″ Amber Crackled
Glass Clyinder

No. 0415 *Five-Light*
No. 0414 Four-Light
Depth 5½″ Spread 18″

No. 0432 *Two-Light*
No. 0433 Three-Light
Length 42″ Spread 13½″

BRONZLUME — FLORALUME

"Two Beautiful Finishes."

"Wired complete — Packed one to a box."

No.	Price Wired Complete	No.	Price Wired Complete
0403	$10.50	0433	6.30
0415	8.90	0432	5.00
0414	6.90		

MELETIO ELECTRICAL SUPPLY COMPANY, DALLAS, TEXAS

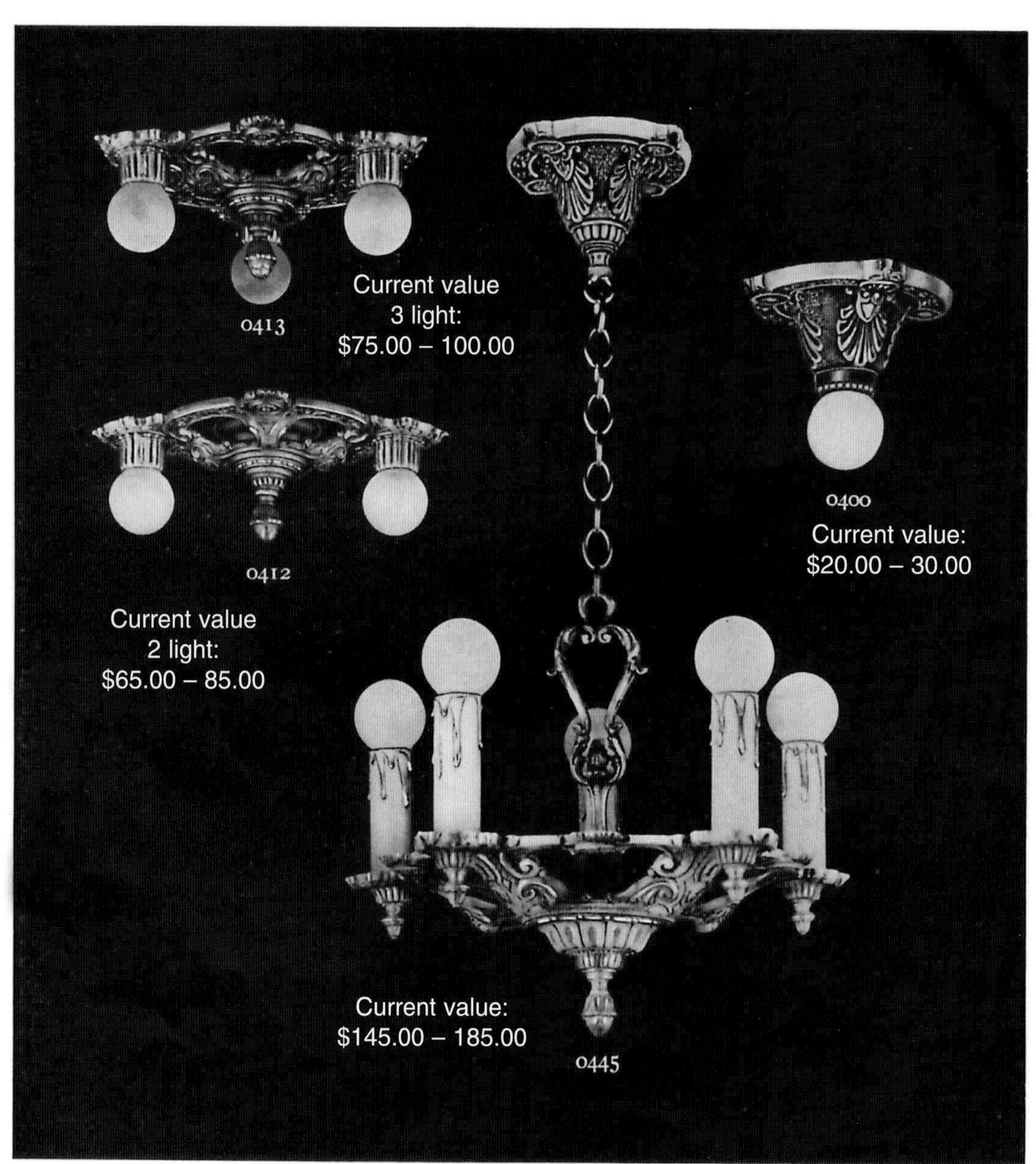

No. 0413 *Three-Light*
No. 0412 Two-Light
Depth 4½″ Spread 12½″

No. 0445 *Five-Light*
Length 42″ Spread 16½″

No. 0400 *One-Light*
Depth 3″
Diameter 6½″

BRONZLUME — FLORALUME

"Two Beautiful Finishes."

"Exceedingly moderate in price — yet appealing in design and finish."

No.	Price Wired Complete
0413	$4.05
0412	3.00
0400	1.50
0445	9.90

MELETIO ELECTRICAL SUPPLY COMPANY, DALLAS, TEXAS

LIGHTING EQUIPMENT FOR THE KITCHEN AND BATH

No. K-408

CEILING UNIT

Diameter of Glass: 8½ inches.
Holder: White Enamel.
Keyless.

Wired Complete..........................**$2.00**
Glass Only.................................... **1.30**

Current value: $50.00 – 60.00

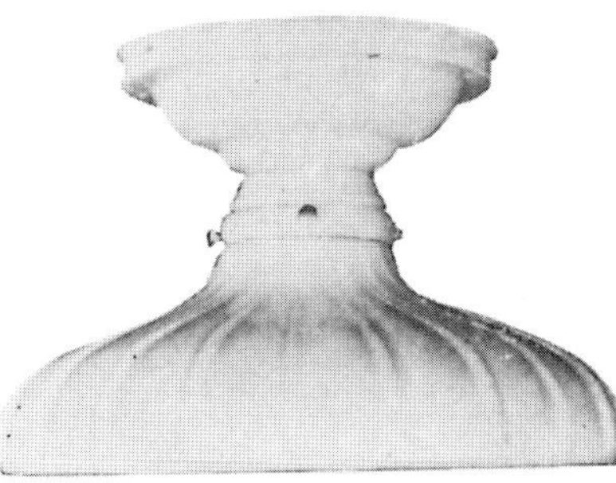

No. K-1008

CEILING UNIT

Diameter of Glass: 8 inches.
Holder: White Enamel
Keyless.

Wired Complete..........................**$1.50**

Current value: $35.00 – 45.00

No. K-408-D

CEILING UNIT

Diameter of Glass: 8½ inches.
Holder: White Enamel.
Keyless.

Glass is Striped in any of the Following Colors:
Red, Blue, Black, Apple Green, Orange.

SPECIFY COLOR WHEN ORDERING.

Wired Complete..........................**$2.40**

Current value: $70.00 – 90.00

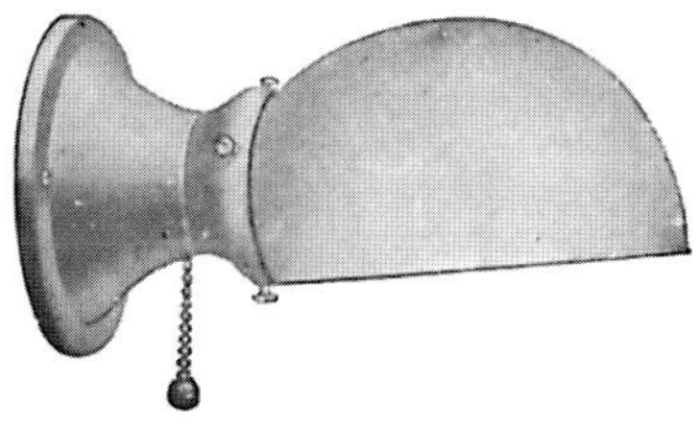

No. P-10
WALL BRACKET
Holder: White Enamel.
Pull Chain

Wired Complete..........................**$1.80**

K-10
WALL BRACKET
Holder: White Enamel.
Keyless.

Wired Complete..........................**$1.50**

Current value: $35.00 – 45.00

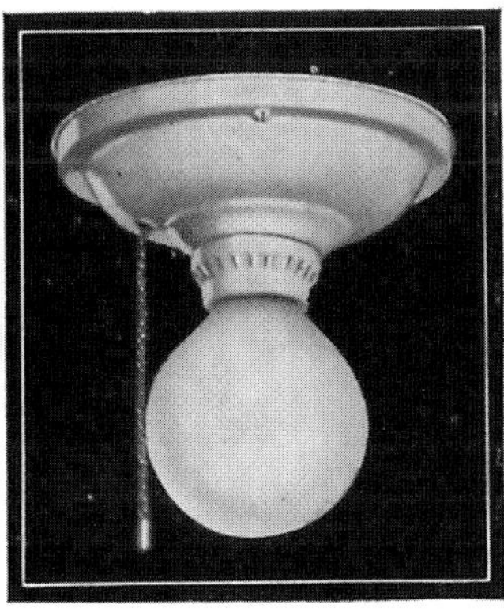

No. P-8117
CEILING LIGHT
White Enamel. Pull Chain

Wired Complete..........................**$1.00**

No. K-8117
CEILING LIGHT
White Enamel. Keyless.

Wired Complete..........................**$ .50**

Current value: $25.00 – 30.00

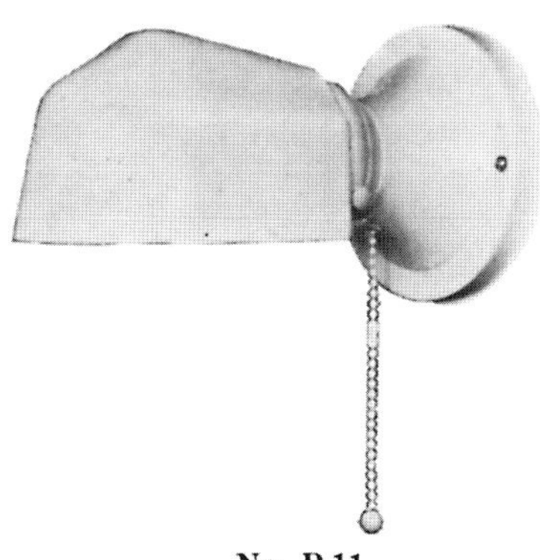

No. P-11
WALL BRACKET
Holder: White Enamel.
Pull Chain

Wired Complete..........................**$2.10**

No. K-11
WALL BRACKET
Holder: White Enamel.
Keyless.

Wired Complete..........................**$1.80**

Current value: $40.00 – 50.00

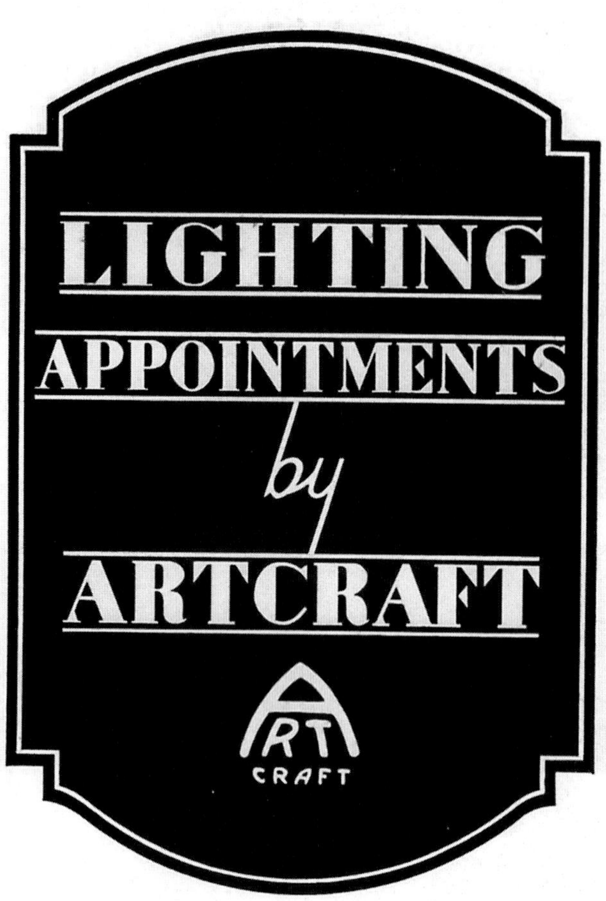

ORIGINAL IN DESIGN

In addition to the careful consideration always given to the matter of design, especial thought has been devoted to the selection of a wide range of beautiful color combinations so that every individual taste in decorative color harmony might be satisfied.

All of these fixtures are made entirely of brass and only the best lacquers and enamels obtainable are employed to give them their beautiful and lasting finish.

We feel certain that among the designs and color combinations shown on the preceding pages are many items that will be of definite interest to you and your clients.

ARTCRAFT BEDROOM LINE

---EXCLUSIVE---

* See opposite page for names of finishes illustrated below.

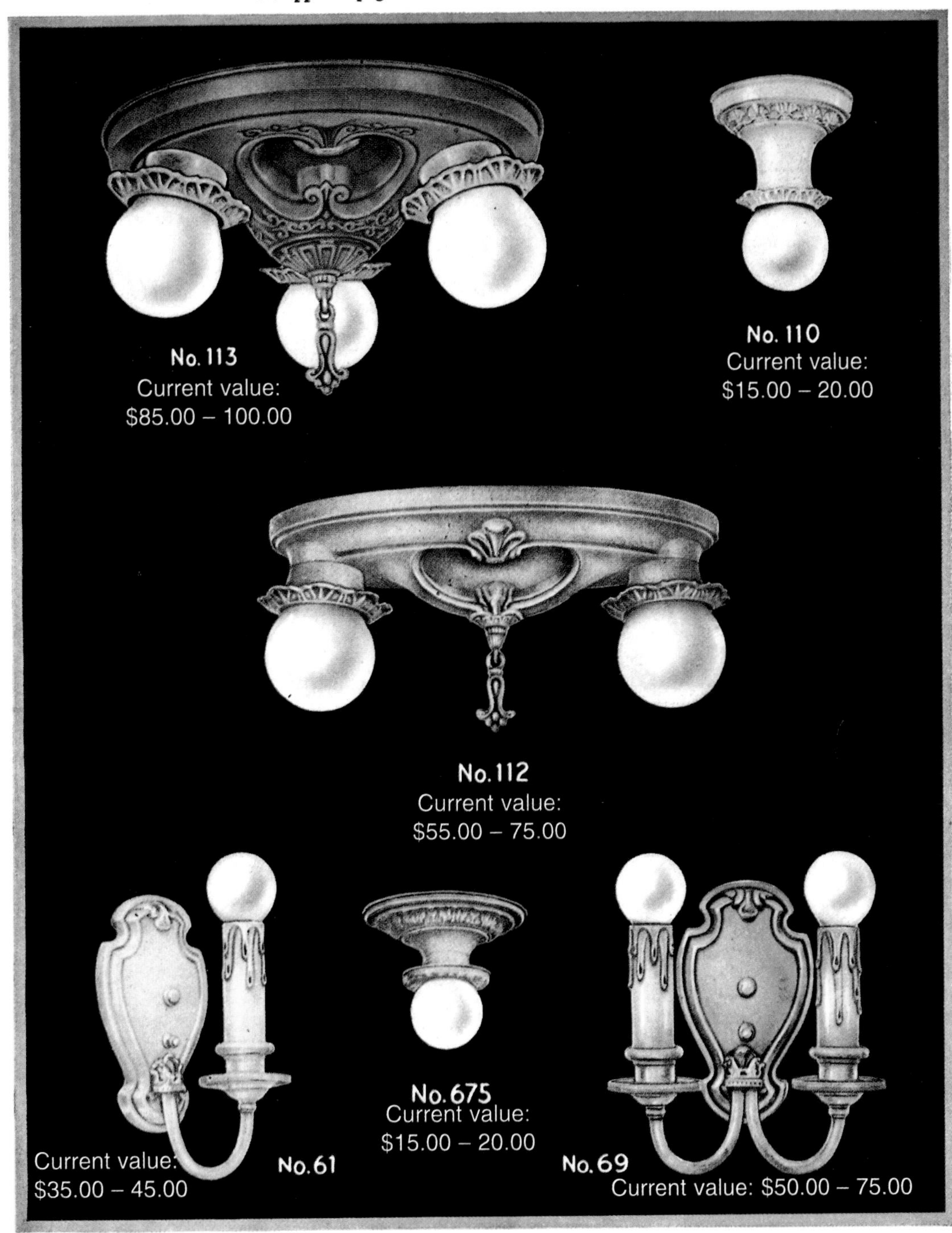

No. 113—3 Lights
Spread 11 inches

No. 112—2 Lights
12 inch Oval

No. 110—1 Light
Diameter at top 5¼ inches

No. 61—1 Light
Extension 4½ inches

No. 675—1 Light
Diameter at top 7 inches

No. 69—2 Lights
Spread 6½ inches

MELETIO ELECTRICAL SUPPLY COMPANY, DALLAS, TEXAS

EXTERIOR LANTERNS

NO. 2010-L

Flemish Copper

Lantern 6 inches wide
Wired Complete........................$10 00

Current value: $145.00 – 175.00

No. 2020-B-102

A BRONZE LANTERN

of Rare Beauty, Designed for use where a Large Lantern is Needed. Leaded Panels of Amber Glass.

Wired Complete........................$24.00

Current value: $250.00 – 300.00

NO. 2010-B-100

Flemish Copper

Lantern 6 inches wide
Wired Complete........................$12.00

Current value: $155.00 – 185.00

NO. 1092-B-29

Antique Copper

Length Over All 10¾ inches.
Lantern 6½ inches wide.

Wired Complete........................$14.50

Current value: $150.00 – 200.00

Current value:
$150.00 – 175.00
each

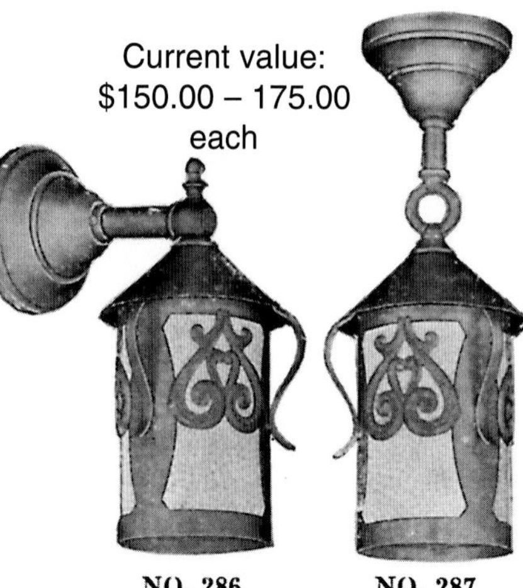

NO. 286 NO. 287

Antique Copper
Amber Glass
Lantern size 8½" x 6".
No. 286—Wired Complete..$6.30
No. 287—Wired Complete.. 6.30

Current value:
$165.00 – 225.00

NO. 1095-L

Antique Copper

Length Over All 12½ inches.
Lantern 6½ inches wide.
Wired Complete $14.50

MELETIO ELECTRICAL SUPPLY COMPANY, DALLAS, TEXAS

EXTERIOR LANTERNS

NO. 1041-B-15
Made of Rustless Metal
Finished in Natural Swedish Iron with Amber Glass.
Length Over All 10¾ inches
Wired Complete **$5.90**
Current value: $65.00 – 85.00

Current value:
$100.00 – 125.00

NO. 337-C
WALL BRACKET
NO. 336-C
CEILING LANTERN
Made of Copper. Finished in Antique Copper, with Amber Glass.
Wired Complete..........................**$4.80**

NO. 8-B-39
Made of Rustless Metal. Finished Verde Green, with Amber Glass.
Length Over All 11¾ inches
Globe 6 inches wide
Wired Complete..........................**$4.90**
Current value: $100.00 – 135.00

NO. 1043
Made of Rustless Metal. Finished in Natural Swedish Iron, with Amber Glass
Length over all 9¾ inches.
Wired Complete..........**$4.40**
Current value:
$65.00 – 85.00

Current value:
$150.00 – 195.00

NO. 1509
LANTERN AND HOUSE NUMBER
Made of Iron. Finished in Mottled Green. Number Plate is Illuminated by Lantern above. Numbers included.
Wired Complete **$14.80**
Please Specify Numbers Desired

NO. 228½
Diameter: 10 inches; Depth: 6 inches
Antique Copper, with Amber Glass
Wired Complete **$7.50**
Current value: $140.00 – 175.00

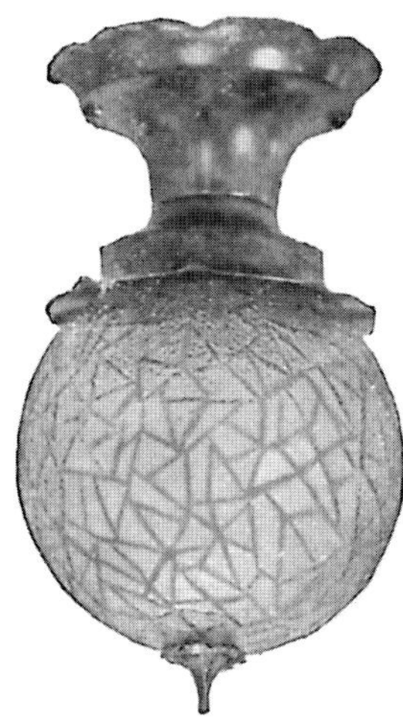

NO. 9
Made of Rustless Metal. Finished Verde Green, with Amber Glass
Length Over All 10 inches.
Globe 6 inches wide
Wired Complete......... **$4.50**
Current value:
$85.00 – 115.00

Gillinder and Sons, Inc.

GILLINDER & SONS, Inc.

PHILADELPHIA

ESTABLISHED 1861

Aerograph of factory of "Gillinder" Products, Philadelphia
(Registered)

Erected 1902. Enlarged 1912 and again 1914. Rebuilt 1920. Covers ten acres.

CATALOGUE No. 34

Our Trade Names

Gillinder *(Registered)*	Finest quality of Lead Glass.
Nebulite *(Registered)*	A fine quality of Opal Glass.
Nemalite *(Registered)*	Same grade as Nebulite with Bisque Finish.
Micra *(Registered)*	A translucent Glass with very little absorption of light.
Melilite *(Registered)*	A Cased Glass with powerful reflecting qualities, known all over the country for high-class commercial and street lighting.
Alabaster	A Cased Glass well known by all Gas and Electric Companies. Nothing better made for Street Lighting.
Glassilk *(Registered)*	A Glass moulded to resemble folds of silk and decorated in various colors showing the sheen of silk.

PLEASE OBSERVE THE FOLLOWING INSTRUCTIONS

Write all Orders plainly and avoid errors.

When referring to Orders always give the number and date of your Order.

Great care is used in packing goods properly, and delivery to the Transportation Companies in good condition, and our liability for breakage or losses ceases after we have carrier's receipt.

We cannot be responsible for delays by reason of strikes, fires, accidents or other causes beyond our control.

Our terms are One Per Cent for Cash in fifteen days or thirty days net, f. o. b. Philadelphia.

If goods are to be sent C. O. D., a sufficient amount must accompany Order to cover transportation charges both ways.

It is understood that this catalogue is loaned, so please do not alter or mutilate in any way; if you have no use for it, kindly return at our expense.

Hoping to be favored with your Orders, we are

Yours very truly,

GILLINDER & SONS, Inc.

GILLINDER & SONS, Inc., PHILADELPHIA

ESTABLISHED 1861

PLATE No. 1

Prices will vary depending on shade sizes.

No. 6671 UNIT
Plain

Current value: $15.00 – 45.00

No. 6633 UNIT
Plain

Current value: $20.00 – 60.00

No. D-1058 UNIT
Tan Decoration
Flat Etched—Italian

Current value: $35.00 – 90.00

No. D-1059 UNIT
Tan Decoration
Flat Etched—Colonial

Current value: $30.00 – 100.00

No. D-1057 UNIT
Tan Decoration
Flat Etched—French

Current value: $35.00 – 90.00

No. D-1060 UNIT
Tan Decoration
Flat Etched—Classic

Current value: $30.00 – 100.00

COMMERCIAL UNITS

Nos. 6671—D-1057—D-1058

Diameter	Height	Fitter	Wattage Recommended
9″	6½″	4″	75–100
10″	6⅜″	4″–5″	100
12″	7¾″	5″–6″	100–150
14″	8½″	6″	150–200
16″	10 ″	6″	200–300

Nos. 6633—D-1059—D-1060

Diameter	Height	Fitter	Wattage Recommended
9″	6½″	4″	75–100
10″	6⅛″	4″	100
12″	7 ″	6″	150
14″	8 ″	6″	200
16″	8½″	6″	300
18″	10¾″	6″	500

GILLINDER & SONS, Inc., PHILADELPHIA

ESTABLISHED 1861

Prices will vary depending on shade sizes.

PLATE No. 2

No. 5453 UNIT
Plain
Current value: $20.00 – 50.00

Current value:
$30.00 – 75.00

No. D-2045 UNIT
Tan Decoration
Flat Ecthed

No. 6759 UNIT
Plain
Current value: $20.00 – 50.00

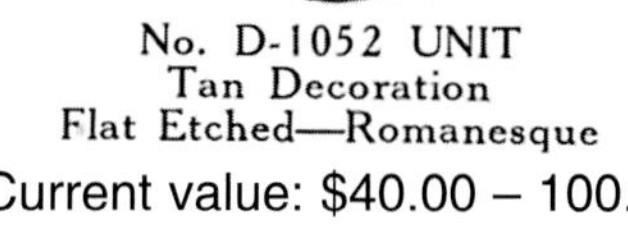

No. D-1052 UNIT
Tan Decoration
Flat Etched—Romanesque
Current value: $40.00 – 100.00

No. D-1050 UNIT
Tan Decoration
Flat Etched—Gothic
Current value: $40.00 – 100.00

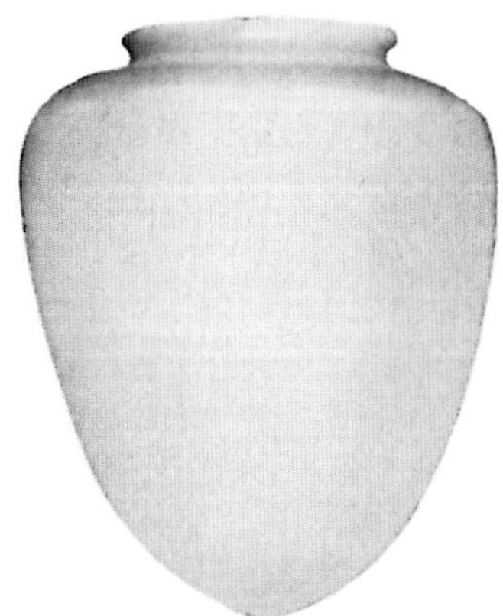

No. 6637 UNIT
Plain
Current value: $30.00 – 60.00

D-902 UNIT
Tan Decoration
Flat Etched
Current value:
$40.00 – 100.00

COMMERCIAL UNITS

Nos. 5453 — D-2045

Diam.	Height	Fitter	Wattage Recom-mended
8½"	6 "	4"	75
9 "	6½"	4"	75–100
10 "	5¾"	4"	100
12 "	7 "	6"	150
14 "	8½"	6"	200
16 "	9 "	6"	300
18 "	10⅞"	6"	500

Nos. 6637 — D-902

Height	Fitter	Wattage Recom-mended
6"	3¼"	50
8"	4 "	75
10"	5 "	100
12"	6 "	150
14"	6 "	200
16"	6 "	300

Nos. 6759 — D-1050 — D-1052

Diam.	Height	Fitter	Wattage Recom-mended
8"	5⅞"	3¼"	50
8"	5⅞"	4 "	75–100
9"	7 "	4 "	100–150
10"	7⅜"	4 "	150
13"	9½"	6 "	200
16"	11 "	6 "	300

GILLINDER & SONS, Inc., PHILADELPHIA

ESTABLISHED 1861

PLATE No. 3

Prices will vary depending on shade sizes.

No. D-930 UNIT
Tan or Gray Decoration
Flat Etched

No. 6669 UNIT—Plain

Current value: $45.00 – 115.00

No. D-933 UNIT
Flat Etched

No. 6685 UNIT—Plain

Current value
Flat etched: $125.00
Plain: $20.00 – 150.00

No. D-928 UNIT
Tan, Blue, Pink or Gray Decoration
Flat Etched

No. 6727 UNIT—Plain
Fixture Not Included

Current value
Flat etched: $35.00 – 75.00
Plain: $15.00 – 25.00

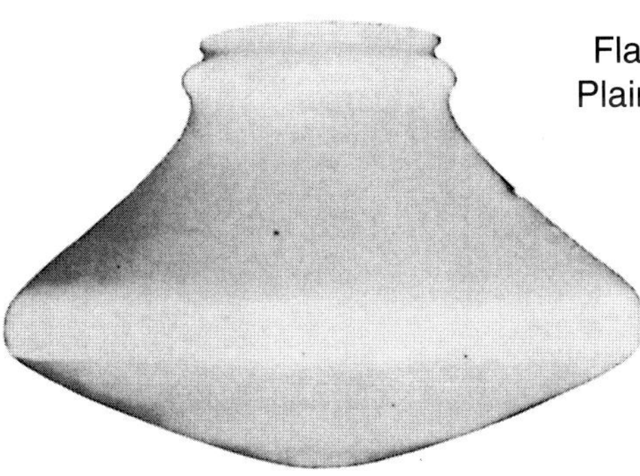

No. 6599 UNIT
Plain

Current value: $25.00 – 50.00

No. 5383 UNIT
Figured

Current value: $35.00 – 75.00

COMMERCIAL UNITS

Nos. 6599 — 5383

Diam.	Height	Fitter	Wattage Recommended
10″	8 ″	4″	100–150
12″	9 ″	5″	150–200
14″	9½″	6″	200
16″	10½″	6″	200–500

Nos. 6669 — D-930

Height	Fitter	Wattage Recommended
12″	6″	150
14″	6″	200
16″	6″	300

Nos. 6685 — D-933

Diam.	Height	Fitter	Wattage Recommended
16″	11″	6″	200–300

Nos. 6727 — D-928

Diam.	Height	Fitter	Wattage Recommended
9″	6¼″	4″	100–150

GILLINDER & SONS, Inc., PHILADELPHIA

ESTABLISHED 1861

PLATE No. 4

Prices will vary depending on shade sizes.

No. 6759 UNIT
9″ x 4″

No. 6727 UNIT
9″ x 4″

No. 6633 UNIT
9″ x 4″

No. 5453 UNIT
9″ x 4″

No. 6671 UNIT
9″ x 4″

No. 6627 UNIT
8″ x 4″

No. 6758 UNIT
9″ x 4″

No. 6626 UNIT
8″ x 4″

Current value for each:
$15.00 – 25.00

KITCHEN OR BATH UNITS

No.	Diam.	Height	Fitter	No.	Diam.	Height	Fitter
5453	9″	6½″	4″	6671	9″	6½″	4″
6626	8″	6¾″	4″	6727	9″	6¼″	4″
6627	8″	6¾″	4″	6758	9″	7 ″	4″
6633	9″	6½″	4″	6759	9″	7 ″	4″

GILLINDER & SONS, Inc., PHILADELPHIA

ESTABLISHED 1861

PLATE No. 5

Prices will vary depending on shade sizes.

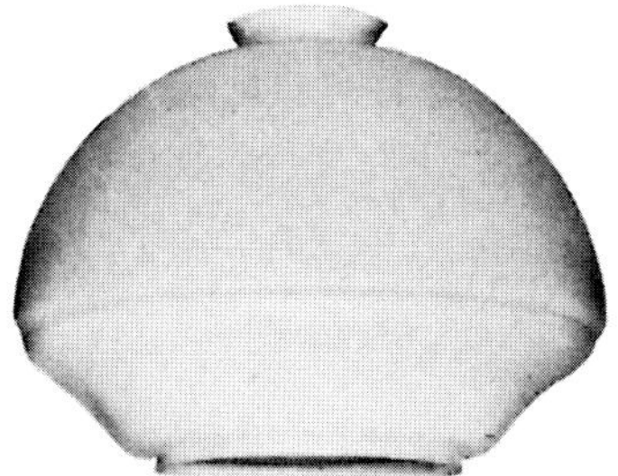

No. 6720 UNIT
8″ x 2¼″
Current value: $15.00 – 25.00

No. 6648 UNIT
8″ x 2¼″
Current value: $15.00 – 25.00

No. 6739 UNIT
9½″ x 2¼″
Current value: $20.00 – 35.00

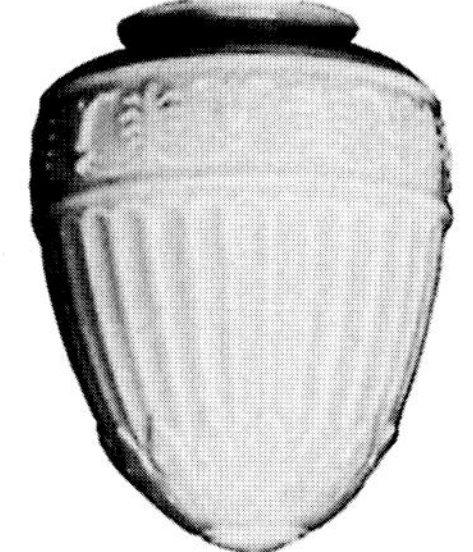

No. 5245 UNIT
6″ x 3¼″ and 8″ x 4″
Current value: $20.00 – 35.00

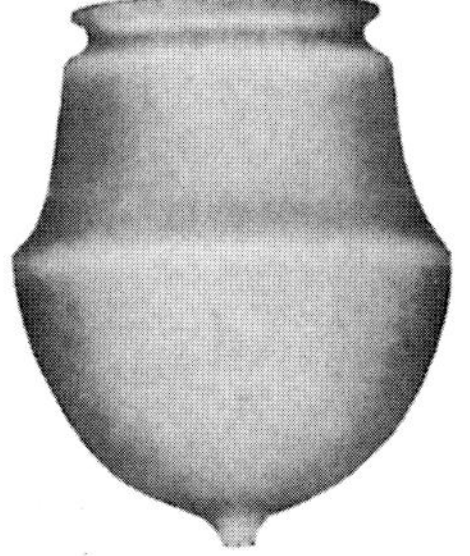

No. 6693 UNIT
8½″ x 5″
Current value: $25.00 – 35.00

No. 6726 UNIT
8½″ x 5″
Current value: $20.00 – 35.00

KITCHEN OR BATH AND STORE UNITS

No.	Diameter	Height	Fitter
5245	..	6 ″	3¼″
5245	..	8 ″	4 ″
6648	8 ″	5½″	2¼″
6693	..	8½″	5 ″
6720	8 ″	6 ″	2¼″
6726	..	8½″	5 ″
6739	9½″	7¼″	2¼″

GILLINDER & SONS, Inc., PHILADELPHIA

ESTABLISHED 1861

PLATE No. 6

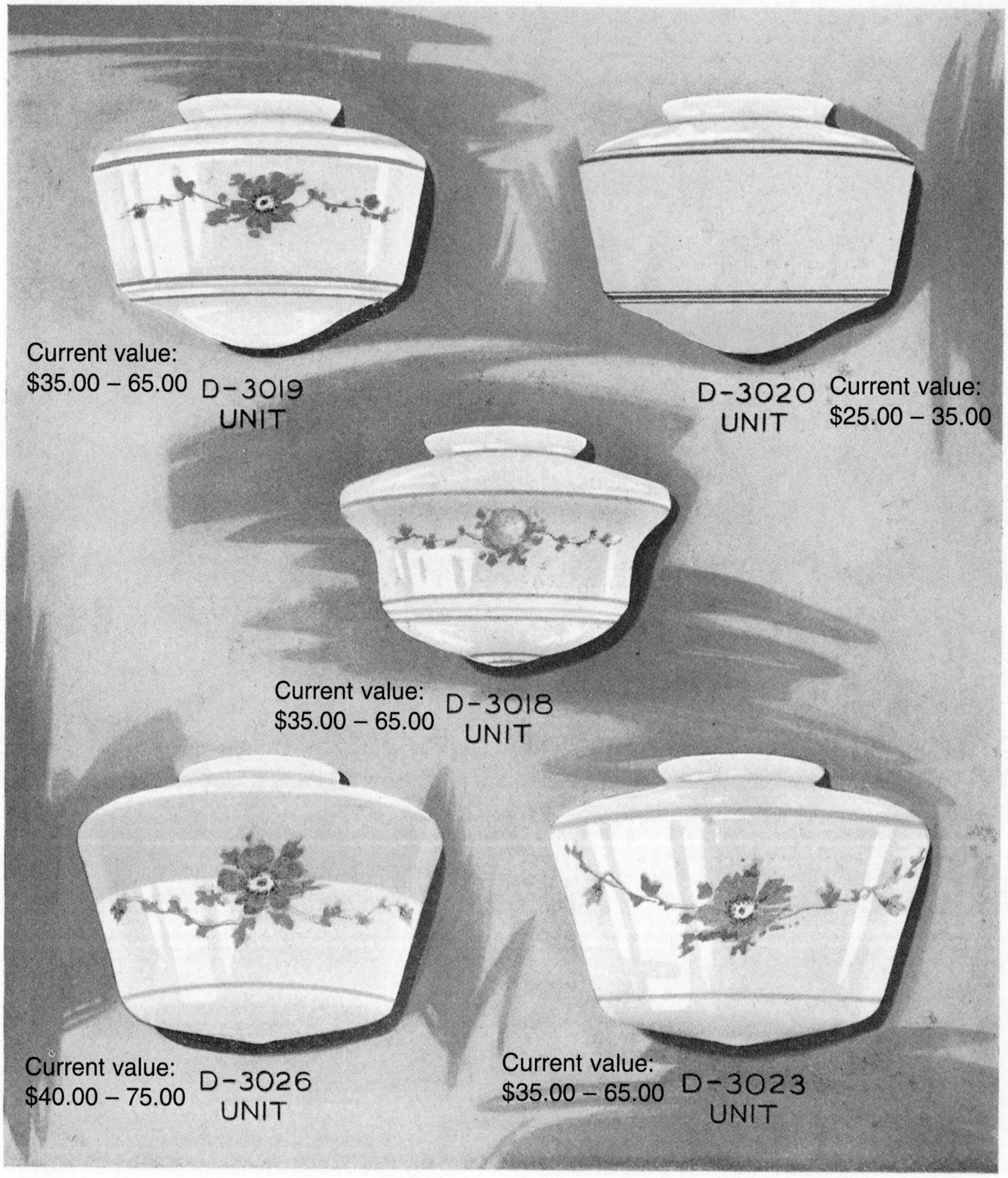

Current value:
$35.00 – 65.00 D-3019
UNIT

D-3020 Current value:
UNIT $25.00 – 35.00

Current value:
$35.00 – 65.00 D-3018
UNIT

Current value:
$40.00 – 75.00 D-3026
UNIT

Current value:
$35.00 – 65.00 D-3023
UNIT

BEDROOM UNITS

No.		Diameter	Height	Fitter
D-3018	Unit	9″	6½″	4″
D-3019	Unit	9″	6½″	4″
D-3020	Unit	9″	6½″	4″
D-3023	Unit	9″	6½″	4″
D-3026	Unit	9″	6½″	4″

GILLINDER & SONS, Inc., PHILADELPHIA

ESTABLISHED 1861

PLATE No. 7

Note: Author believes D-2038 has a bird on the shade.

BEDROOM UNITS

No.		Diameter	Height	Fitter
D-1093	Unit	8″	5⅞″	4″
D-1095	Unit	8″	5⅞″	4″
D-1096	Unit	8″	5⅞″	4″
D-2038	Unit	8″	6¾″	4″
D-2039	Unit	8″	6¾″	4″

GILLINDER & SONS, Inc., PHILADELPHIA

ESTABLISHED 1861

PLATE No. 8

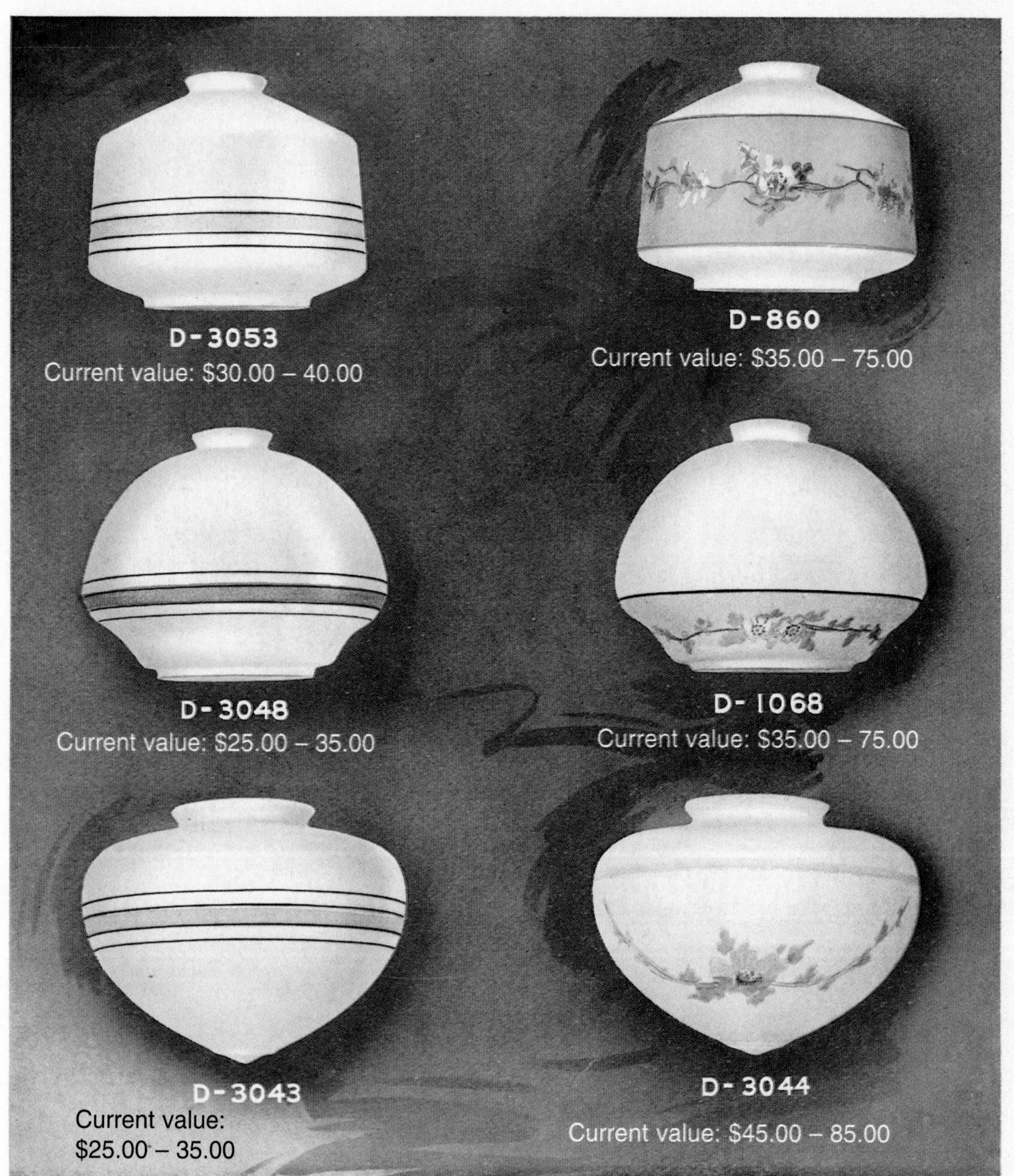

BEDROOM SHADES

No.		Diam.	Height	Fitter
D-860	Unit—Pink Sprays on Blue or Pink Panel	8″	5½″	2¼″
D-1068	Unit—Pink Roses on Tan Band—Top, Plain White	8″	6 ″	2¼″
D-3043	Unit—Ivory Background—Pink, Blue or Red Bands	9″	6¼″	4 ″
D-3044	Unit—Blue Cornflower—Tan Rings	9″	6¼″	4 ″
D-3048	Unit—Ivory Background—Pink, Blue or Red Bands	8″	6 ″	2¼″
D-3053	Unit—Ivory Background—Pink, Blue or Red Bands	8″	5½″	2¼″

GILLINDER & SONS, Inc., PHILADELPHIA

ESTABLISHED 1861

PLATE No. 9

DINING ROOM DOMES

FIXTURES NOT FURNISHED

No.		Decoration	Diameter	Height	Fitter
D-2041	Dome	Blue Parchment—Flowered Band	16″	10¾″	6″–8″
D-2043	Dome	Tan Parchment—Rose Bouquets	16″	10¾″	6″–8″
D-3037	Dome	Ivory Ground—Blue Band	16″	10¾″	6″–8″
D-3038	Dome	Blue Ground—Yellow Brown Band	16″	10¾″	6″–8″

GILLINDER & SONS, Inc., PHILADELPHIA

ESTABLISHED 1861

PLATE No. 10

Current value: $25.00 – 35.00

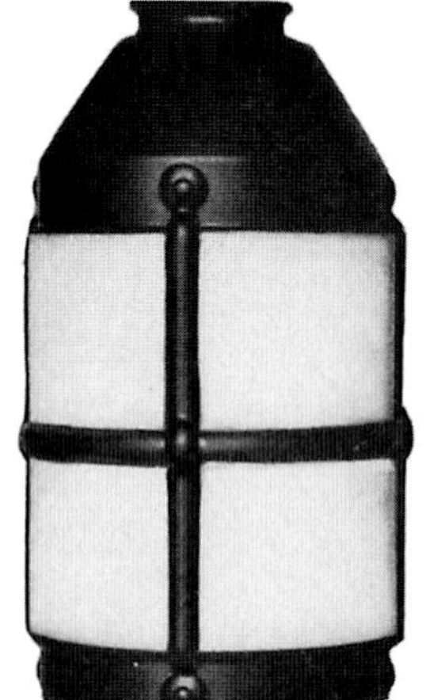

No. 9 Roughed

Current value: $25.00 – 35.00

No. 11 Roughed

Current value each: $30.00 – 40.00

Nos. 15 and 29 Roughed

Current value: $45.00 – 60.00

No. 24 Crystal Roughed, Opal, Plain Amber or Amber Roughed

Current value
10: $30.00 – 40.00
28: $35.00 – 45.00

Nos. 10 and 28 Roughed

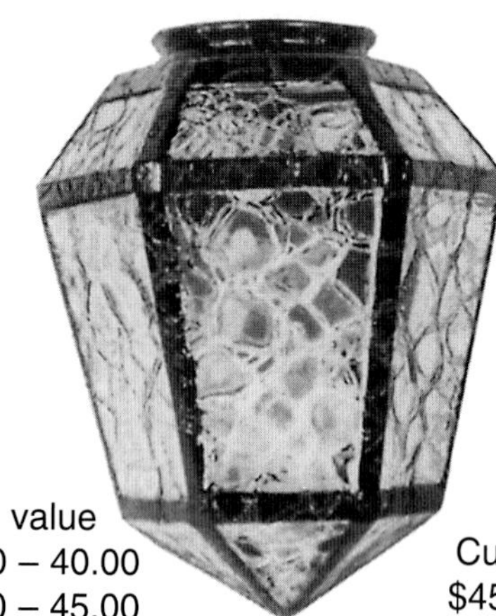

Current value: $45.00 – 60.00

No. 24 Amber Crackled

No. 16 Roughed or Opal

Current value: $40.00 – 50.00

Current value
6: $25.00 – 35.00
14: $25.00 – 35.00

Nos. 6 and 14 Roughed

No. 16 Amber Crackled

Current value: $40.00 – 50.00

ALL GLASS LANTERNS—BLACK FRAMES

No.		Diam.	Height	Fitter
6	Lantern	5⅜"	8 "	3¼"
9	Lantern	5½"	8 "	3¼"
10	Lantern	6¼"	7⅞"	3¼"
11	Lantern	7¼"	8¼"	3¼"
14	Lantern	4 "	6 "	2¼"
15	Lantern	6¼"	9½"	3¼"
16	Lantern	8 "	6½"	3¼ or 4"
24	Lantern	. . .	8 "	3¼ or 4"
28	Lantern	5½"	6¼"	3¼"
29	Lantern	5½"	8 "	3¼"

GILLINDER & SONS, Inc., PHILADELPHIA

ESTABLISHED 1861

PLATE No. 11

11073
TANGERINE

11074
ASHES OF ROSES

11078
AZURE

11086
PONGEE

11081
DAWN

11084
LEMON

ALL SHAPES SHOWN ON PAGES 12, 13, 14 AND 15 IN THIS CATALOGUE ARE DECORATED IN ALL THE ABOVE COLORS

In ordering give color number as indicated above, together with blank number, as shown on following pages, and name of article, to wit: 50/11081 candle shade.

GILLINDER & SONS, Inc., PHILADELPHIA

ESTABLISHED 1861

PLATE No. 12

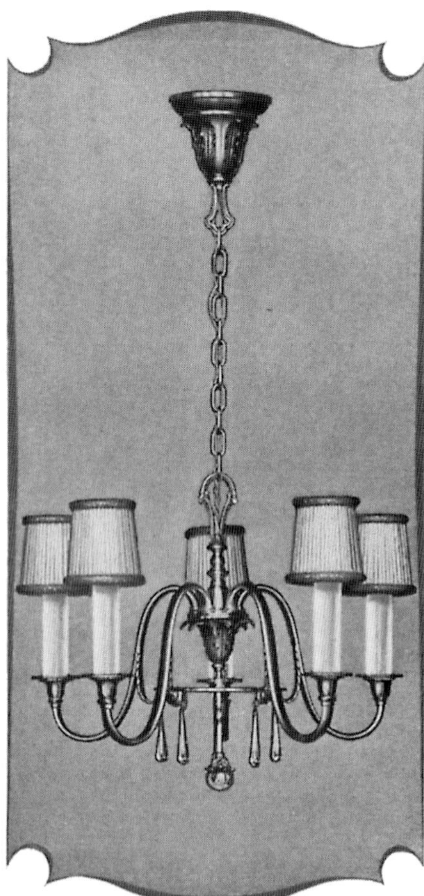

No. 50 GLASSILK CANDLE SHADE
On Pendant Fixture
Current value: $35.00 – 45.00

Pat. Sept. 1, 1925.
No. 51 GLASSILK CANDLE SHADE
Complete with Holder
Current value: $35.00 – 45.00

No. 50 GLASSILK CANDLE SHADE
Complete with Holder
Current value: $35.00 – 45.00

No. 50 GLASSILK CANDLE SHADE
On Bracket Fixture
Current value: $35.00 – 45.00

(Registered)

	Diam.	Height	
No. 50 Glassilk Candle Shade . . .	4″	4″	Holder Included
No. 51 Glassilk Candle Shade . . .	4″	4″	Holder Included

Made in All Colors Shown on Plate 11 — We Do Not Sell Fixtures

GILLINDER & SONS, Inc., PHILADELPHIA

ESTABLISHED 1861

PLATE No. 13

These fiber holder shades rested on the light bulb.

Current value: $35.00 – 45.00

Pat. Sept. 1, 1925.
No. 53 GLASSILK BALL LAMP SHADE
Complete with Fibre Holder

No. 52 GLASSILK BALL LAMP SHADE
Complete with Fibre Holder
Current value: $35.00 – 45.00

No. 53 GLASSILK BALL LAMP SHADES
On Ceiling Fixture

Current value: $35.00 – 45.00

No. 53 GLASSILK BALL LAMP SHADE
On Bracket Fixture

Current value: $35.00 – 45.00

Pat. Sept. 1, 1925.
No. 54 GLASSILK ELECTRIC

Current value: $35.00 – 45.00

(Registered)

		Diam.	Height	Fitter	
No. 52	Glassilk Ball Lamp Shade	4 "	4 "	. . .	Holder Included
No. 53	Glassilk Ball Lamp Shade	3½"	3½"	. . .	Holder Included
No. 54	Glassilk Electric . . .	4 "	4½"	2¼"	

Made in All Colors Shown on Plate 11

We Do Not Sell Fixtures

GILLINDER & SONS, Inc., PHILADELPHIA

ESTABLISHED 1861

PLATE No. 14

Pat. Sept. 1, 1925.

No. 55 GLASSILK HALL GLOBE

Pat. Sept. 1, 1925.

No. 56 GLASSILK HALL GLOBE

Pat. Sept. 1, 1925.

No. 57 HALL GLOBE OR SLIP-IN CYLINDER

(Registered)

Current value
Each: $45.00 – 55.00

		Diam.	Height	Fitter
No. 55	Glassilk Hall Globe—¼″ Hole in Bottom	6″	8 ″	3¼–4″
No. 56	Glassilk Hall Globe—Open Bottom . .	6″	7½″	3¼–4″
No. 57	Glassilk Hall Globe or Slip-In Cylinder .	6″	6½″	. . . . .

Made in All Colors Shown on Plate 11

GILLINDER & SONS, Inc., PHILADELPHIA

ESTABLISHED 1861

PLATE No. 1

Current value:
$50.00 – 60.00

Pat. Sept. 1, 1925.
No. 58 GLASSILK BEDROOM SHADE

Pat. Sept. 1, 1925.
No. 59 GLASSILK BOUDOIR SHADE
Complete with Holder

Current value: $55.00 – 75.00

Current value:
$75.00 – 100.00

Pat. Sept. 1, 1925.
No. 61 GLASSILK PORCH SHADE

Pat. Sept. 1, 1925.
No. 62 GLASSILK PORCH CYLINDER
OR SLIP-IN BOWL

Current value: $75.00 – 100.00

Current value:
$135.00 – 185.00

Pat. Sept. 1, 1925.
No. 63 GLASSILK DINING ROOM DOME

(Registered)

		Diameter	Height	Fitter	
58	Glassilk Bedroom Shade . .	7″	5 ″	2¼″	
59	Glassilk Boudoir Shade . .	7″	4¼″	. . .	Holder Included
61	Glassilk Porch Shade . . .	10″	6¾″	2¼″	
62	Glassilk Porch Cylinder . .	10″	5¾″	. . .	
63	Glassilk Dining Room Dome .	16″	11 ″	8 ″	

Made in All Colors Shown on Plate 11, Excepting No. 63,
Which is Only Made in 11074, 11078 and 11081.

GILLINDER & SONS, Inc., PHILADELPHIA

ESTABLISHED 1861

PLATE No. 16

D-506 ASSORTMENT

CREAM GROUND WITH BROWN BANDS—FLORAL DECORATION

No.		Diameter	Height	Fitter	
D-506	Unit	10 "	7 "	4 "	Tassel Not Included
D-506	Bedroom Shade .	7 "	5 "	2¼"	
D-506	Candle Shade . .	4 "	4 "		Complete with Holder
D-506	Bell Lamp Shade .	3½"	3½"		Complete with Holder
D-506	Electric . . .	4 "	4½"	2¼"	

GILLINDER & SONS, Inc., PHILADELPHIA

ESTABLISHED 1861

PLATE No. 17

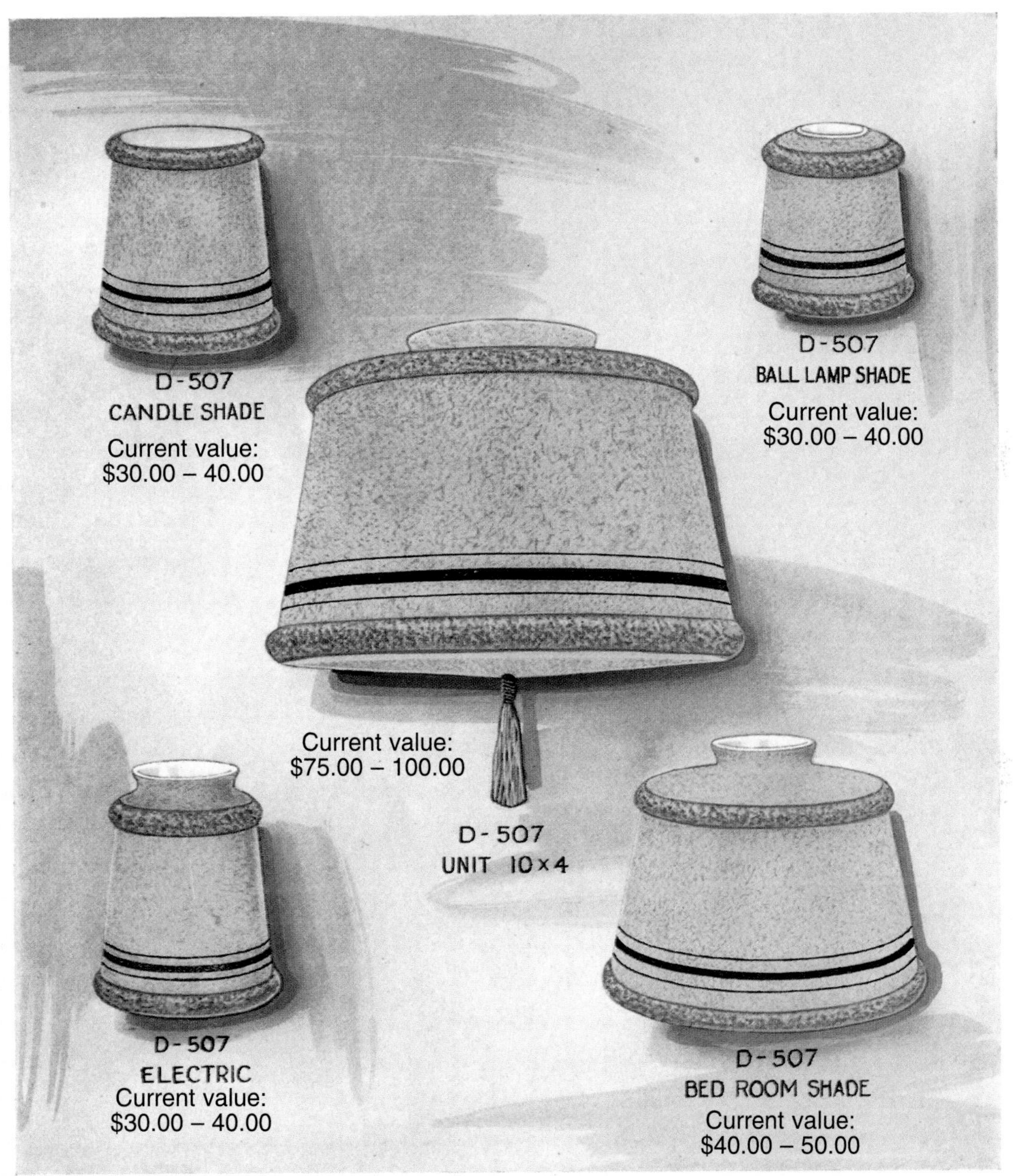

D-507 ASSORTMENT

PARCHMENT FINISH WITH BLACK LINES

No.		Diameter	Height	Fitter	
D-507	Unit	10 "	7 "	4 "	Tassel Not Included
D-507	Bedroom Shade .	7 "	5 "	2¼"	
D-507	Candle Shade . .	4 "	4 "		Complete with Holder
D-507	Ball Lamp Shade .	3½"	3½"		Complete with Holder
D-507	Electric . . .	4 "	4½"	2¼"	

GILLINDER & SONS, Inc., PHILADELPHIA

ESTABLISHED 1861

PLATE No. 18

NURSERY ASSORTMENT

No.		Diameter	Height	Fitter	
D-505	Unit	9 "	6½"	4 "	
D-505	Bedroom Shade .	8 "	5½"	2¼"	
D-505	Candle Shade . .	4 "	4 "		Complete with Holder
D-505	Ball Lamp Shade .	3½"	3½"		Complete with Holder
D-505	Electric . . .	4 "	4½"	2¼"	

GILLINDER & SONS, Inc., PHILADELPHIA

ESTABLISHED 1861

PLATE No. 19

D-508 ASSORTMENT

BATH OR KITCHEN SHADES—OPAL GLASS WITH BLUE BANDS

No.		Diameter	Height	Fitter	Length
D-508	Unit	9 "	7 "	4 "	
D-508	Electric	4⅞"	4⅜"	2¼"	
D-508	Bathroom	..	4 "	2¼"	5¾"
D-508	Bowl	10 "	3⅛"	..	
D-508	Candle	1 "	4 "	..	
D-508	Bobesche	3¼"	..	..	

GILLINDER & SONS, Inc., PHILADELPHIA

ESTABLISHED 1861

PLATE No. 20

D-509 ASSORTMENT

BATH OR KITCHEN SHADES—OPAL GLASS WITH BROWN BANDS

No.		Diameter	Height	Fitter	
D-509	Unit	9 "	8 "	4 "	
D-509	Electric . . .	4¼"	4⅛"	2¼"	
D-509	Candle Shade . .	4 "	4 "		Complete with Holder
D-509	Ball Lamp Shade .	3½"	3 "		Complete with Holder
D-509	Bedroom Shade .	8 "	5 "	2¼"	
D-509	Candle . . .	1 "	4 "	. .	
D-509	Bobesche . . .	3¼"	. .	. .	

GILLINDER & SONS, Inc., PHILADELPHIA

ESTABLISHED 1861

PLATE No. 21

6746/D-502 BREAKFAST ROOM
Current value: $55.00 – 85.00

6684/D-502 BEDROOM
Current value: $40.00 – 50.00

6648/D-502 BEDROOM
Current value: $40.00 – 50.00

6403/D-502 URN 7 x 3¼"
8 x 4 "

Current value
7 x 3½: $40.00 – 50.00
8 x 4: $45.00 – 55.00

6650/D-502 BALL LAMP SHADE
6651/D-502 BALL LAMP SHADE
Current value
6650: $25.00 – 35.00
6651: $30.00 – 35.00

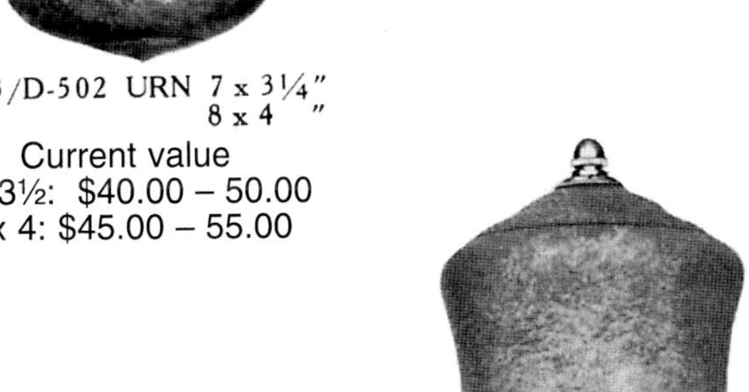

6786/D-502 CANDLE SHADE
Current value: $25.00 – 30.00

D-502 ASSORTMENT

TAN PARCHMENT FINISH WITH BLACK LINES

No.		Diameter	Height	Fitter
6746/D-502	Breakfast Room . .	10 "	7¾"	2¼"
6403/D-502	Urn	7 "	6½"	3¼"
6403/D-502	Urn	8 "	7¾"	4 "
6684/D-502	Bedroom	8 "	5 "	2¼"
6648/D-502	Bedroom	8 "	5½"	2¼"
6650/D-502	Ball Lamp Shade . .	3½"	3 "	Complete with Holder
6651/D-502	Ball Lamp Shade . .	4⅛"	3⅞"	Complete with Holder
6786/D-502	Candle Shade . . .	3⅝"	3⅞"	Complete with Holder

GILLINDER & SONS, Inc., PHILADELPHIA

ESTABLISHED 1861

PLATE No. 22

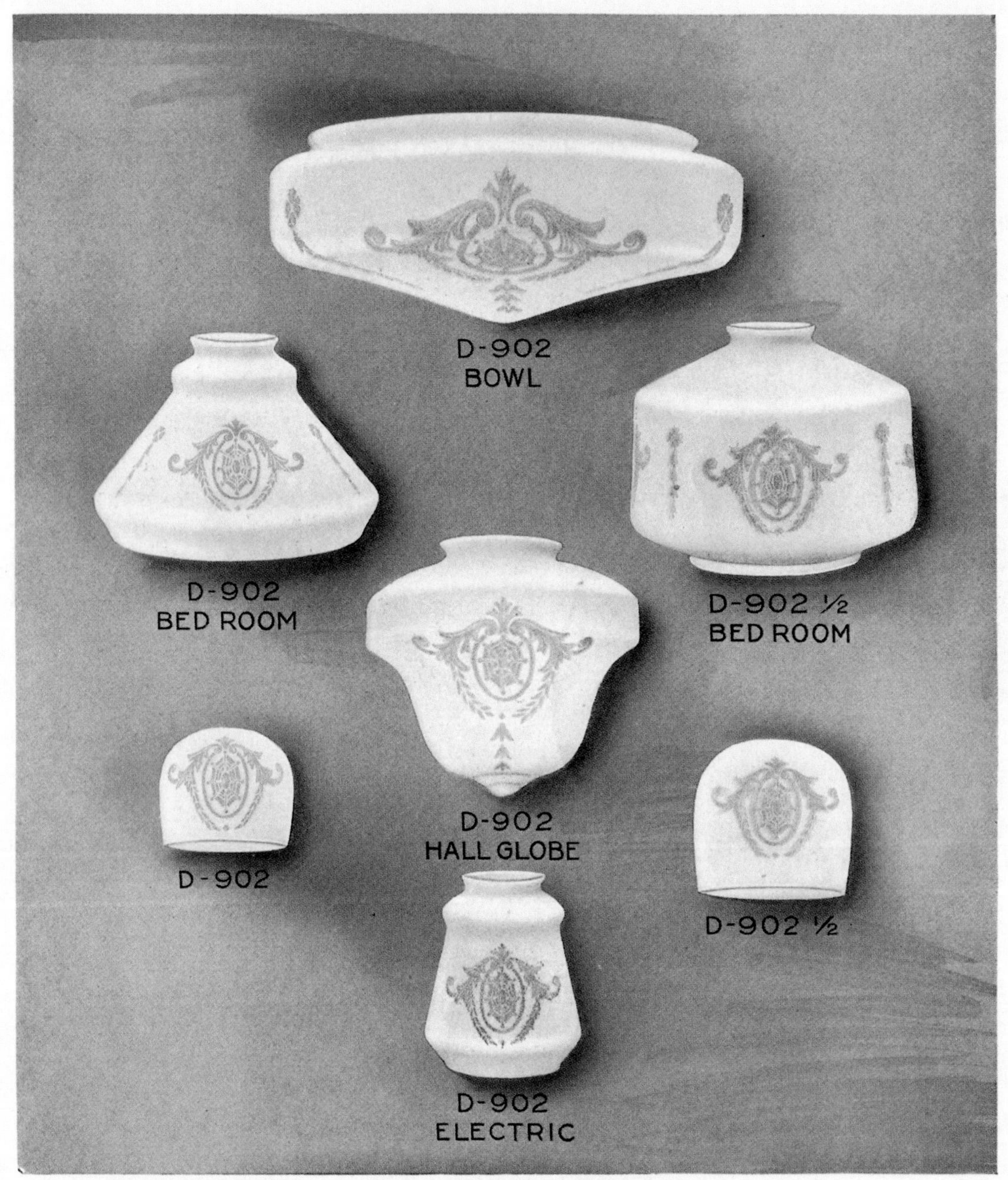

D-902 ASSORTMENT

FLAT ETCHED DECORATION—TAN, BLUE, GRAY OR PINK

No.		Diameter	Height	Fitter		Current values:
D-902	Bowl . . .	12 "	$4\frac{1}{8}$"	10 "		\$65.00 – 85.00
D-902	Bowl . . .	14 "	$4\frac{5}{8}$"	12 "		\$75.00 – 100.00
D-902	Bowl . . .	15 "	$5\frac{3}{8}$"	14 "		\$100.00 – 135.00
D-902	Hall Globe . .	7 "	$6\frac{1}{2}$"	$3\frac{1}{4}$"		\$30.00 – 40.00
D-902	Hall Globe . .	8 "	$7\frac{3}{4}$"	4 "		\$35.00 – 45.00
D-902	Bedroom Shade .	8 "	5 "	$2\frac{1}{4}$"		\$35.00 – 45.00
D-902½	Bedroom Shade .	8 "	$5\frac{1}{2}$"	$2\frac{1}{4}$"		\$20.00 – 25.00
D-902	Ball Lamp Shade	$3\frac{1}{2}$"	3 "		Complete with Holder	\$20.00 – 25.00
D-902½	Ball Lamp Shade	$4\frac{1}{8}$"	$3\frac{7}{8}$"		Complete with Holder	\$25.00 – 30.00
D-902	Electric . . .	$4\frac{1}{4}$"	5 "	$2\frac{1}{4}$"		\$25.00 – 30.00

GILLINDER & SONS, Inc., PHILADELPHIA

ESTABLISHED 1861

PLATE No. 23

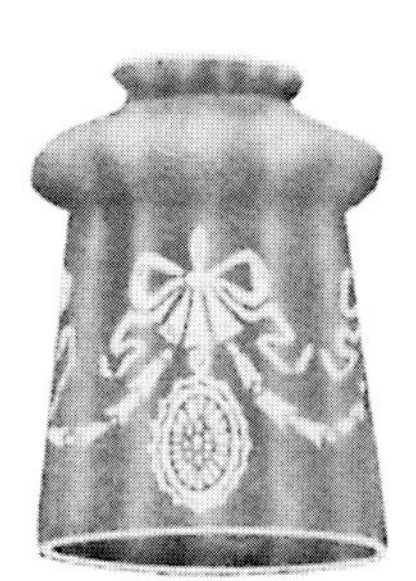

6725/3076 ELECTRIC

3076 BOWL

3076½ BALL

3076 ASSORTMENT—SILVER-ETCHED, RIBBED, IRIDESCENT

D-675 HALL GLOBE

D-675 BOWL

D-675 BEDROOM

D-675 ELECTRIC

D-675 ASSORTMENT—TAN DECORATION—DEEP ETCHED

No.		Diameter	Height	Fitter	Current values:
3076	Bowl	12 "	5⅝"	10 "	$185.00 – 225.00
6725/3076	Electric	4 "	5 "	2¼"	$30.00 – 45.00
3076½	Ball	6 "	4½"	3¼"	$50.00 – 60.00
3076½	Ball	7 "	5 "	3¼"	$60.00 – 70.00
3076½	Ball	8 "	5½"	3¼–4"	$70.00 – 85.00
D-675	Bowl	12 "	6 "	10 "	$125.00 – 150.00
D-675	Bowl	15 "	6½"	14 "	$145.00 – 185.00
D-675	Bedroom	8 "	5½"	2¼"	$65.00 – 85.00
D-675	Electric	4¼"	4½"	2¼"	$30.00 – 40.00
D-675	Urn	7 "	6½"	3¼"	$50.00 – 60.00

GILLINDER & SONS, Inc., PHILADELPHIA

ESTABLISHED 1861

PLATE No. 24

D-511
CANDLE SHADE
Current value: $30.00 – 35.00

D-511
BALL LAMP SHADE
Current value: $30.00 – 35.00

D-510
BALL LAMP SHADE
Current value: $35.00 – 45.00

D-510
CANDLE SHADE
Current value: $35.00 – 45.00

DECORATED CANDLE AND BALL LAMP SHADES

No.		Diameter	Height	
D-510	Candle Shade . . .	4 "	4 "	Complete with Holder
D-510	Ball Lamp Shade . . .	3½"	3½"	Complete with Holder
D-511	Candle Shade . . .	4 "	4 "	Complete with Holder
D-511	Ball Lamp Shade . . .	3½"	3½"	Complete with Holder

GILLINDER & SONS, Inc., PHILADELPHIA

ESTABLISHED 1861

PLATE No. 25

D-877 BALL LAMP
D-878 " "
Current value each: $55.00 – 75.00

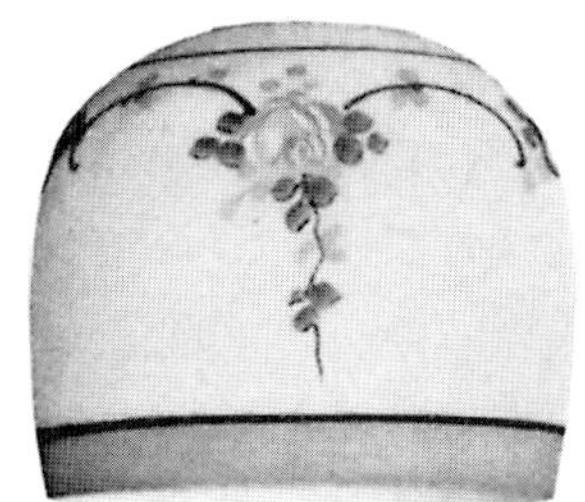

D-879 BALL LAMP
D-880 " "
Current value each: $50.00 – 60.00

D-881 BALL LAMP
D-882 " "
Current value each: $55.00 – 75.00

D-885 BALL LAMP
D-886 " "
Current value each: $50.00 – 65.00

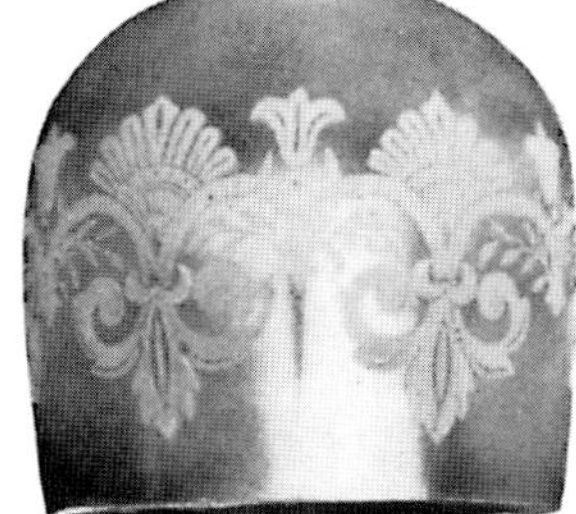

3134 BALL LAMP
3135 " "
Current value each: $50.00 – 70.00

D-887 BALL LAMP
D-888 " "
Current value each: $50.00 – 65.00

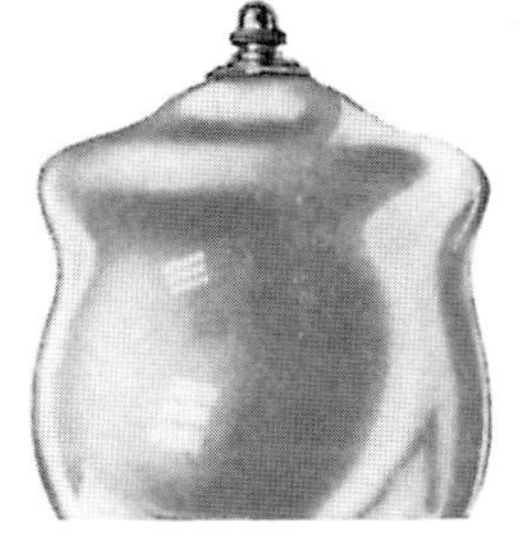

11045 CANDLE SHADE
11049 " "
11050 " "
11051 " "
Current value each: $30.00 – 35.00

D-889 BALL LAMP
D-890 " "
Current value each: $35.00 – 40.00

11035 BALL LAMP
11039 " "
11040 " "
11041 " "
Current value each: $25.00 – 30.00

Note: Filter holder used because the shade rests on the light bulb.

BALL LAMP AND CANDLE SHADES

BALL LAMP SHADES

No.	Diam.	Height	
D-877	3½"	3 "	Country Scene on
D-878	4⅛"	3⅞"	Buff Background
D-879	3½"	3 "	Pink Roses on White,
D-880	4⅛"	3⅞"	Tan Band at Bottom
D-881	3½"	3 "	
D-882	4⅛"	3⅞"	House Scene
D-885	3½"	3 "	Deep Etched
D-886	4⅛"	3⅞"	Tan Design
D-887	3½"	3 "	Deep Etched—Tan,
D-888	4⅛"	3⅞"	Pink and Green Design
D-889	3½"	3 "	Star Cut,
D-890	4⅛"	3⅞"	Iridescent

BALL LAMP SHADES

No.	Diam.	Height	
3134	3½"	3 "	Silver Etched
3135	4⅛"	3⅞"	Iridescent
11035	3⅝"	3⅛"	Shell Pink
11039	3⅝"	3⅛"	Golden Yellow
11040	3⅝"	3⅛"	Powder Blue
11041	3⅝"	3⅛"	Cirese

CANDLE SHADES

No.	Diam.	Height	
11045	3⅝"	3⅞"	Shell Pink
11049	3⅝"	3⅞"	Golden Yellow
11050	3⅝"	3⅞"	Powder Blue
11051	3⅝"	3⅞"	Cirese

All Ball Lamp Shades and Candle Shades Furnished with Holders.

GILLINDER & SONS, Inc., PHILADELPHIA

ESTABLISHED 1861

PLATE No. 26

D-1061 PORCH UNIT, 12″
Current value: $100.00 – 125.00

D-1061½ BALL, 6″
Current value: $35.00 – 50.00

D-1062 PORCH UNIT, 12″
Current value: $100.00 – 125.00

D-1062½ BALL, 6″
Current value: $35.00 – 50.00

30 PORCH UNIT, 12″
Current value: $45.00 – 60.00

30½ BALL, 6″
Current value: $25.00 – 35.00

PORCH AND BREAKFAST ROOM UNITS

		Diameter	Height	Fitter	
D-1061	Porch Unit . . .	12″	7 ″	4 ″	Tan, Pink or Blue
D-1061½	Ball	6″	5½″	3¼″	" " "
D-1062	Porch Unit . . .	12″	7 ″	4 ″	" " "
D-1062½	Ball	6″	5½″	3¼″	" " "
30	Porch Unit . . .	12″	7 ″	4 ″	Opal, Black Lines
30½	Ball	6″	5½″	3¼″	" " "

GILLINDER & SONS, Inc., PHILADELPHIA

ESTABLISHED 1861

PLATE No. 27

D-100 ASSORTMENT

TAN, BLUE OR PINK TINTS WITH BOUQUET ON PANEL

No.		Diameter	Height	Fitter
D-100	Bowl	12 "	5½"	10 "
D-100	Bowl	15 "	6⅛"	14 "
D-100	Hall Globe	7 "	6½"	3¼"
D-100	Bedroom Shade . . .	8 "	5 "	2¼"
D-100	Electric	4⅜"	4⅜"	2¼"

GILLINDER & SONS, Inc., PHILADELPHIA

ESTABLISHED 1861

PLATE No. 28

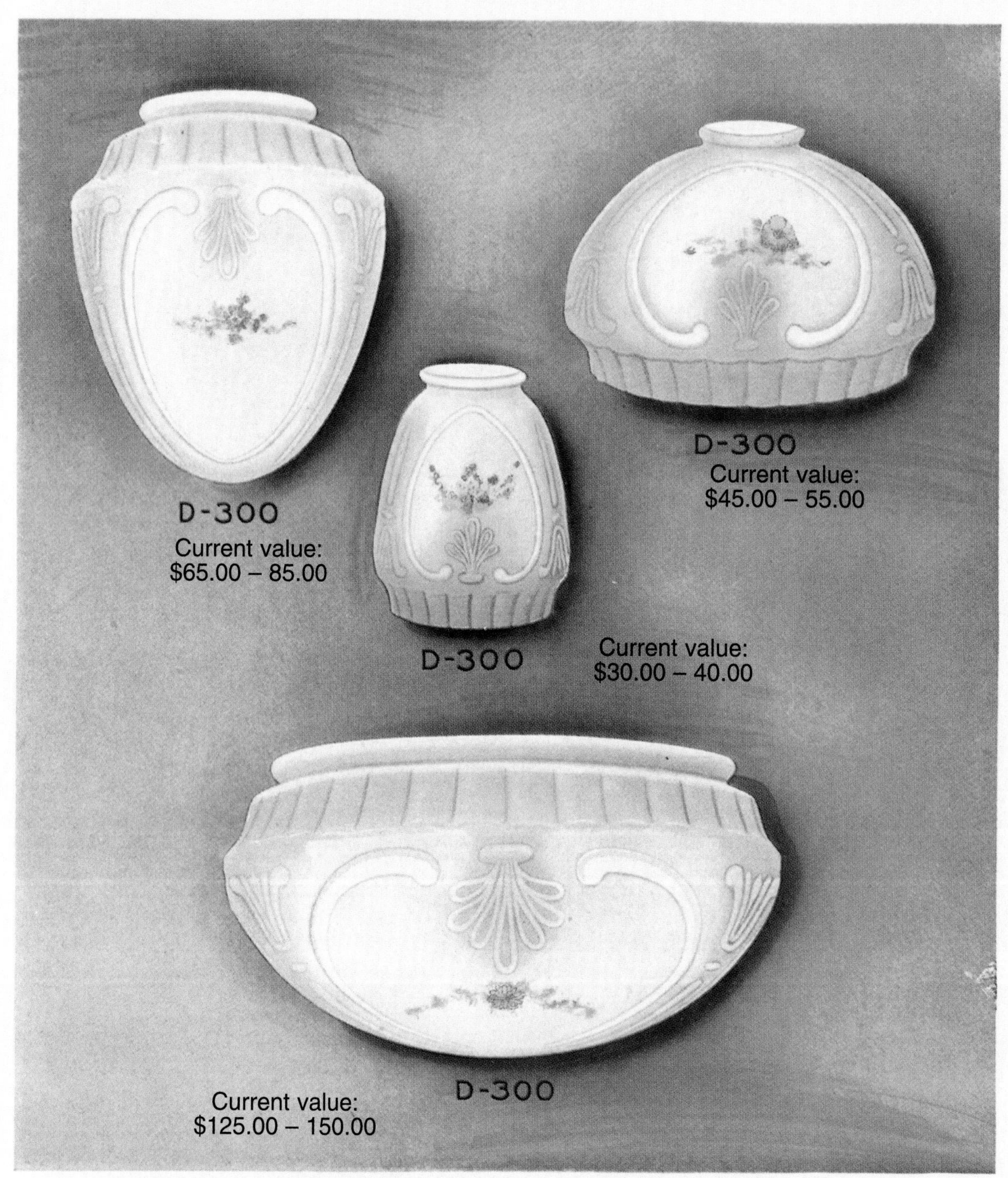

D-300 ASSORTMENT

TAN, BLUE OR PINK TINTS WITH BOUQUET ON PANEL

No.		Diameter	Height	Fitter
D-300	Bowl	11½"	6"	10 "
D-300	Hall Globe	. .	8"	4 "
D-300	Bedroom Shade	8 "	5"	2¼"
D-300	Electric	4¼"	5"	2¼"

GILLINDER & SONS, Inc., PHILADELPHIA

ESTABLISHED 1861

PLATE No. 29

5230 BOWL
11001 "
Current value: $125.00 – 200.00

5230 BEDROOM
11001 "
Current value: $35.00 – 45.00

5230 ELECTRIC
11001 "
Current value: $25.00 – 30.00

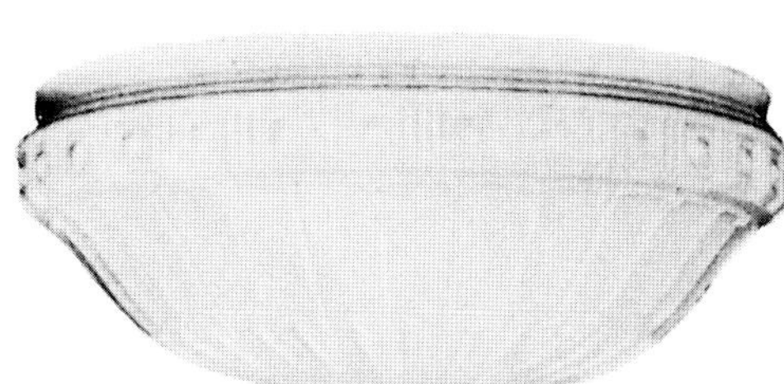

5283 BOWL
11005 "
Current value: $100.00 – 150.00

5283 BEDROOM
11005 "
Current value: $35.00 – 45.00

5283 ELECTRIC
11005 "
Current value: $25.00 – 30.00

5283 URN
11005 "
Current value: $50.00 – 65.00

NEMALITE AND TINTED GLASSWARE

5230 AND 5283 FURNISHED IN NEMALITE

11001 AND 11005 ARE SAME AS ABOVE BUT TINTED EITHER TAN, BLUE OR PINK

Nemalite	Tinted		Diam.	Height	Fitter
5230	11001	Bowl	12 "	6⅛"	10 "
5230	11001	Bowl	15 "	6½"	14 "
5230	11001	Bowl	18 "	8 "	16 "
5230	11001	Bedroom	7½"	5 "	2¼"
5230	11001	Electric	4½"	5 "	2¼"

Nemalite	Tinted		Diam.	Height	Fitter
5283	11005	Bowl	12 "	5½"	10 "
5283	11005	Bowl	15 "	6⅛"	14 "
5283	11005	Urn	7 "	6½"	3¼"
5283	11005	Bedroom	8 "	5 "	2¼"
5283	11005	Electric	4⅜"	4⅜"	2¼"

GILLINDER & SONS, Inc., PHILADELPHIA

ESTABLISHED 1861

PLATE No. 30

D-705 BOWL
Current value: $250.00 – 300.00

6725/D-705 ELECTRIC
Current value: $50.00 – 85.00

6725/D-704 ELECTRIC
Current value: $50.00 – 85.00

D-704 BOWL
Current value: $250.00 – 300.00

D-760 ELECTRIC
Current value: $40.00 – 50.00

D-759 ELECTRIC
Current value: $40.00 – 50.00

D-758 ELECTRIC
Current value: $40.00 – 50.00

		Diam.	Height	Fitter	
D-704	Bowl	12 "	5⅝"	10 "	Decorated Blue, Black Tints—Sunset Ground
6725/D-704	Electric	4 "	5 "	2¼"	Decorated Blue, Black Tints—Sunset Ground
D-705	Bowl	12 "	5⅝"	10 "	Decorated Yellow, Brown and Green—Sunset Ground
6725/D-705	Electric	4 "	5 "	2¼"	Decorated Yellow, Brown and Green—Sunset Ground
D-758	Electric	4⅝"	4⅞"	2¼"	Pink Tints—Bouquet Around Center
D-759	Electric	4⅝"	4⅞"	2¼"	Blue Tints—Bouquet Around Center
D-760	Electric	4⅝"	4⅞"	2¼"	Tan Tints—Bouquet Around Center

GILLINDER & SONS, Inc., PHILADELPHIA

ESTABLISHED 1861

PLATE No. 31

5083 BALL CRYSTAL
Current value: $30.00 – 60.00

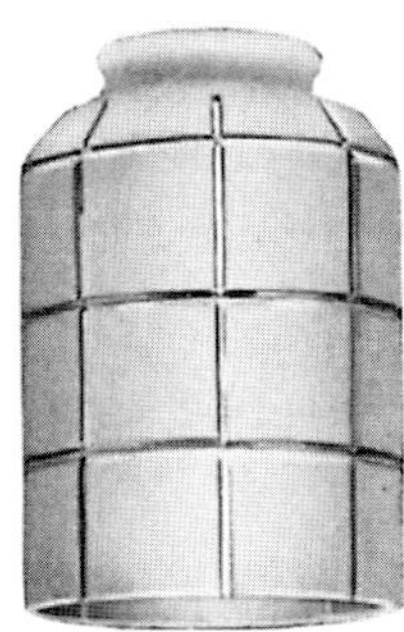

5078 ELECTRIC, Clear Lines
5078 ELECTRIC, Black Lines
Current value: $25.00 – 50.00

5210 URN
Current value: $40.00 – 75.00

5083 BALL, Black Lined
Crystal or Amber
Current value: $30.00 – 70.00

6213 CONE CYLINDER
Current value: $20.00 – 25.00

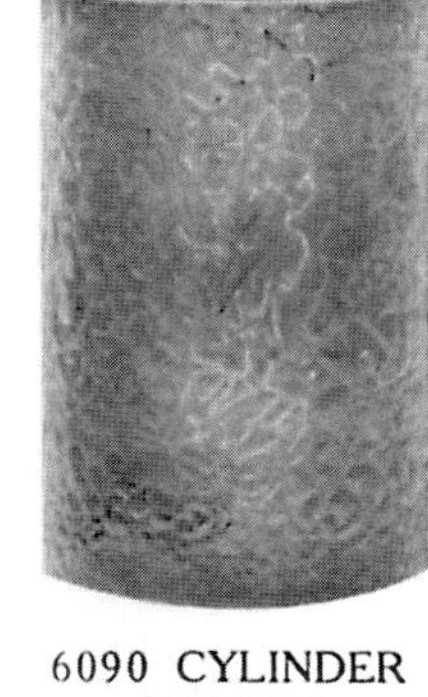

6090 CYLINDER CHIPPED
Current value: $45.00 – 75.00

6090 CYLINDER PLAIN
Current value: $35.00 – 45.00

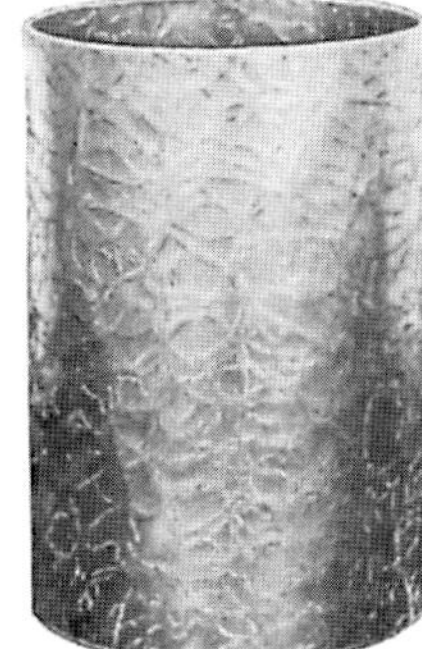

6090 CYLINDER CRACKLED
Current value: $45.00 – 75.00

	Diam.	Height	Fitter	
5078 Electric	3⅝″	5″	2¼″	Roughed Clear Lines
5078 Electric	3⅝″	5″	2¼″	Roughed Black Lines
5083 Ball .	6″	6″	3¼″	Roughed Clear Lines
5083 Ball .	6″	6″	3¼″	Roughed Black Lines
5083 Ball .	6″	6″	3¼″	Amber Black Lines
5210 Urn .	6″	6″	3¼″	Roughed Clear Lines
5210 Urn .	8″	8″	4 ″	Roughed Clear Lines

	D.	H.	Furnished in
6090 Cylinder	4″	6″	Clear
	3″	8″	Clear Chipped
	4″	8″	Clear Crackled
	5″	7″	C. R. I.
	6″	8″	Amber
	7″	9″	Amber Chipped
			Amber Crackled

Other Sizes Upon Application

	Diam.	Ht.	Top
6213 Cone Cylinder, C. R. I.	6″	6″	3″

GILLINDER & SONS, Inc., PHILADELPHIA

ESTABLISHED 1861

PLATE No. 33

Note: Prices will vary depending on shade size.

4156 MICRA REFLECTORS 4159
4157 SHALLOW TYPE 4160
4158

Current value
4156: $20.00 – 35.00 4159: $30.00 – 45.00
4157: $20.00 – 35.00 4160: $50.00 – 75.00
4158: $20.00 – 35.00

4150 MICRA REFLECTORS 4153
4151 BOWL TYPE 4156
4152

Current value
4150: $25.00 – 45.00 4153: $25.00 – 45.00
4151: $25.00 – 45.00 4156: $20.00 – 35.00
4152: $25.00 – 45.00

5158 OPAL BLOWN 5162
5160 REFLECTORS 5165
5161 BOWL TYPE 5166

Current value
5158: $25.00 – 60.00 5162: $25.00 – 60.00
5160: $25.00 – 60.00 5165: $25.00 – 60.00
5161: $25.00 – 60.00 5166: $25.00 – 60.00

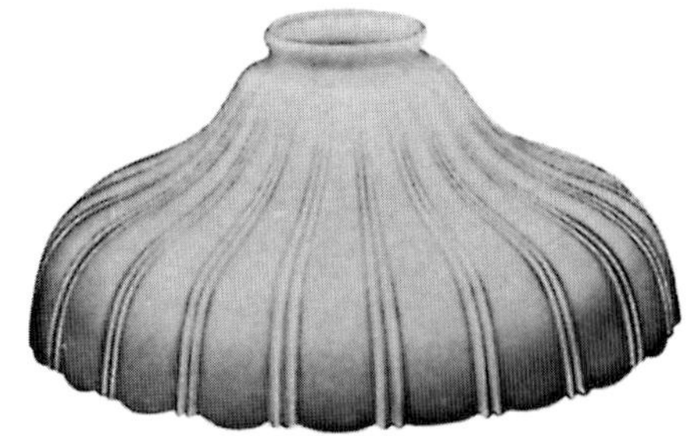

5179 OPAL BLOWN 5171
5169 REFLECTORS 5186
5170 SHALLOW TYPE

Current value
5179: $30.00 – 50.00 5171: $35.00 – 75.00
5169: $30.00 – 50.00 5184: $35.00 – 75.00
5170: $30.00 – 50.00

TUNGSTEN REFLECTORS

Micra Reflectors

No.		Diam.	Height	Fitter	Watt
4150	Bowl	5⅝"	4 "	2¼"	25
4151	Bowl	6 "	4½"	2¼"	40
4152	Bowl	6⅞"	4¾"	2¼"	60
4153	Bowl	7½"	5½"	2¼"	100
4154	Bowl	9 "	6¾"	3¼"	150
4155	Bowl	10 "	7¾"	3¼"	250
4156	Shallow	7 "	2¾"	2¼"	25
4157	Shallow	7½"	3¼"	2¼"	40
4158	Shallow	8½"	3¾"	2¼"	60
4159	Shallow	11 "	4⅜"	2¼"	100
4160	Shallow	14 "	5 "	3¼"	250

Opal Blown Reflectors

No.		Diam.	Height	Fitter	Watt
5158	Bowl	5¼"	3⅞"	2¼"	25
5160	Bowl	6 "	4⅝"	2¼"	40
5161	Bowl	7 "	5¼"	2¼"	60
5162	Bowl	8 "	5¾"	2¼"	100
5165	Bowl	9⅛"	6¾"	3¼"	150
5166	Bowl	11⅛"	7¾"	3¼"	250
5179	Shallow	7 "	2¾"	2¼"	25
5169	Shallow	7⅜"	3½"	2¼"	40
5170	Shallow	9 "	3⅞"	2¼"	60
5171	Shallow	11 "	4¾"	2¼"	100
5184	Shallow	14 "	5¼"	3¼"	250

GILLINDER & SONS, Inc., PHILADELPHIA

ESTABLISHED 1861

Note: Prices will vary depending on shade sizes.

PLATE No. 34

6052 BOWL

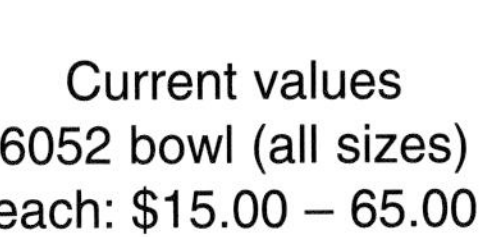

Current values
6052 bowl (all sizes)
each: $15.00 – 65.00

97 BALL

Current values
97 ball:
6" to 12":
$10.00 – 25.00
14" to 20":
$25.00 – 50.00

6408 BALL 6073
6041 6074
6042

Current values
6408:
$10.00 – 25.00
6041:
$10.00 – 25.00
6042:
$10.00 – 25.00
6073:
$10.00 – 25.00
6074:
$10.00 – 25.00

6392 BOWL 6237 BOWL
6303 " 6164 "
6335 " 6375 "

Current values
6392:
$25.00 – 55.00
6303:
$25.00 – 55.00
6335:
$60.00 – 100.00
6237:
$25.00 – 55.00
6164:
$60.00 – 100.00
6375:
$60.00 – 100.00

6064 BOWL 6382
6067 6567

Current values
6064:
$20.00 – 50.00
6067:
$20.00 – 50.00
6382:
$20.00 – 50.00
6567:
$20.00 – 50.00

210 BOWL

Current values
210 bowl (all sizes)
each: $15.00 – 30.00

CEILING BOWLS AND BALLS

No.		Diam.	Height	Fitter
97	Ball	6"	6 "	3¼"
		7"	7 "	3¼–4"
		8"	8 "	3¼–4"
		10"	10 "	4–5–6"
		12"	12 "	4–5–6–7–8"
		14"	14 "	6–7–8"
		16"	16 "	6–7–8"
		18"	18 "	6–8–10–12"
		20"	20 "	6–8–10–12"
6408	Ball	6"	4½"	3¼"
6041	"	7"	5 "	3¼"
6042	"	8"	5½"	3¼–4"
6073	"	10"	6 "	5"
6074	"	12"	6¾"	6"
210	Bowl	9"	4¼"	7"
		10"	4¾"	8"
		12"	5⅝"	10"
		14"	5⅝"	12"

No.		Diam.	Height	Fitter
6052	Bowl	8"	4 "	8"
		10"	5 "	10"
		12"	6 "	12"
		14"	7 "	14"
		16"	8 "	16"
6064	Bowl	10"	3⅛"	10"
6067	"	12"	3⅛"	12"
6382	"	14"	4 "	14"
6567	"	16"	5 "	16"
6392	Bowl	12"	4 "	12"
6237	"	14"	5 "	14"
6303	"	16"	6 "	16"
6164	"	18"	7 "	18"
6335	"	20"	7½"	20"
6375	"	22"	8½"	22"

GILLINDER & SONS, Inc., PHILADELPHIA

ESTABLISHED 1861

PLATE No. 35

MELILITE BOWLS

Note: Prices will vary depending on shade sizes.

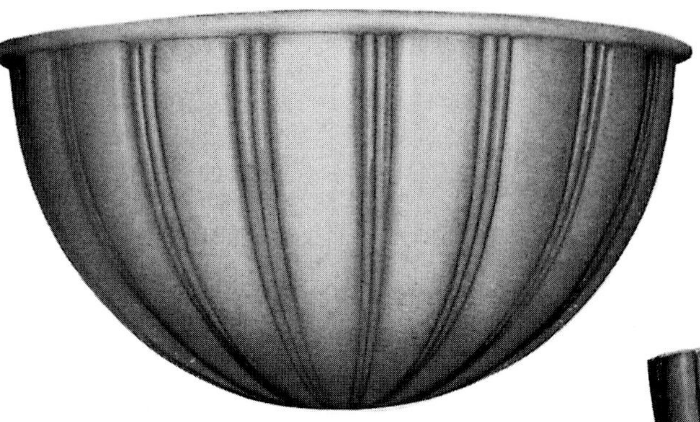

5141 BOWL 5143
5142 5148

Current values
5141, 5142, 5143, 5148
each: $35.00 – 65.00

5141½ BOWL 5143½
5142½ 5148½

Current values
5141½, 5142½, 5143½,
5148½ each: $50.00 – 100.00

5191 BOWL 5192
5189 5193

Current values
5191, 5189, 5192, 5193
each: $40.00 – 85.00

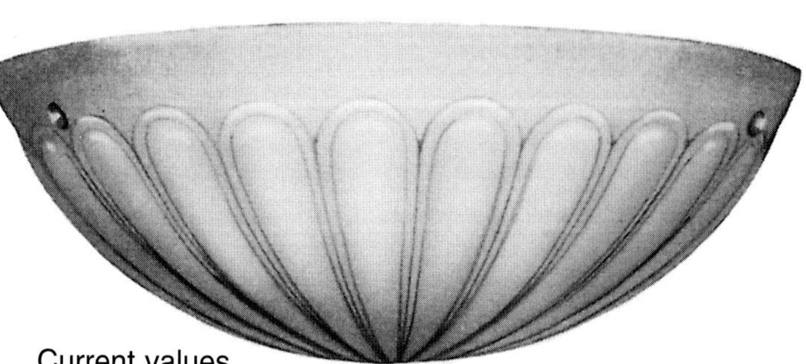

Current values
5191½, 5192½, 5189½, 5193½
each: $75.00 – 150.00

5191½ BOWL 5192½
5189½ 5193½

BOWLS FOR SLIP-IN COLLAR
BOWLS WITH 3 HOLES FOR CHAIN SUSPENSION

5141	Bowl	10″	5 ″	With Lip
5142	Bowl	12″	6 ″	With Lip
5143	Bowl	14″	7 ″	With Lip
5148	Bowl	16″	8 ″	With Lip
5191	Bowl	14″	4½″	With Lip
5189	Bowl	16″	5¼″	With Lip
5192	Bowl	18″	6 ″	With Lip
5193	Bowl	20″	6¾″	With Lip

No.		Diam.	Height	
5141½	Bowl	9⅜″	4⅝″	No Lip, 3 Holes
5142½	Bowl	11⅜″	5⅝″	No Lip, 3 Holes
5143½	Bowl	13¼″	6¾″	No Lip, 3 Holes
5148½	Bowl	15⅛″	7¾″	No Lip, 3 Holes
5191½	Bowl	13⅜″	4¼″	No Lip, 3 Holes
5189½	Bowl	15⅜″	5 ″	No Lip, 3 Holes
5192½	Bowl	17⅜″	5¾″	No Lip, 3 Holes
5193½	Bowl	19⅜″	6½″	No Lip, 3 Holes

GILLINDER & SONS, Inc., PHILADELPHIA

ESTABLISHED 1861

Note: Prices will vary depending on shade sizes.

PLATE No. 37

6002/881 ASTRAL
Current value: $35.00 – 55.00

6002/848 ASTRAL
Current value: $35.00 – 55.00

6002/9113 ASTRAL
Current value: $35.00 – 55.00

239/881 ASTRAL
240/881 "
Current value: $30.00 – 60.00

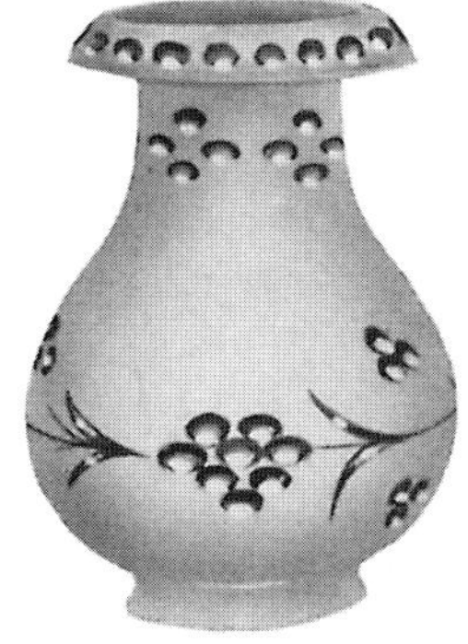

239/880 ASTRAL
240/880 "
Current value: $30.00 – 60.00

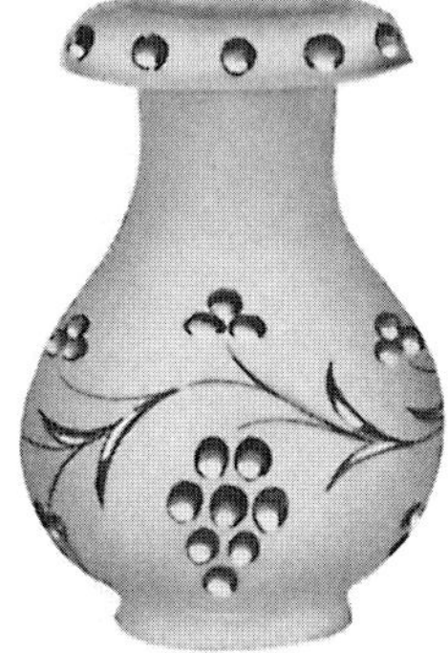

239/9112 ASTRAL
240/9112 "
Current value: $30.00 – 60.00

290/881 ASTRAL
Current value: $45.00 – 75.00

6002/880 ASTRAL
Current value: $35.00 – 55.00

6104/881 ASTRAL
6205/881 "
Current value: $40.00 – 65.00

ASTRALS—CRYSTAL ROUGHED OUTSIDE AND CUT

No.		Diam.	Height	Fitter
239/880	Astral	5½"	7 "	3¼"
240/880	Astral	5½"	8¼"	3¼"
239/881	Astral	5½"	7 "	3¼"
240/881	Astral	5½"	8¼"	3¼"
239/9112	Astral	5½"	7 "	3¼"
240/9112	Astral	5½"	8¼"	3¼"
290/881	Astral	6½"	7 "	3¼"

No.		Diam.	Height	Fitter
6002/848	Astral	5 "	6"	3¼"
6002/880	Astral	5 "	6"	3¼"
6002/881	Astral	5 "	6"	3¼"
6002/9113	Astral	5 "	6"	3¼"
6104/881	Astral	6½"	6"	4 "
6205/881	Astral	6½"	6"	3¼"

GILLINDER & SONS, Inc., PHILADELPHIA

ESTABLISHED 1861

Note: Prices will vary depending on shade size.

PLATE No. 38

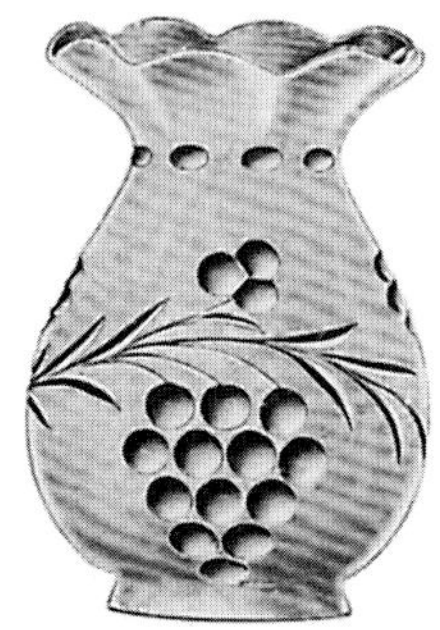

6085/881 HARP
6086/881 "
6087/881 "
Current value: $35.00 – 50.00

7001/881 ASTRAL
7002/881 "
7003/881 "
Current value
9": $85.00 – 120.00
11": $135.00 – 185.00
14": $200.00 – 275.00

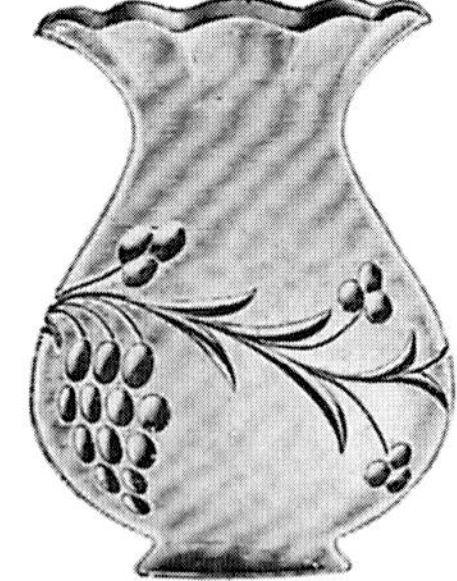

6085/849 HARP
6086/849 "
6087/849 "
Current value: $35.00 – 50.00

6143/8009½ ELECTRIC
Current value: $40.00 – 60.00

273/881 CANDLE SHADE
Current value: $30.00 – 40.00

6143/8009 ELECTRIC
Current value: $40.00 – 60.00

6182/8057 HARP
Current value: $45.00 – 70.00

218/881 ELECTRIC
Current value: $30.00 – 40.00

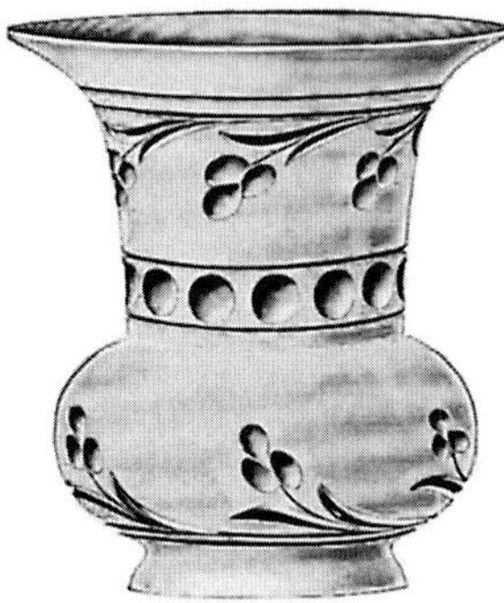

6182/8058 HARP
Current value: $40.00 – 50.00

ASTRALS, ELECTRICS AND HARPS—ROUGHED OUTSIDE AND CUT

No.		Diam.	Height	Fitter
218/881	Electric . .	5½"	4 "	4 "
273/881	Candle Shade	5⅝"	3¼"	5⅛" Bottom
6085/849	Harp . .	4¼"	5¾"	2¼"
6086/849	Harp . .	4¼"	5¾"	2¾" Princess
6087/849	Harp . .	4¼"	5¾"	3¼"
6085/881	Harp . .	4¼"	5¾"	2¼"
6086/881	Harp . .	4¼"	5¾"	2¾" Princess
6087/881	Harp . .	4¼"	5¾"	3¼"

No.		Diam.	Height	Fitter
6143/8009	Electric	5⅝"	6¼"	2¼"
6143/8009½	Electric	5⅝"	6¼"	2¼"
6182/8057	Harp	5¾"	6⅛"	3¼"
6182/8058	Harp	5¾"	6⅛"	3¼"
7001/881	Astral	9 .	7 "	6 "
7002/881	Astral	11 "	7½"	8 "
7003/881	Astral	14 "	8 "	10 "

GILLINDER & SONS, Inc., PHILADELPHIA

ESTABLISHED 1861

Note: Prices will vary depending on shade size.

PLATE No. 39

289/9115 ELECTRIC
Current value: $35.00 – 45.00

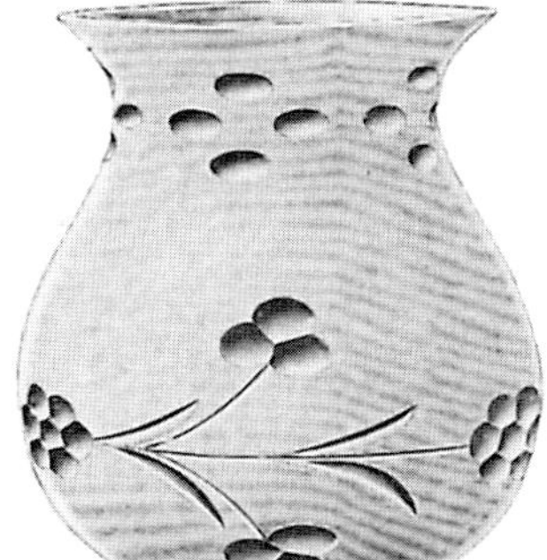

289/880 ELECTRIC
295/880 "

Current value
289/880: $35.00 – 45.00
295/880: $25.00 – 35.00

289/881 ELECTRIC
Current value: $35.00 – 45.00

6096/9117 ELECTRIC
Current value: $20.00 – 30.00

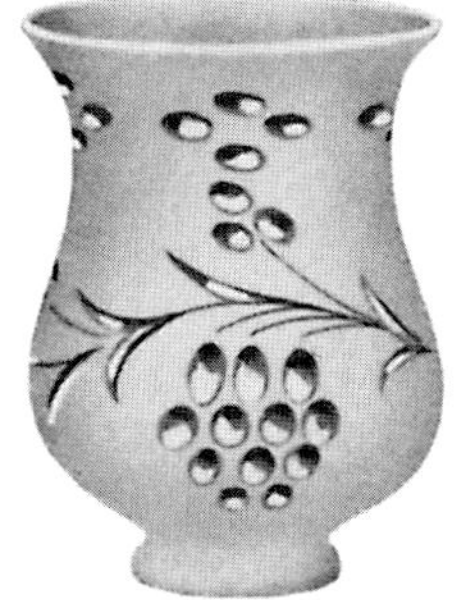

295/881 ELECTRIC
Current value: $25.00 – 35.00

6096/849 ELECTRIC
Current value: $20.00 – 30.00

6075/881 HARP
6013/881 "
Current value: $30.00 – 40.00

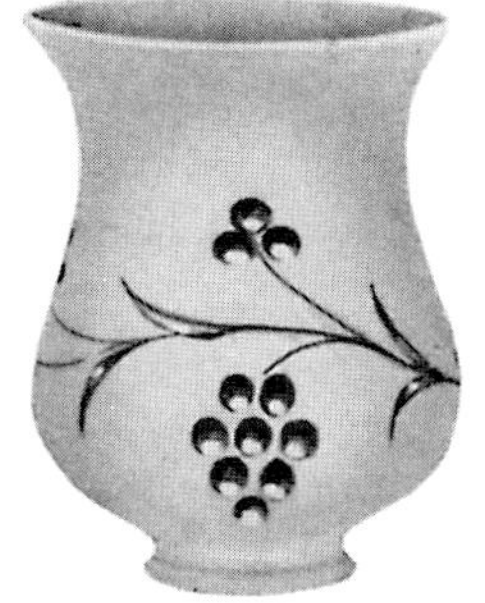

295/9118 ELECTRIC
Current value: $25.00 – 35.00

6075/848 HARP
6013/848 "
Current value: $30.00 – 40.00

ELECTRICS—ROUGHED OUTSIDE AND CUT

No.		Diam.	Height	Fitter
289/880	Electric	5″	6″	2¼″
289/881	Electric	5″	6″	2¼″
289/9115	Electric	5″	6″	2¼″
295/880	Electric	4″	5″	2¼″
295/881	Electric	4″	5″	2¼″
295/9118	Electric	4″	5″	2¼″

No.		Diam.	Height	Fitter	
6013/848	Harp	6¼″	5⅜″	4″	Straight
6075/848	Harp	6 ″	5½″	3¼″	
6013/881	Harp	6¼″	5⅜″	4″	Straight
6075/881	Harp	6 ″	5½″	3¼″	
6096/9117	Electric	4⅜″	4⅜″	2¼″	
6096/849	Electric	4⅜″	4⅜″	2¼″	

GILLINDER & SONS, Inc., PHILADELPHIA

ESTABLISHED 1861

Note: Prices will vary depending on shade size.

PLATE No. 40

6110/1944
6169/1944
CANDLE GLOBES
White Etched Pattern

Current value: $40.00 – 55.00

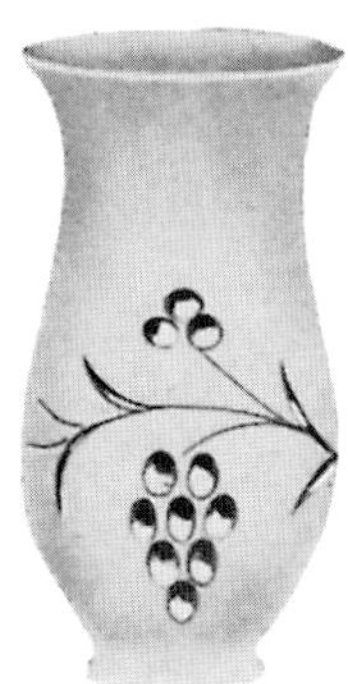

6033/9116
ELECTRIC

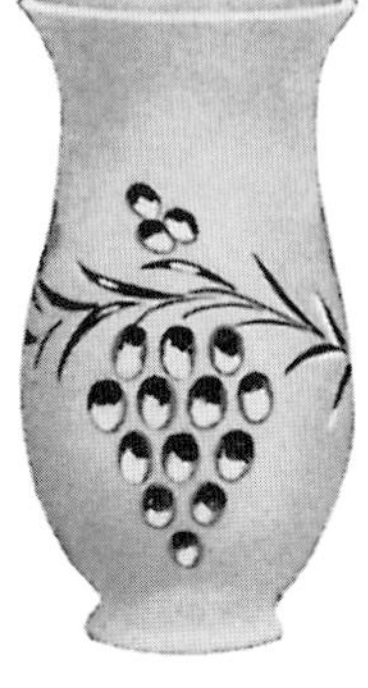

6033/881
ELECTRIC

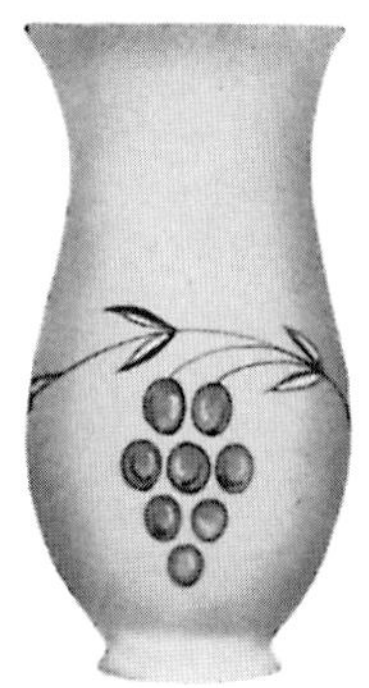

6033/9160
ELECTRIC

Current value
6033/9116, 6033/881, 6033/9160 each: $25.00 – 35.00

6110/1945
6169/1945
CANDLE GLOBES
White Etched Pattern

Current value: $40.00 – 55.00

6102/8009
WIND GUARD

Current value: $35.00 – 45.00

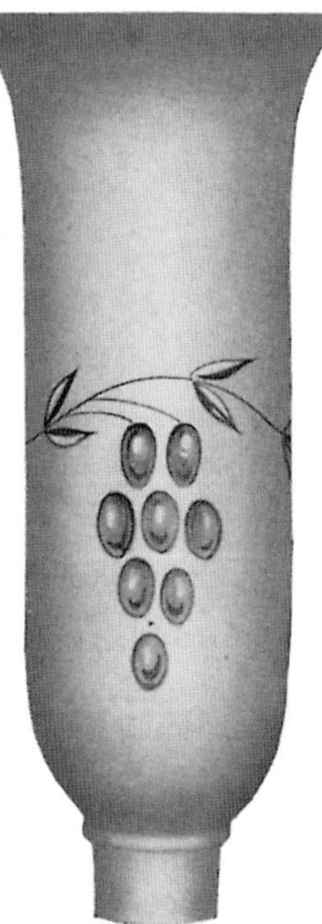

6110/9160
6169/9160
CANDLE GLOBES

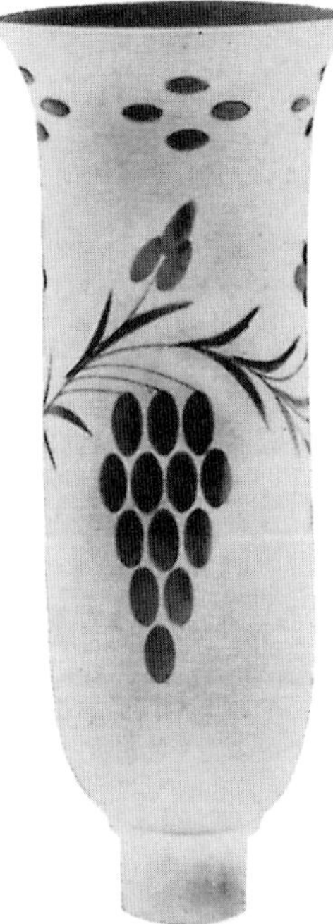

6110/881
6169/881
CANDLE GLOBES

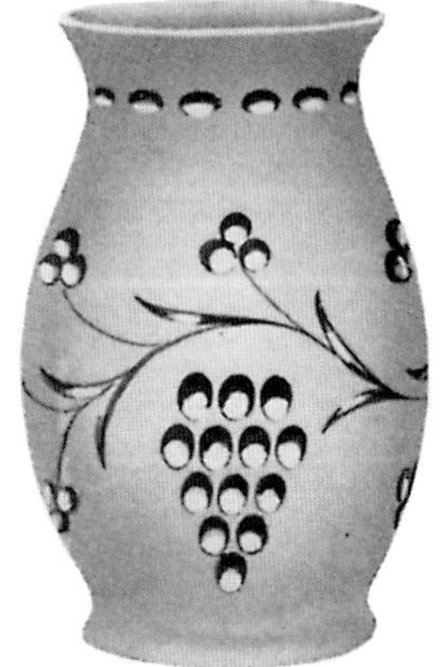

6102/9131
WIND GUARD

Current value: $35.00 – 45.00

Current value 6110/9160 & 881; 6169/9160 & 881: $30.00 – 40.00

ELECTRICS, ETC.—ROUGHED OUTSIDE AND CUT

No.		Diam.	Height	Fitter
6033/881	Electric .	4 "	7 "	2¼"
6033/9116	Electric .	4 "	7 "	2¼"
6033/9160	Electric .	4 "	7 "	2¼"
6102/8009	Wind Guard	5¼"	7¾"	4 "
6102/9131	Wind Guard	5¼"	7¾"	4 "

N.B. All Candle Globes furnished with Brass Ferrule.

No.		Diam.	Height	Fitter
6110/1944	Candle Globe	4½"	10½"	1⅝"
6169/1944	Candle Globe	3¾"	8 "	1⅝"
6110/1945	Candle Globe	4½"	10½"	1⅝"
6169/1945	Candle Globe	3¾"	8 "	1⅝"
6110/881	Candle Globe	4½"	10½"	1⅝"
6169/881	Candle Globe	3¾"	8 "	1⅝"
6110/9160	Candle Globe	4½"	10½"	1⅝"
6169/9160	Candle Globe	3¾"	8 "	1⅝"

GILLINDER & SONS, Inc., PHILADELPHIA

ESTABLISHED 1861

PLATE No. 41

Note: Prices will vary depending on shade size.

6102/808
WIND GUARD
Current value: $25.00 – 35.00

240/808
ASTRAL
Current value: $35.00 – 45.00

239/808
ASTRAL
Current value: $35.00 – 45.00

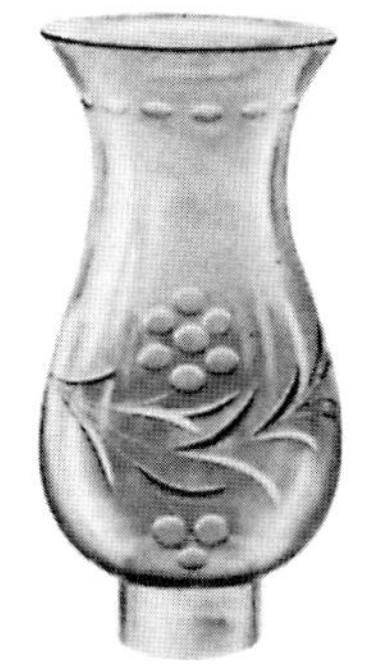

6699/9198
CANDLE GLOBE
Current value: $30.00 – 40.00

6002/808
ASTRAL
Current value: $35.00 – 45.00

6085/808
6086/808
6087/808
HARP
Current value each: $25.00 – 35.00

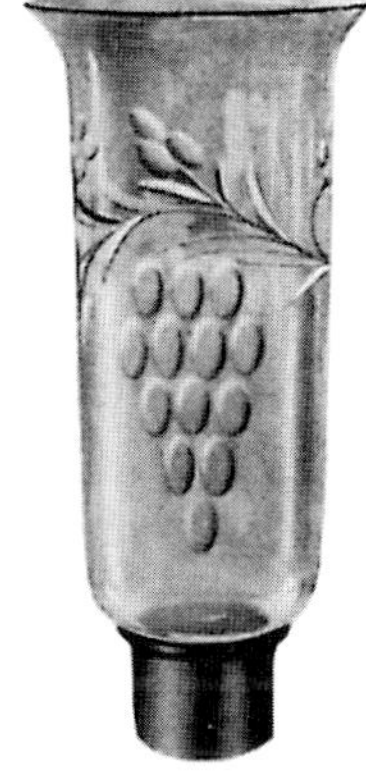

6169/808
CANDLE GLOBE
Brass Ferrule
Current value: $30.00 – 40.00

CLEAR GLASS WITH CUT DESIGN

No.		Diam.	Height	Fitter	
239/808	Astral . .	5½"	7 "	3¼"	
240/808	Astral . .	5½"	8¼"	3¼"	
6002/808	Astral . .	5 "	6 "	3¼"	
6085/808	Harp . .	4¼"	5¾"	2¼"	
6086/808	Harp . .	4¼"	5¾"	2¾"	Princess
6087/808	Harp . .	4¼"	5¾"	3¼"	
6102/808	Wind Guard	5¼"	7¾"	4 "	
6169/808	Candle Globe	3¾"	8 "	1⅝"	
6699/9198	Candle Globe	3¼"	6½"	1⅝"	

GILLINDER & SONS, Inc., PHILADELPHIA

ESTABLISHED 1861

Note: Prices will vary depending on shade size.

PLATE No. 42

289/808
ELECTRIC
Current value:
$30.00 – 40.00

218/808
ELECTRIC
Current value:
$30.00 – 40.00

6013/808
6075/808
HARP
Current value each:
$30.00 – 40.00

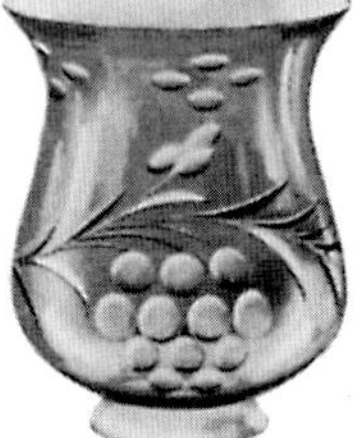

295/808
ELECTRIC
Current value:
$30.00 – 40.00

6096/808
ELECTRIC
Current value:
$30.00 – 40.00

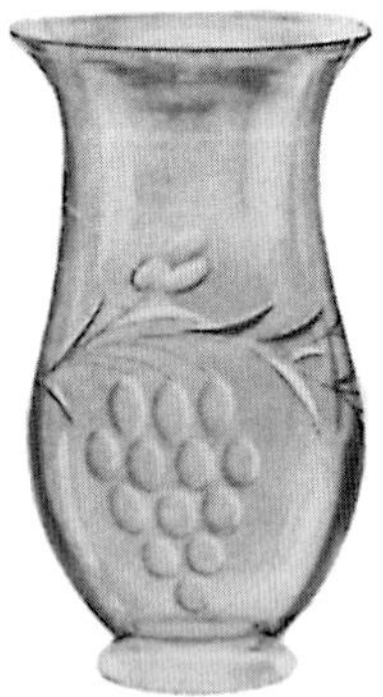

6033/808
ELECTRIC
Current value:
$30.00 – 40.00

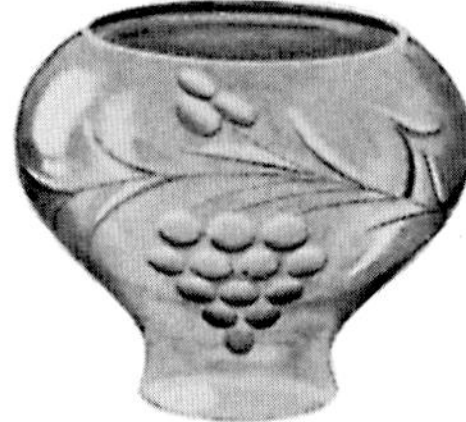

6012/808
ELECTRIC
Current value:
$30.00 – 40.00

6182/808
HARP
Current value:
$30.00 – 40.00

CLEAR GLASS WITH CUT DESIGN

218/808	Electric . .	5½"	4 "	4 "	
289/808	Electric . .	5 "	6 "	2¼"	
295/808	Electric . .	4 "	5 "	2¼"	
6012/808	Electric . .	5 "	4 "	2¼"	
6013/808	Harp . . .	6¼"	5⅜"	4 "	Straight
6033/808	Electric . .	4 "	7 "	2¼"	
6075/808	Harp . . .	6 "	5½"	3¼"	
6096/808	Electric . .	4⅜"	4⅜"	2¼"	
6182/808	Harp . . .	5¾"	6⅛"	3¼"	

GILLINDER & SONS, Inc., PHILADELPHIA

ESTABLISHED 1861

PLATE No. 43

Note: Prices will vary depending on shade size.

249/881 ELECTRIC
6056/881 "
250/881 "

Current value
249/881: $30.00 – 40.00
6056/881: $30.00 – 40.00
250/881: $30.00 – 40.00

6140/881 ELECTRIC
6159/881 "
6160/881 "

Current value
6140/881: $30.00 – 40.00
6159/881: $30.00 – 40.00
6160/881: $30.00 – 40.00

244/881 ELECTRIC

Current value:
$30.00 – 40.00

6688/881 BEDROOM

Current value:
$40.00 – 50.00

6072/881 ELECTRIC

Current value:
$30.00 – 40.00

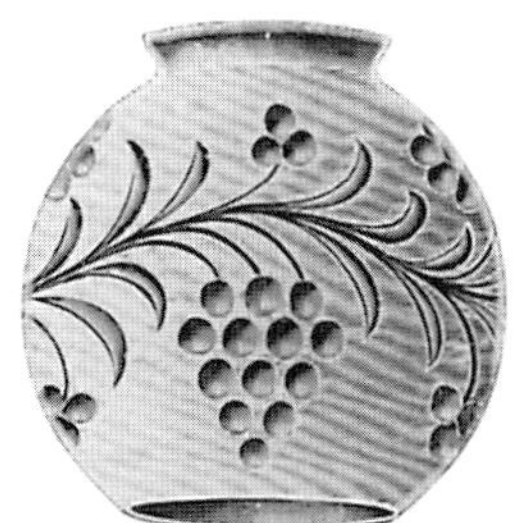

173/881 ELECTRIC

Current value:
$40.00 – 50.00

ELECTRICS ROUGHED OUTSIDE AND CUT

No.		Diam.	Height	Fitter
173/881	Electric	4⅜"	4 "	2¼"
244/881	Electric	6½"	3 "	2¼"
249/881	Electric	6 "	4 "	2¼"
6056/881	Electric	7 "	4½"	2¼"
250/881	Electric	8 "	5 "	2¼"

No.		Diam.	Height	Fitter
6072/881	Electric	5 "	4½"	2¼"
6688/881	Bedroom	8 "	5 "	2¼"
6140/881	Electric	5½"	4½"	2¼"
6159/881	Electric	6½"	4¾"	2¼"
6160/881	Electric	7 "	5¼"	2¼"

GILLINDER & SONS, Inc., PHILADELPHIA

ESTABLISHED 1861

Note: Prices will vary depending on shade size.

PLATE No. 44

Current value each: $40.00 – 75.00

6098/881 CYLINDER
6099/881 "
6100/881 "
6142/881 "

6090/881 CYLINDER
Current value: $40.00 – 65.00

Current value each: $40.00 – 75.00

6094/881 CYLINDER
6095/881 "
6173/881 "

6408/881 BALL
6041/881 "
6042/881 "

Current value each: $45.00 – 75.00

6064/881 BOWL
6067/881 "
6382/881 "

Current value: $85.00 – 150.00

Current value: $75.00 – 200.00

6052/881 BOWL

210/881 BOWL

Current value:
9": $75.00 – 100.00
10": $100.00 – 130.00
12": $130.00 – 175.00
14": $150.00 – 200.00

CYLINDERS AND BOWLS—ROUGHED OUTSIDE AND CUT

No.		Diam.	Height	Fitter
6090/881	Cylinder	4 "	6 "	. . .
		3 "	8 "	. . .
		4 "	8 "	. . .
		5 "	7 "	. . .
		6 "	8 "	. . .
		7 "	9 "	. . .
6094/881	Cylinder	3¼"	5 "	3¼"
6095/881	Cylinder	3¼"	6 "	3¼"
6173/881	Cylinder	5 "	8 "	5 "
6098/881	Cylinder	3¼"	4¾"	2¼"
6099/881	Cylinder	3½"	5¼"	2¼"
6100/881	Cylinder	4 "	6 "	3¼"
6142/881	Cylinder	4 "	5 "	3¼"

No.		Diam.	Height	Fitter
210/881	Bowl	9"	4¼"	7 "
210/881	Bowl	10"	4¾"	8 "
210/881	Bowl	12"	5⅝"	10 "
210/881	Bowl	14"	5⅞"	12 "
6052/881	Bowl	8"	4 "	8 "
6052/881	Bowl	10"	5 "	10 "
6052/881	Bowl	12"	6 "	12 "
6052/881	Bowl	14"	7 "	14 "
6064/881	Bowl	10"	3⅛"	10 "
6067/881	Bowl	12"	3⅛"	12 "
6382/881	Bowl	14"	4 "	14 "
6408/881	Ball	6"	4½"	3¼"
6041/881	Ball	7"	5 "	3¼"
6042/881	Ball	8"	5½"	3¼–4"

GILLINDER & SONS, Inc., PHILADELPHIA

ESTABLISHED 1861

PLATE No. 45

205/881 DOME
Current value: $100.00 – 135.00

211/881 DOME
Current value: $120.00 – 140.00

09829/881 DOME
Current value: $100.00 – 125.00

285/881 DOME
286/881 DOME
Current value
285/881: $85.00 – 100.00
286/881: $100.00 – 125.00

6462/881 DOME
Current value: $75.00 – 95.00

6576/881 DOME
Current value: $65.00 – 75.00

DOMES ROUGHED OUTSIDE AND CUT

205/881	Dome	. . .	11½″	6 ″	10″
211/881	Dome	. . .	12¾″	6¼″	10″
285/881	Dome	. . .	8 ″	5¼″	5″
286/881	Dome	. . .	11 ″	6 ″	8″
6462/881	Dome	. . .	7¾″	5½″	7″
6576/881	Dome	. . .	6 ″	4¼″	6″
09829/881	Dome	. . .	10 ″	6 ″	10″

GILLINDER & SONS, Inc., PHILADELPHIA

ESTABLISHED 1861

Note: Prices will vary depending on shade size.

PLATE No. 46

210/9160 BOWL

Current value: $100.00 – 150.00

97/9160 BALL

Current value: $40.00 – 75.00

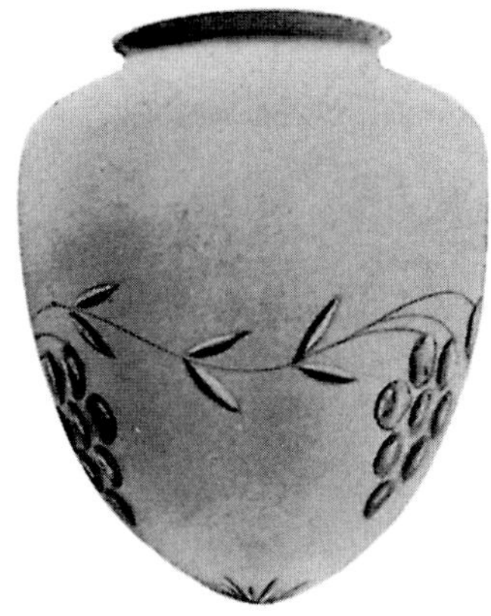

6637/9160 HALL GLOBE

Current value: $85.00 – 100.00

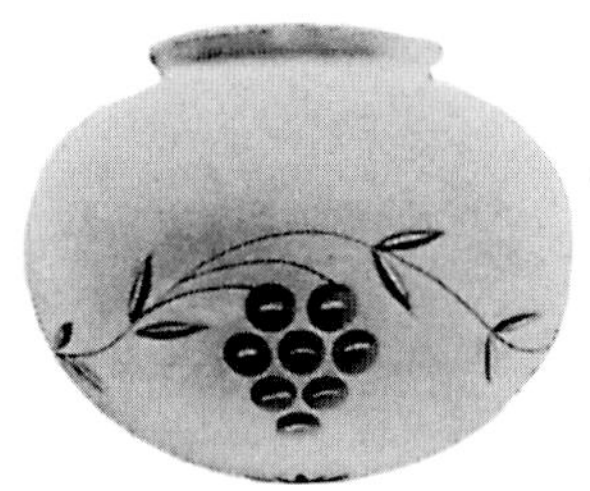

6408/9160 BALL
6041/9160 "
6042/9160 "

Current value: $40.00 – 75.00

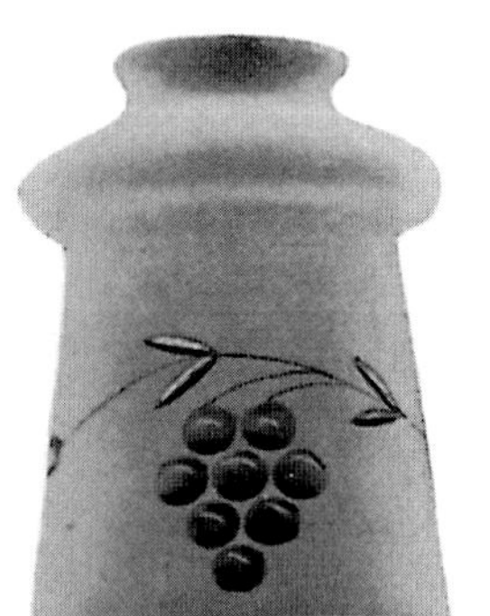

6725/9160 ELECTRIC

Current value: $50.00 – 85.00

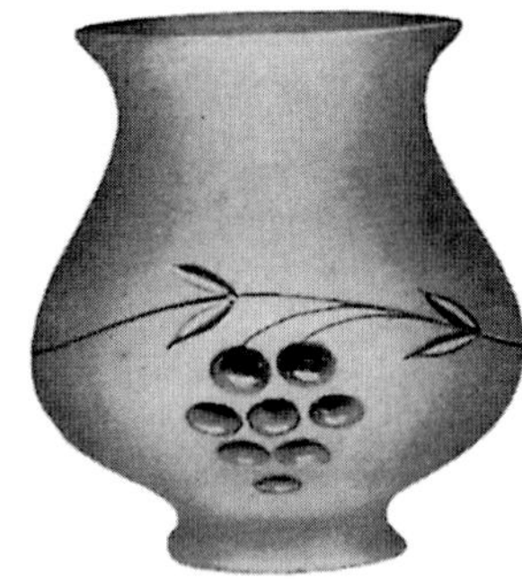

6096/9160 ELECTRIC

Current value: $20.00 – 25.00

ROUGHED OUTSIDE AND CUT

No.		Diam.	Height	Fitter
97/9160	Ball	6 "	6 "	3¼"
97/9160	Ball	7 "	7 "	3¼"
97/9160	Ball	8 "	8 "	3¼–4"
210/9160	Bowl	10 "	4¾"	8 "
210/9160	Bowl	12 "	5⅝"	10 "
210/9160	Bowl	14 "	6 "	12 "
6096/9160	Electric	4⅜"	4⅜"	2¼"

No.		Diam.	Height	Fitter
6408/9160	Ball . .	6"	4½"	3¼"
6041/9160	Ball . .	7"	5 "	3¼"
6042/9160	Ball . .	8"	5½"	3¼–4"
6637/9160	Hall Globe	. .	6 "	3¼"
6637/9160	Hall Globe	. .	8 "	4 "
6725/9160	Electric .	4"	5 "	2¼"

GILLINDER & SONS, Inc., PHILADELPHIA

ESTABLISHED 1861

PLATE No. 47

Note: Prices will vary depending on shade size.

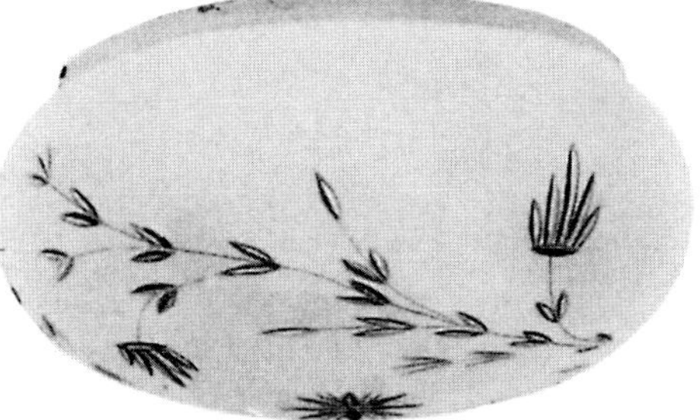

210/9154 BOWL
Current value: $50.00 – 100.00

97/9154 BALL
Current value: $35.00 – 65.00

6408/9154 BALL
6041/9154 "
6042/9154 "
Current value: $35.00 – 65.00

6096/9154 ELECTRIC
Current value: $25.00 – 30.00

6725/9154 ELECTRIC
Current value: $25.00 – 30.00

6230/9154 ELECTRIC
Current value: $25.00 – 30.00

ROUGHED OUTSIDE AND CUT

No.		Diam.	Height	Fitter	No.		Diam.	Height	Fitter
97/9154	Ball	6″	6 ″	3¼″	210/9154	Bowl	10 ″	4¾″	8 ″
97/9154	Ball	7″	7 ″	3¼″	210/9154	Bowl	12 ″	5⅝″	10 ″
97/9154	Ball	8″	8 ″	3¼–4″	210/9154	Bowl	14 ″	6 ″	12 ″
6408/9154	Ball	6″	4½″	3¼″	6096/9154	Electric	4⅜″	4⅜″	2¼″
6041/9154	Ball	7″	5 ″	3¼″	6230/9154	Electric	4⅜″	4⅝″	2¼″
6042/9154	Ball	8″	5½″	3¼–4″	6725/9154	Electric	4 ″	5 ″	2¼″

GILLINDER & SONS, Inc., PHILADELPHIA

ESTABLISHED 1861

PLATE No. 48

Note: Prices will vary depending on shade size and lettering.

5260

FLAT-SIDED BALLS FOR ADVERTISING

No.	Diam.	Width	Fitter
5260 Ball Opal	6″	3¼″	3¼″
	8″	4 ″	4 ″
	10″	5 ″	4–5″
	12″	6 ″	4–6″
	14″	7 ″	6–7″
	16″	8 ″	8 ″
	18″	8 ″	8 ″

Current value each: $50.00 – 175.00

No.	Lettering	Size
5260 Ball Lettered	"Up" . . .	6x3¼″
	"Down" . .	6x3¼″
	"Beauty Parlor"	10x4–5″
	"Beauty Parlor"	12x4–6″
	"Hair Bobbing"	10x4–5″
	"Hair Bobbing"	12x4–6″
	"Barber Shop"	12x4″

Current value each: $135.00 – 350.00

GILLINDER & SONS, Inc., PHILADELPHIA

ESTABLISHED 1861

PLATE No. 49

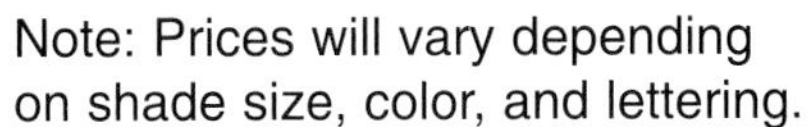

Note: Prices will vary depending on shade size, color, and lettering.

Current value each:
$150.00 – 250.00

11026/A6

Current value
5260: $150.00 – 200.00
11026/A1, A2, A6: $250.00 – 350.00

11026/A2

11026/A1

FLAT-SIDED BALLS FOR ADVERTISING

5260	Ball Opal, Lettered	"Free Air"	10x4–5″
		"Free Air"	12x5–6″
		"Gasoline"	10x4–5″
		"Gasoline"	12x5–6″
		"Garage"	12x6″
5260	Ball Opal, Lettered	"Elevator"	10x5″
		"Elevator"	12x6″
*11026/A1	Ball, Lettered	"Fire Escape"	
*11026/A2	Ball, Lettered	"Stairs"	
*11026/A6	Ball, Lettered	"Exit"	

* Red Ball—White Enameled Letters.

GILLINDER & SONS, Inc., PHILADELPHIA

ESTABLISHED 1861

Note: Prices will vary depending on shade size and color.

PLATE No. 50

1939 SQUAT, 7½x4"

Current value all Squat: $135.00 – 185.00

175/1941 ELECTRIC

Current value all 175 Electric: $125.00 – 150.00

5450 GLOBE, LETTERED "MEN"

Current value 5450: $200.00 – 300.00

97/1940 BALL

Current value
6 x 3¼": $165.00 – 195.00
7 x 3½": $165.00 – 195.00
8 x 3¼": $195.00 – 225.00

5450 GLOBE, LETTERED "WOMEN"

Either lettering or background etched 1939 and 1940: $200.00 – 285.00

97/1939	Ball,	6x3¼"	Lettered "Exit"
97/1940	Ball,	6x3¼"	Lettered "Fire Escape"
97/1941	Ball,	6x3¼"	Lettered "Up"
97/1942	Ball,	6x3¼"	Lettered "Down"
97/1939	Ball,	7x3¼"	Lettered "Exit"
97/1940	Ball,	7x3¼"	Lettered "Fire Escape"
97/1941	Ball,	7x3¼"	Lettered "Up"
97/1942	Ball,	7x3¼"	Lettered "Down"
97/1939	Ball,	8x3¼–4"	Lettered "Exit"
97/1940	Ball,	8x3¼–4"	Lettered "Fire Escape"
97/1941	Ball,	8x3¼–4"	Lettered "Up"
97/1942	Ball,	8x3¼–4"	Lettered "Down"

175/1939	Electric,		Lettered "Exit"
175/1940	Electric,		Lettered "Fire Escape"
175/1941	Electric,		Lettered "Up"
175/1942	Electric,		Lettered "Down"
1939	Squat,	7½x4",	Lettered "Exit"
1940	Squat,	7½x4",	Lettered "Fire Escape"
1941	Squat,	7½x4",	Lettered "Up"
1942	Squat,	7½x4",	Lettered "Down"

1939 and 1940 Made in Ruby Glass
Either Lettering or Background Etched

5450 Ball Lettered "Men," black with white letters
5450 Ball Lettered "Women," blue with white letters

GILLINDER & SONS, Inc., PHILADELPHIA

ESTABLISHED 1861

PLATE No. 51

0518 GAS
Current value: $45.00 – 60.00

0518 ELECTRIC
Current value: $25.00 – 35.00

1977 GAS
Current value: $30.00 – 40.00

1977 ELECTRIC
Current value: $20.00 – 25.00

4102 GAS
Current value: $45.00 – 60.00

4102 ELECTRIC
Current value: $30.00 – 45.00

			Diam.	Height	Fitter
0518	Gas	White Acid . .	7½"	4¼"	4 "
0518	Electric	White Acid . .	4 "	4¼"	2¼"
1977	Gas	White Acid . .	7½"	4¼"	4 "
1977	Electric	White Acid . .	4 "	4¼"	2¼"
4102	Gas	Roughed, Clear Lines	7¼"	4 "	4 "
4102	Electric	Roughed, Clear Lines	5 "	4⅜"	2¼"

GILLINDER & SONS, Inc., PHILADELPHIA

ESTABLISHED 1861

PLATE No. 52

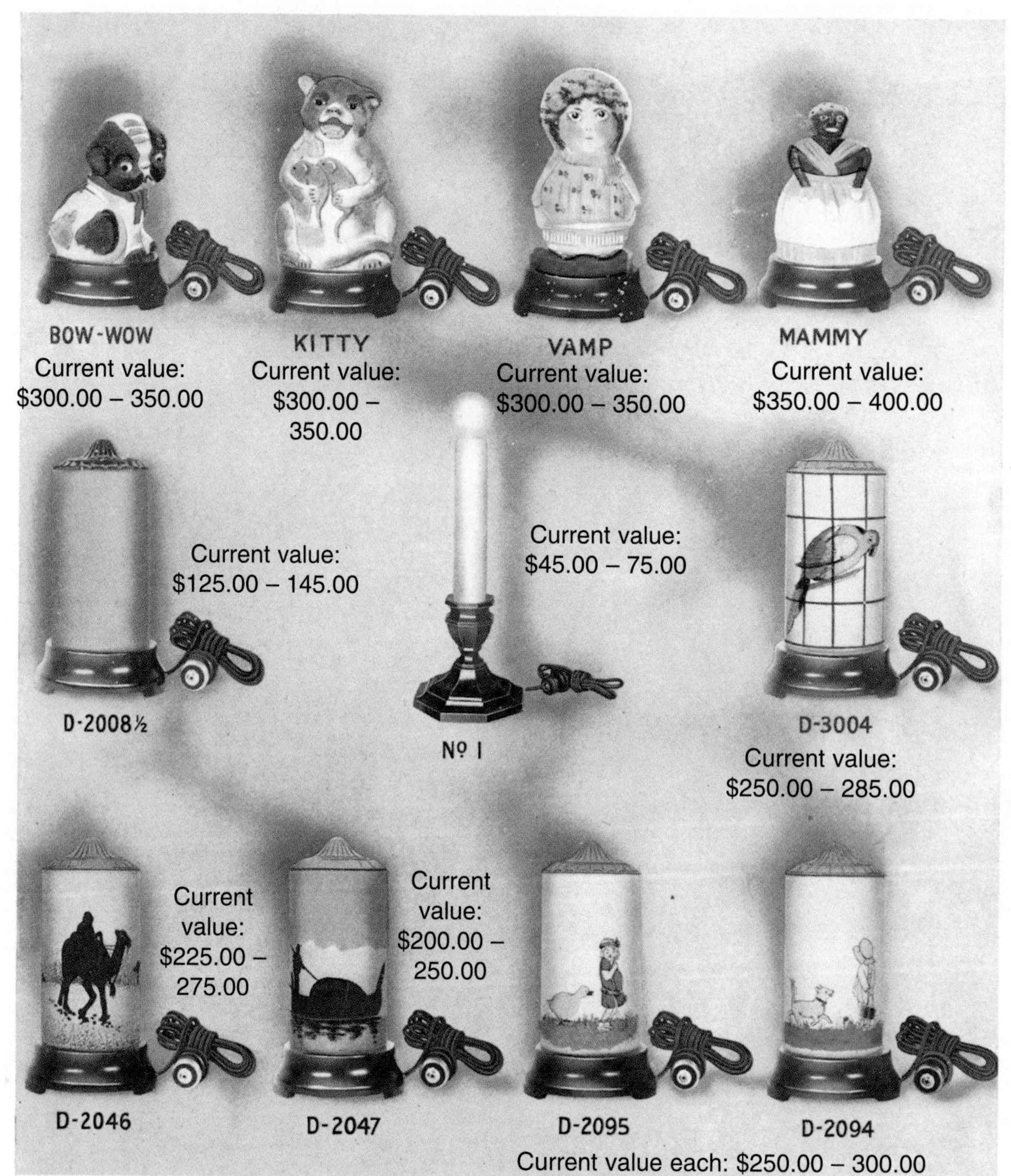

NOVELTY NIGHT LAMPS AND TORCHIERES

Bow-wow Night Lamp	6½"	Overall—Black Glass Base—
Vamp Night Lamp	8½"	Overall—Black Glass Base—
Mammy Night Lamp	7½"	Overall—Black Glass Base—
Kitty Night Lamp	8 "	Overall—Black Glass Base—
No. 1 Electric Candlestick	13½"	Overall—Black Glass Base—Opal Candle
D-2008½ Torchiere	9 "	Overall—Black Glass Base—Blue, Gray or Tan Parchment
D-2046 Torchiere	9 "	Overall—Black Glass Base—Camel Scene
D-2047 Torchiere	9 "	Overall—Black Glass Base—Gondola Scene
D-2094 Torchiere	9 "	Overall—Black Glass Base—Nursery Scene—Schoolgirl and Dog
D-2095 Torchiere	9 "	Overall—Black Glass Base—Nursery Scene—Duck Chasing Girl
D-3004 Torchiere	9 "	Overall—Black Glass Base—Parrot in Cage

Complete with Cord, Plug and Socket—No Lamp. Through Switch on Cord Extra.

Halcolite Company, Inc.

On the following pages, we take pleasure in presenting the latest creations and designs by HALCOLITE.

Cable Address:
Halcolite, New York

Telephones: Canal
6020 6021

HALCOLITE COMPANY, INC.

Manufacturers of Lighting Equipment
100 Grand St. New York

April 12, 1929

United Ltg. Fix. Co.
San Francisco, Cal.

Gentlemen:

Our latest Lighting Equipment Catalogue "J" has been mailed out to you to-day.

In this catalogue you will find illustrated a very complete line of lighting equipment at a wide range of prices.

Your discount from the price list included with this catalogue is 50% and 20%.

We have gone to considerable expense and labor in compiling this catalogue for your use, and would like very much to receive from you an acknowledgement of same, and also any comments you may wish to make.

Very truly yours,
HALCOLITE COMPANY INC.

M. Aaron

MA:RH

Sales Manager

SEVILLE HALCOLITES

SEVILLE HALCOLITES; the result of an intensive study of present day requirements in the residential lighting field.

These Halcolites are simple in design and yet retain the rugged appearance and sturdy features which make them so entirely suitable for the Spanish and English types of home now at the height of their popularity.

Particular attention is called to the finishes, i.e., Stained Bronze or Swedish Iron, both heretofore used only on much more expensive lighting fixtures than these surprisingly moderate priced Seville Halcolites.

SEVILLE HALCOLITES are the exclusive creation of the Halcolite Company, Inc., and are covered by United States Design Patents and applications therefor.

No. 1518
Made of Cast Metal
Plate 8¼" x 4½" – Extension 4"
Length over all 18½"
Wired with Pin Switch
Finish: Stained Bronze
Swedish Iron
Current value: $50.00 – 65.00
1518
1519
No. 1519
Made of Cast Metal
Plate 8¾" x 4½" – Extension 4½"
Length over all 18½"
Wired with Pin Switch
Finish: Stained Bronze
Swedish Iron
Current value: $75.00 – 120.00
1510
No. 1510
Made of Cast Metal
Length over all 36" – Width over all 21"
Wired Keyless
Finish: Stained Bronze
Swedish Iron
Current value: $140.00 – 185.00

No. 1529
Made of Cast Metal
Plate 10″x4¼″—Extension 3¾″
Wired with pin switch
Finish: Stained Bronze
Swedish Iron
Current value: $65.00 – 85.00

No. 1528
Made of Cast Metal
Plate 4½″x10″—Extension 4½″
Wired with pin switch
Finish: Stained Bronze
Swedish Iron
Current value: $40.00 – 55.00

No. 1515
Made of Cast Metal
Length over all 36″—Width over all 21″
Wired Keyless
Finish: Stained Bronze
Swedish Iron
Current value: $140.00 – 185.00

No. 1520
Made of Cast Metal
Equipped with half frosted cut shades
Length over all 36"—Width over all 21"
Wired Keyless
Finish: *Stained Bronze*
Swedish Iron

No. 1521
Made of Cast Metal
Equipped with half frosted cut shade
Plate 8¾" x 4½"—Extension 4"
Wired with Pin Switch
Finish: *Stained Bronze*
Swedish Iron

No. 1522
Made of Cast Metal
Equipped with half frosted cut shades
Plate 8¾" x 4½"—Extension 4½"
Wired with Pin Switch
Finish: *Stained Bronze*
Swedish Iron

No. 1517
Made of Cast Metal
Length over all 12″—Width over all 21″
Wired Keyless
Finish: Stained Bronze
Swedish Iron
Current value: $100.00 – 125.00

No. 1501
Made of Cast Metal
Diameter of top 7″
Length over all 6″
Wired Keyless
Finish: Stained Bronze
Swedish Iron
Current value: $25.00 – 35.00

No. 1511
Made of Cast Metal
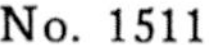
Length over all 30″—Width over all 8″
Wired Keyless
Finish: Stained Bronze
Swedish Iron
Current value: $135.00 – 185.00

No. 1512
Made of Cast Metal
Length over all 18″—Width over all 8″
Wired Keyless
Finish: Stained Bronze
Swedish Iron
Current value: $125.00 – 175.00

OXFORD LINE

The OXFORD series is our answer to the ever-increasing demand for lighting equipment of simple designs and conservative finishes.

These Halcolites are particularly adaptable for those who prefer the Old English type of architecture.

The simple beauty and lifelong durability of the Antique Brass finish in which these Halcolites come to you are the principle reasons for the extreme popularity of the OXFORD series.

OXFORD HALCOLITES are the exclusive creation of the Halcolite Co., Inc., and are covered by United States Design Patent Nos. 76945, 77014, 77015 and 77016.

No. 1849
Made of Cast Brass
Plate 10⅜" x 4⅝" – Extension 4¼"
Wired with Pin Switch
Finish: Burnt Brass
Current value: $135.00 – 175.00

No. 1848
Made of Cast Brass
Plate 10⅜" x 4⅝" – Extension 4½"
Wired with Pin Switch
Finish: Burnt Brass
Current value: $85.00 – 115.00

No. 1840
Made of Cast Brass
Length over all 36" – Width over all 20"
Wired Keyless
Finish: Burnt Brass
Current value: $175.00 – 225.00

No. 1828
Made of Cast Brass
Plate 10″ x 4⅛″—Extension 4¼″
Wired with Pin switch
Finish: Burnt Brass
Current value: $80.00 – 1115.00

No. 1829
Made of Cast Brass
Plate 10″ x 4⅛″—Extension 4⅛″
Wired with Pin Switch
Finish: Burnt Brass
Current value: $135.00 – 175.00

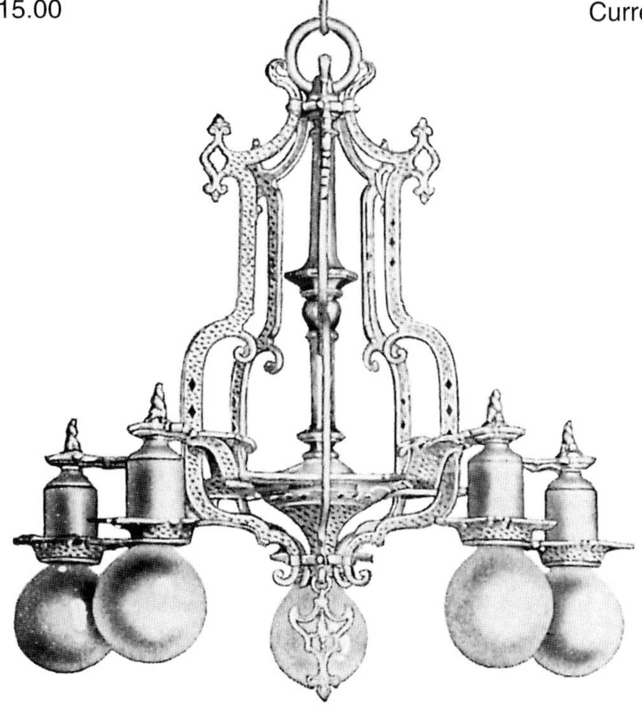

No. 1845
Made of Cast Brass
Width over all 20″—Length over all 36″
Wired Keyless
Finish: Burnt Brass
Current value: $175.00 – 225.00

No. 1839
Made of Cast Brass
Equipped with frosted shades
with clear borders.
Plate 10⅜" x 4⅝"—Extension 4½"
Wired with Pin Switch
Finish: Burnt Brass
Current value: $150.00 – 200.00

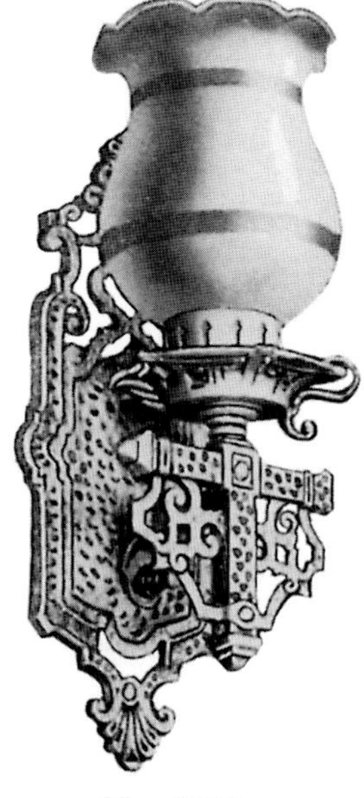

No. 1838
Made of Cast Brass
Equipped with frosted shade
with clear borders.
Plate 10⅜" x 4⅝"—Extension 4¾"
Wired with Pin Switch
Finish: Burnt Brass
Current value: $120.00 – 145.00

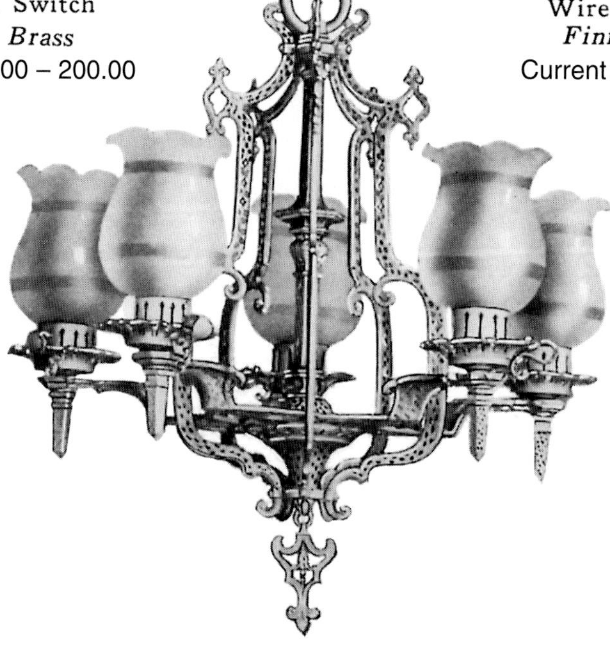

No. 1835
Made of Cast Brass
Equipped with frosted shades
with clear borders.
Length over all 36"—Width over all 20"
Wired Keyless
Finish: Burnt Brass
Current value: $175.00 – 235.00

No. 1864

Made of Cast Brass

Equipped with hand painted mica shade
Length over all 36″—Width over all 17½″

Wired Keyless

Finish: Burnt Brass
Current value: $400.00 – 500.00

No. 1863

Made of Cast Brass

Equipped with hand painted mica shade
Length over all 36″—Width over all 10″

Wired Keyless

Finish: Burnt Brass
Current value: $350.00 – 400.00

No. 1847
Made of Cast Brass
Length over all 22"—Width over all 20"
Wired Keyless
Finish: Burnt Brass
Current value: $175.00 – 200.00

No. 1844
Made of Cast Brass
Length over all 36"—Width over all 14½"
Wired Keyless
Finish: Burnt Brass
Current value: $150.00 – 185.00

No. 1824
Made of Cast Brass
Length over all 36"--Width over all 14½"
Wired Keyless
Finish: Burnt Brass
Current value: $150.00 – 185.00

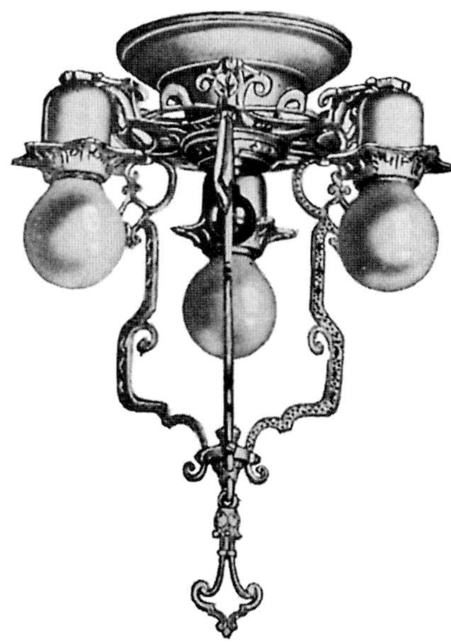

No. 1833
Length over all 13½″
Width over all 11½″
Wired Keyless
Finish: Burnt Brass
Current value: $175.00 – 200.00

No. 1841
Made of Cast Brass
Equipped with 5″x7″
amber crackled cylinder
Length over all 27″
Width over all 7½″
Wired Keyless
Finish: Burnt Brass
Current value: $200.00 – 250.00

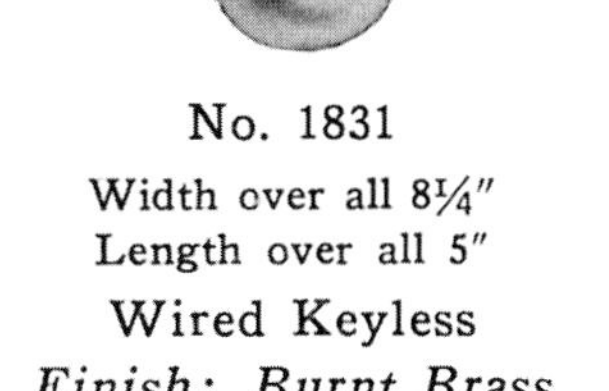

No. 1831
Width over all 8¼″
Length over all 5″
Wired Keyless
Finish: Burnt Brass
Current value: $25.00 – 40.00

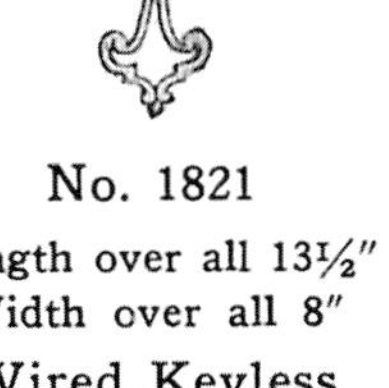

No. 1821
Length over all 13½″
Width over all 8″
Wired Keyless
Finish: Burnt Brass
Current value: $130.00 – 150.00

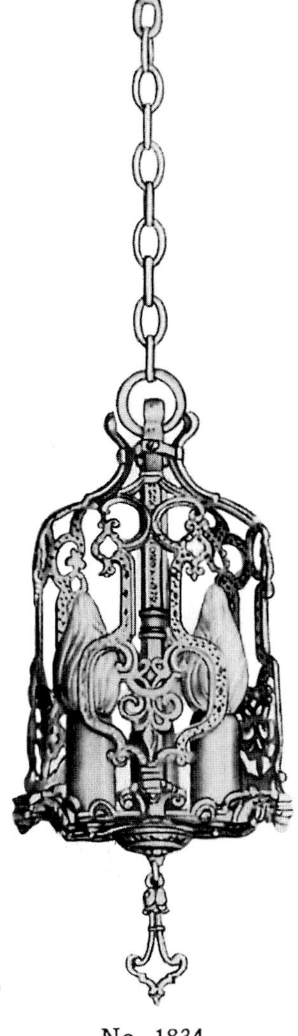

No. 1834
Made of Cast Brass
Width over all 9½″
Length over all 36″
Wired Keyless
Finish: Burnt Brass
Current value: $195.00 – 225.00

PLYMOUTH LINE

For the rugged type of interiors so frequently employed in English, Spanish, Colonial and Italian types of architecture we suggest PLYMOUTH HALCOLITES.

Made of hammered iron, finished in Swedish Iron with slight gold relief, the resulting effect of sturdy construction and beautiful simplicity is extremely refreshing. Note also the attractive prices at which Plymouth Halcolites are being offered.

PLYMOUTH HALCOLITES are the exclusive creation of the Halcolite Co., Inc., and are covered by United States Design Patents and applications therefor.

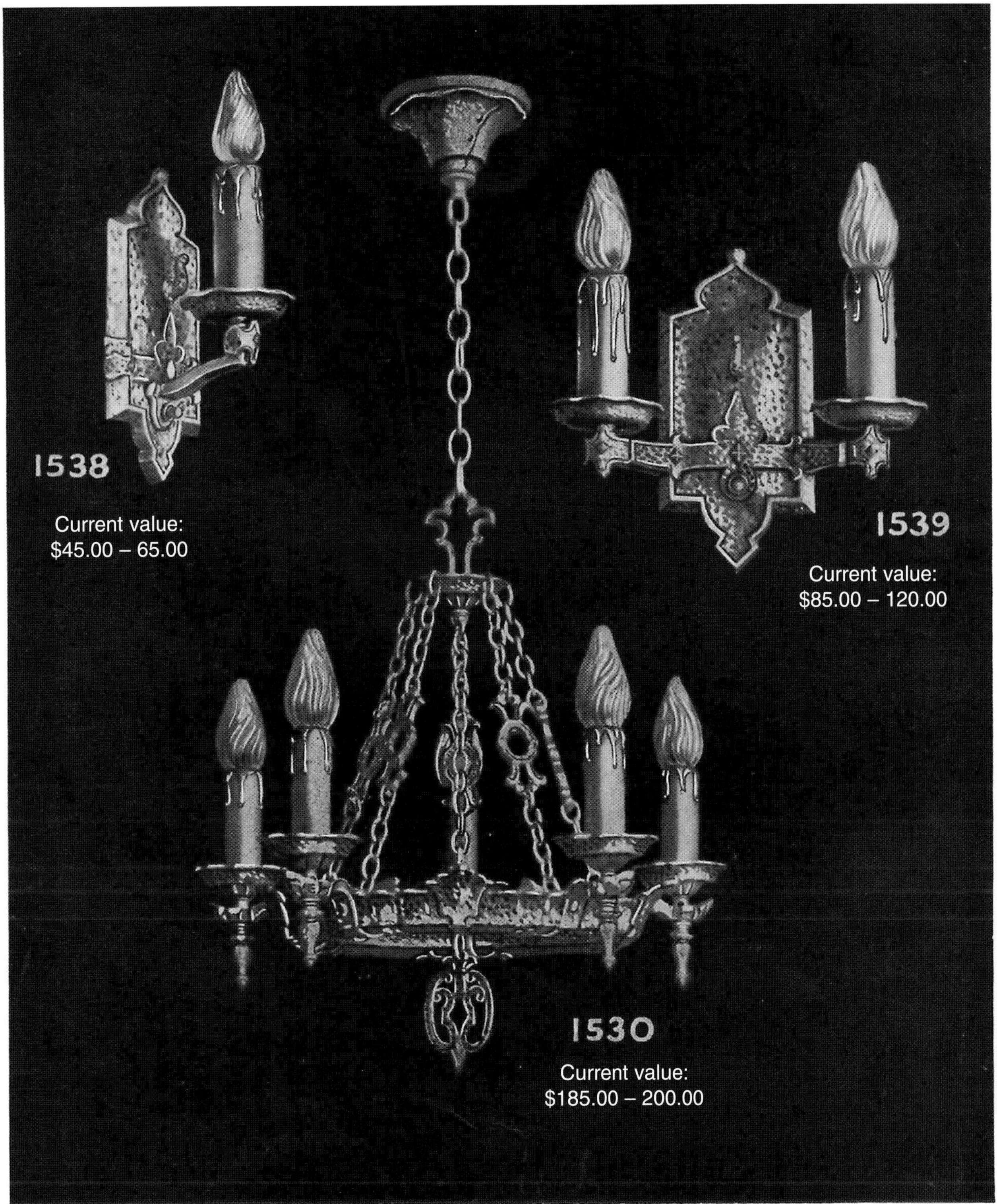

No. 1530
Made of Cast Metal
Length over all 36″—Width over all 20″
Wired Keyless
Finish: Swedish Iron and Gold

No. 1538
Made of Cast Metal
Plate 9″x4¼″—Extension 4¾″
Wired with Pin Switch
Finish: Swedish Iron and Gold

No. 1539
Made of Cast Metal
Plate 9″x4¼″—Extension 3½″
Wired with Pin Switch
Finish: Swedish Iron and Gold

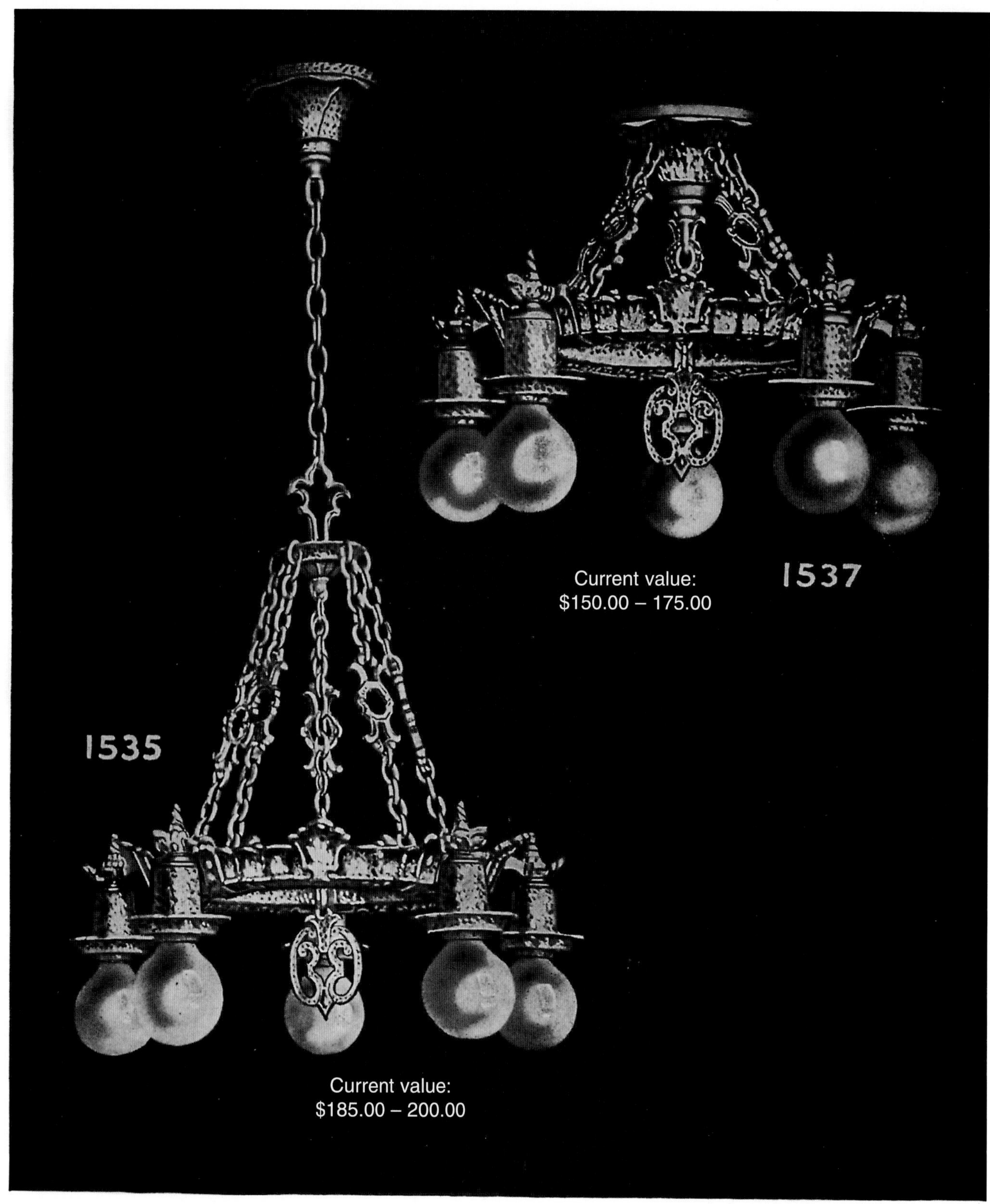

No. 1535
Made of Cast Metal
Length over all 36″—Width over all 20″
Wired Keyless
Finish: Swedish Iron and Gold

No. 1537
Made of Cast Metal
Length over all 13½″—Width over all 20″
Wired Keyless
Finish: Swedish Iron and Gold

No. 1533
Made of Cast Metal
Length over all 32″—Width over all 9″
Wired Keyless
Finish: Swedish Iron and Gold

No. 1541
Made of Cast Metal
Length over all 6½″
Width over all 5¾″
Wired Keyless
Finish: Swedish Iron and Gold

No. 1531
Made of Cast Metal
Length over all 32″—Width over all 8″
Wired Keyless
Finish: Swedish Iron and Gold

Canterbury Line

In an effort to create a line of fixtures which would fit gracefully into rooms of every description, we brought forth the CANTERBURY line. Never before have utility and beauty been combined to better advantage.

These fixtures come wired with approved wiring devices and completely assembled ready to install. CANTERBURY HALCOLITES are made of cast brass and finished in Pewter with a slight relief of gold, producing an unusually rich effect.

CANTERBURY HALCOLITES are the exclusive creation of the Halcolite Company, Inc., and are covered by United States Design Patents No. 74181, No. 74313, No. 74232, No. 74270, No. 74269, No. 74268.

No. 2552
Made of Cast Brass
Plate 10" x 6" – Extension 4½"
Wired with Pin Switch
Finish: Pewter and Gold
Current value: $125.00 – 150.00

No. 2551
Made of Cast Brass
Plate 10" x 6" – Extension 4½"
Wired with Pin Switch
Finish: Pewter and Gold
Current value: $100.00 – 125.00

No. 2550
Made of Cast Brass
Length over all 42" – Width over all 19"
Wired Keyless
Finish: Pewter and Gold
Current value: $200.00 – 250.00

No. 2557

Made of Cast Brass

Length over all 23"—Width over all 19"

Wired Keyless

Finish: Pewter and Gold

Current value: $190.00 – 225.00

No. 2555

Made of Cast Brass

Length over all 42"—Width over all 19"

Wired Keyless

Finish: Pewter and Gold

Current value: $200.00 – 250.00

No. 2563

Made of Cast Brass

Plate 7¼"x10"—Extension 3¼"

Wired with Pin Switch

Finish: Pewter and Gold

Current value: $200.00 – 250.00

Note: Six light fixtures were unusual as not many companies made them.

No. 2560

SIX LIGHT FIXTURE

Made of Cast Brass

Length over all 42"—Width over all 20"

Wired Keyless

Finish: Pewter and Gold

Current value: $275.00 – 325.00

No. 2544
Made of Cast Brass
Length over all 15"—Width over all 10"
Wired Keyless
Finish: Pewter and Gold
Current value: $150.00 – 200.00

Note: Six light fixtures were unusual as not many companies made them.

No. 2566
SIX LIGHT FIXTURE
Made of Cast Brass
Length over all 42"—Width over all 20"
Wired Keyless
Finish: Pewter and Gold
Current value: $275.00 – 325.00

No. 2570
FIVE LIGHT FIXTURE
Made of Cast Brass
Equipped with 20″ amber mica shade
Length over all 42″
Wired Keyless
Finish: Pewter and Gold
Current value: $350.00 – 450.00

No. 2553
Made of Cast Brass
Equipped with 10″ Parchment Shade
Wired with Three Keyless Sockets
Finish: Ivory Polychrome
Green Polychrome
Current value: $300.00 – 350.00

No. 2561

Made of Brass

Length over all 10¼"—Diameter of canopy 7½"

Wired Keyless

Finish: Pewter and Gold

Current value: $25.00 – 40.00

No. 2548

Made of Cast Brass

Length over all 26"—Width over all 10"

Wired Keyless

Finish: Pewter and Gold

Current value: $195.00 – 250.00

No. 2543

Made of Cast Brass

Length over all 36"—Width over all 9"

Wired Keyless

Finish: Pewter and Gold

Current value: $215.00 – 250.00

No. 2585

Length over all 16″
Diameter of plate 16″
Wired Keyless
Finish: Pewter and Gold

Current value
If made of brass: $225.00 – 285.00
If made of metal: $150.00 – 185.00

Note: Description doesn't give kind of metal used so two prices are given.

No. 2583

Length over all 13″
Diameter of plate 14″
Wired Keyless
Finish: Pewter and Gold

Current value
If made of brass: $200.00 – 250.00
If made of metal: $135.00 – 165.00

CRYSTAL LINE

The vogue for crystal fixtures led us to present what we consider a complete line of crystals suitable for any room.

Metal parts are made of cast brass and only a very high grade of crystals is used.

CRYSTAL HALCOLITES come wired with approved wiring devices and packed one to a carton.

Made in three finishes.

Silver and Black—A soft silver finish with a slight relief of black.

Green and Gold—An apple green finish with a slight relief of old gold.

Lustrogold—A polished gold background with a slight relief of umber.

No. 529
Made of Cast Brass
Equipped with Glass Candle Cups
Plate 9″x4¾″
Extension 4″—Spread 6¼″
Wired with Pin Switch
Finish: Silver and Black, Lustrogold, Green and Gold

No. 517
Made of Cast Brass
Length over all 54″—Dia. of ring 18″
Fitter 14″
Wired with Four Keyless Sockets
Finish: Silver and Black, Lustrogold, Green and Gold

No. 528
Made of Cast Brass
Equipped with Glass Candle Cup
Plate 9″x4¾″—Extension 4½″
Wired with Pin Switch
Finish: Silver and Black, Lustrogold, Green and Gold

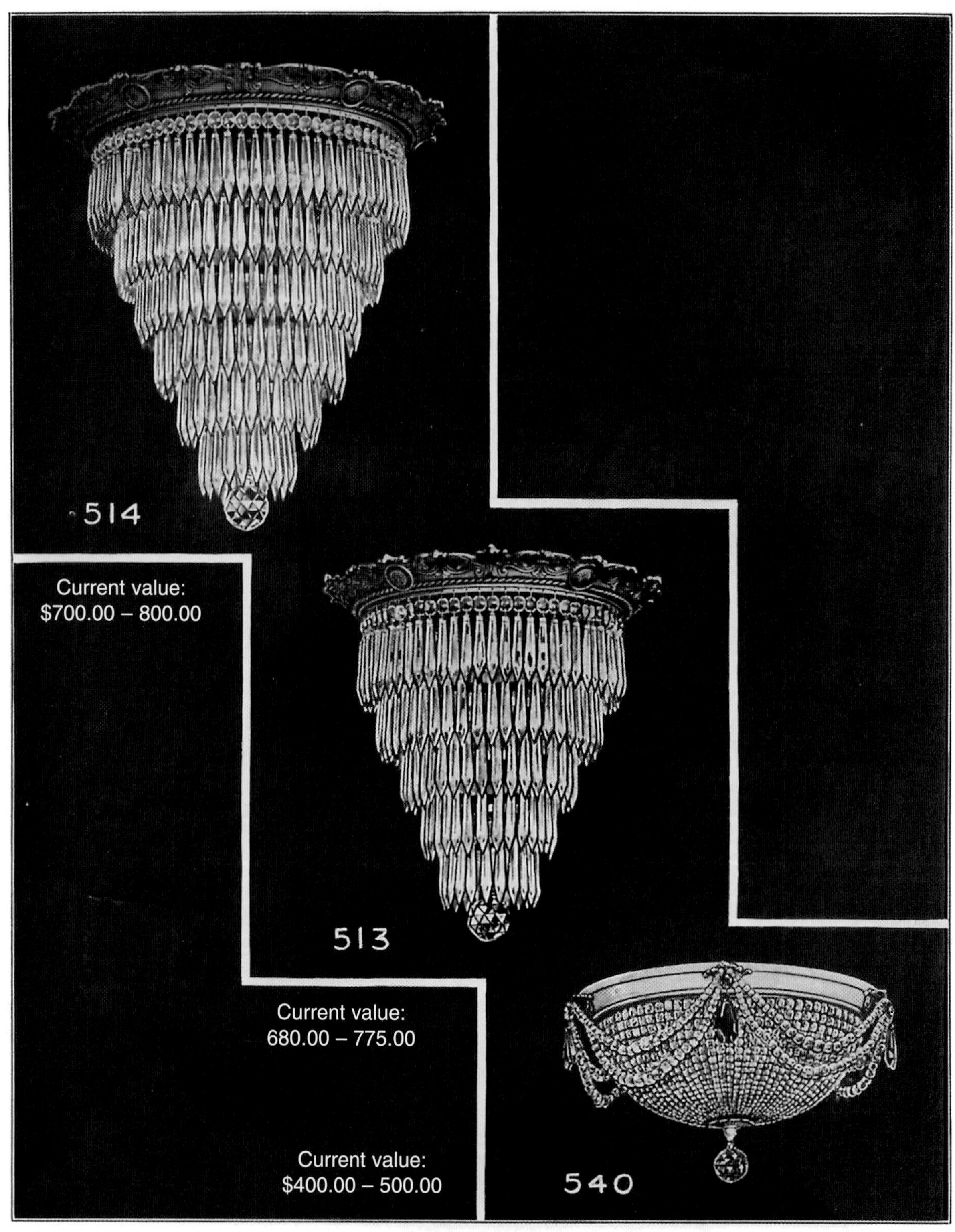

No. 514

Made of Cast Brass

Length over all 18″
Diameter of ring 18″—Fitter 14″

Wired with Four Keyless Sockets

Finish: Silver and Black, Lustrogold, Green and Gold

No. 513

Made of Cast Brass

Length over all 16″
Diameter of ring 15″—Fitter 12″

Wired with Three Keyless Sockets

Finish: Silver and Black, Lustrogold, Green and Gold

No. 540

Diameter of top 13½″
Fitter 12″—Depth 8½″

Wired with Two Keyless Sockets

Finish: Silver and Black, Lustrogold, Green and Gold

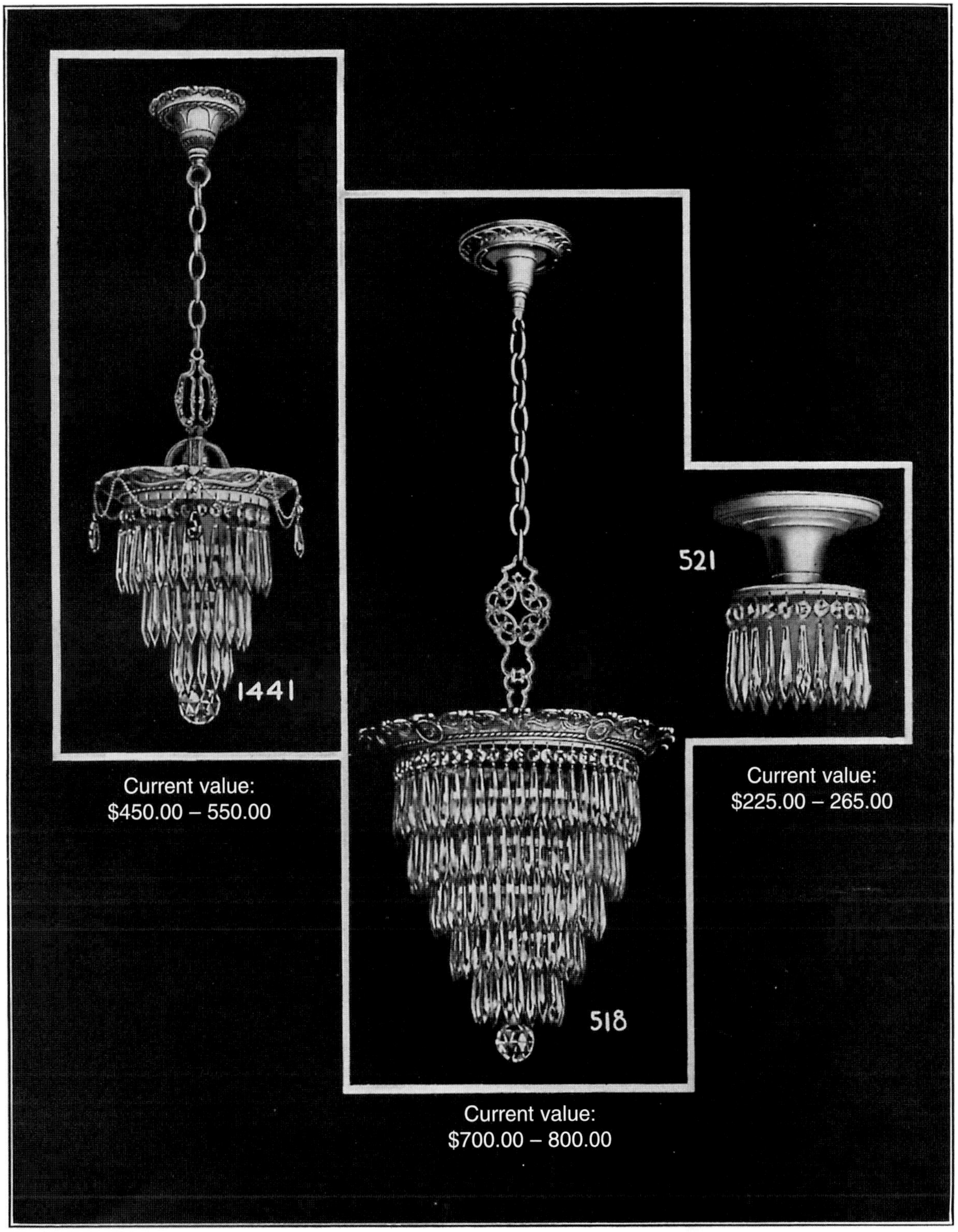

No. 1441
Made of Cast Brass
Length over all 36″—Diameter 9″
Fitter 6″
Wired Keyless
Finish: Silver and Black, Lustrogold, Green and Gold

No. 518
Made of Cast Brass
Length over all 42″
Diameter of ring 15″—Fitter 12″
Wired with Three Keyless Sockets
Finish: Silver and Black, Lustrogold, Green and Gold

No. 521
Made of Brass
Diameter of top 6½″—Length over all 7½″
Wired Keyless
Finish: Silver and Black, Lustrogold, Green and Gold

MARWOOD LINE

We herewith present a line of HALCOLITES which for value and practicability cannot be surpassed.

This line is particularly adaptable for the popular priced home where there is a specified allowance made for the lighting fixtures.

These fixtures come wired with approved wiring devices, and completely assembled ready to install.

MARWOOD HALCOLITES are made of cast brass and finished in Verdigold—a metallic Gold background with hilite of pale Green.

MARWOOD HALCOLITES are the exclusive creation of the Halcolite Company, Inc., and are covered by United States Design Patents and applications therefor.

No. 1381

Made of Cast Brass

Depth over all 6″—Diameter of top 5¾″

Wired Keyless

Finish: Verdigold

Current value: $35.00 – 45.00

No. 1385

Made of Cast Brass

Length over all 36″—Width over all 18½″

Wired Keyless

Finish: Verdigold

Current value: $285.00 – 350.00

No. 1388

Made of Cast Brass

Plate 9½"x5"—Extension 3"

Wired with Pin Switch

Finish: Verdigold

Current value: $100.00 – 125.00

No. 1389

Made of Cast Brass

Plate 9½"x5"—Extension 4"

Wired with Pin Switch

Finish: Verdigold

Current value: $135.00 – 175.00

No. 1380

Made of Cast Brass

Length over all 36"—Width over all 19½"

Wired Keyless

Finish: Verdigold

Current value: $285.00 – 350.00

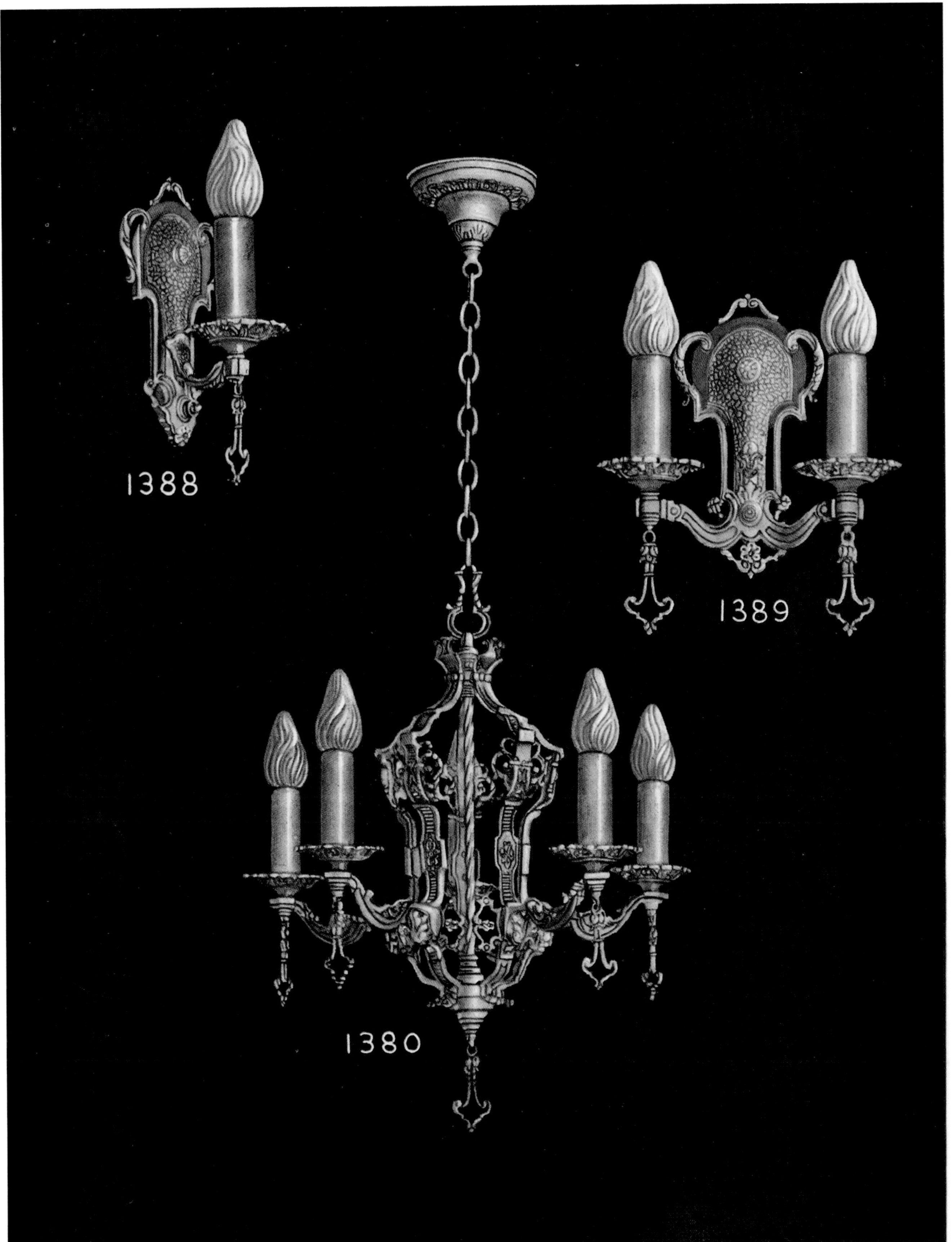
1388
1389
1380

No. 1387
Made of Cast Brass
Length over all 25″—Width over all 18½″
Wired Keyless
Finish: Verdigold
Current value: $265.00 – 300.00

No. 1383
Made of Cast Brass
Length over all 36″—Width over all 8″
Wired Keyless
Finish: Verdigold
Current value: $150.00 – 185.00

WOODSTOCK LINE

The finely wrought details of superb craftsmanship but serve to heighten the charming simplicity of this line. Being made of brass with all castings of cast brass, it enables us to apply a finish particularly suitable to this type of fixture, i.e., Pewter and Burnt Brass.

All WOODSTOCK HALCOLITES come completely wired and assembled, packed one to a carton.

WOODSTOCK HALCOLITES are the exclusive creation of the Halcolite Company, Inc., and are covered by United States Design Patents and applications therefor.

No. 1988

Made of Cast Brass

Plate 10″ x 4½″—Extension 4½″

Wired with Pin Switch

Finish: Pewter and Burnt Brass

Current value: $100.00 – 125.00

No. 1989

Made of Cast Brass

Plate 10″ x 4¼″—Extension 3¾″

Wired with Pin Switch

Finish: Pewter and Burnt Brass

Current value: $130.00 – 175.00

No. 1980

Made of Brass with Cast Brass Ornamentations

Length over all 36″—Width over all 20″

Wired Keyless

Finish: Pewter and Burnt Brass

Current value: $200.00 – 245.00

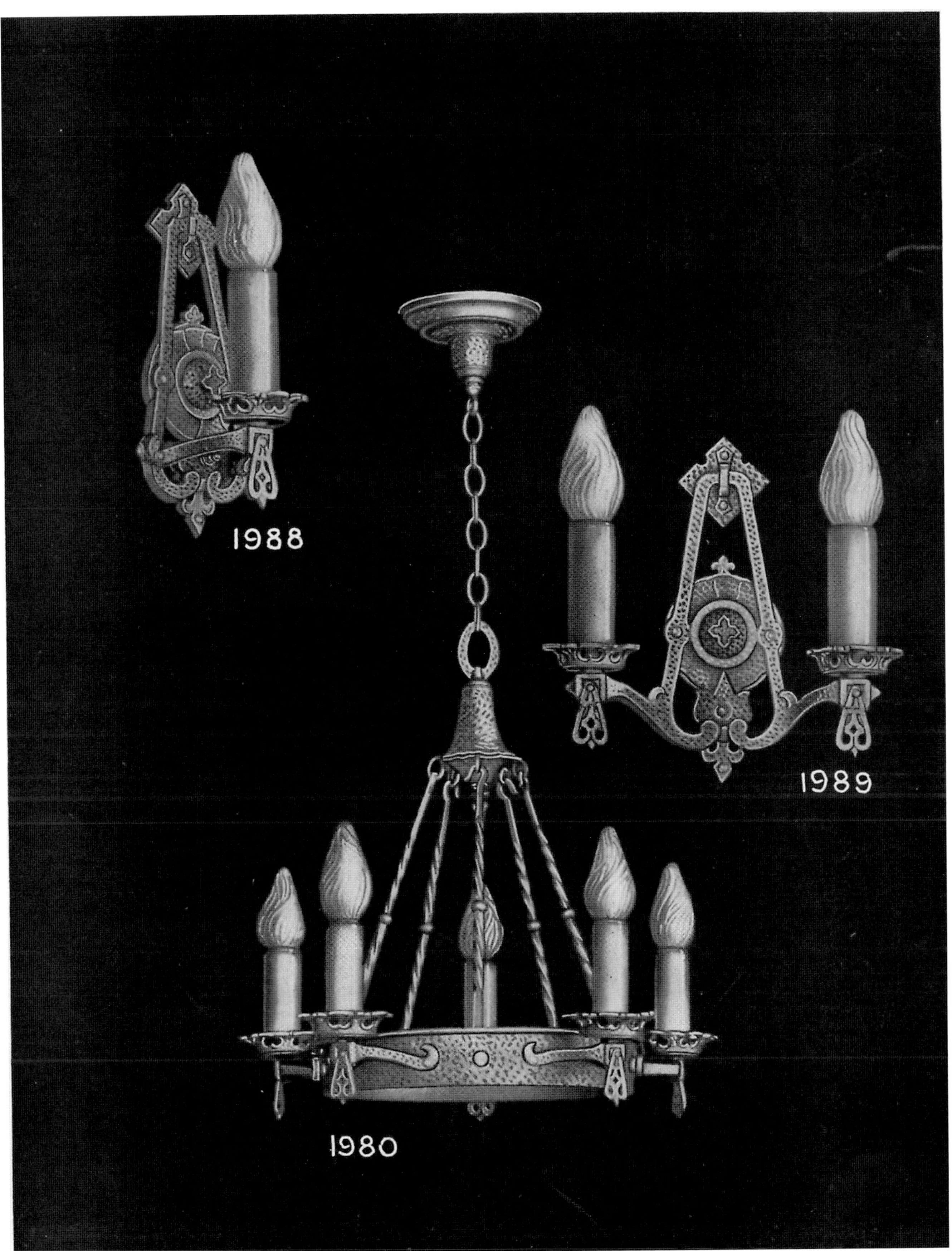
1988
1989
1980

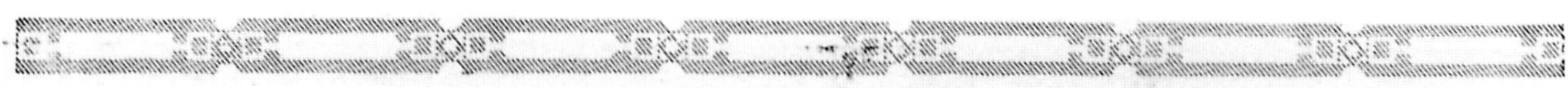

No. 1987
Made of Brass with Cast Brass Ornamentations
Length over all 20"—Width over all 20"
Wired Keyless
Finish: Pewter and Burnt Brass
Current value: $185.00 – 225.00

No. 1985
Made of Brass with Cast Brass Ornamentations
Length over all 36"—Width over all 20"
Wired Keyless
Finish: Pewter and Burnt Brass
Current value: $200.00 – 245.00

MADRINA LINE

In introducing the MADRINA LINE, we offer for your approval a group of fixtures which for sheer beauty of line and grace of contour can hardly be surpassed.

The MADRINA LINE is made of cast bronze and finished in stained bronze, which is a polished bronze finish with just a slight relief of color.

All fixtures come wired with approved wiring devices and completely assembled, ready to hang.

MADRINA HALCOLITES are the exclusive creation of the Halcolite Co., Inc., and are covered by United States Design Patents and applications therefor.

No. 1768

Made of Solid Bronze

Plate 9¼"x4½"—Extension 4½"

Wired Pull Chain

Finish: Stained Bronze

Current value: $135.00 – 175.00

No. 1769

Made of Solid Bronze

Plate 6¼"x4½"—Extension 4"

Wired with Pin Switch

Finish: Stained Bronze

Current value: $185.00 – 225.00

No. 1780

Made of Solid Bronze

Length over all 42"—Width over all 20"

Wired Keyless

Finish: Stained Bronze

Current value: $325.00 – 475.00

1769
1768
1780

No. 1787

Made of Solid Bronze

Length over all 24″—Width over all 20″

Wired Keyless

Finish: Stained Bronze

Current value: $325.00 – 400.00

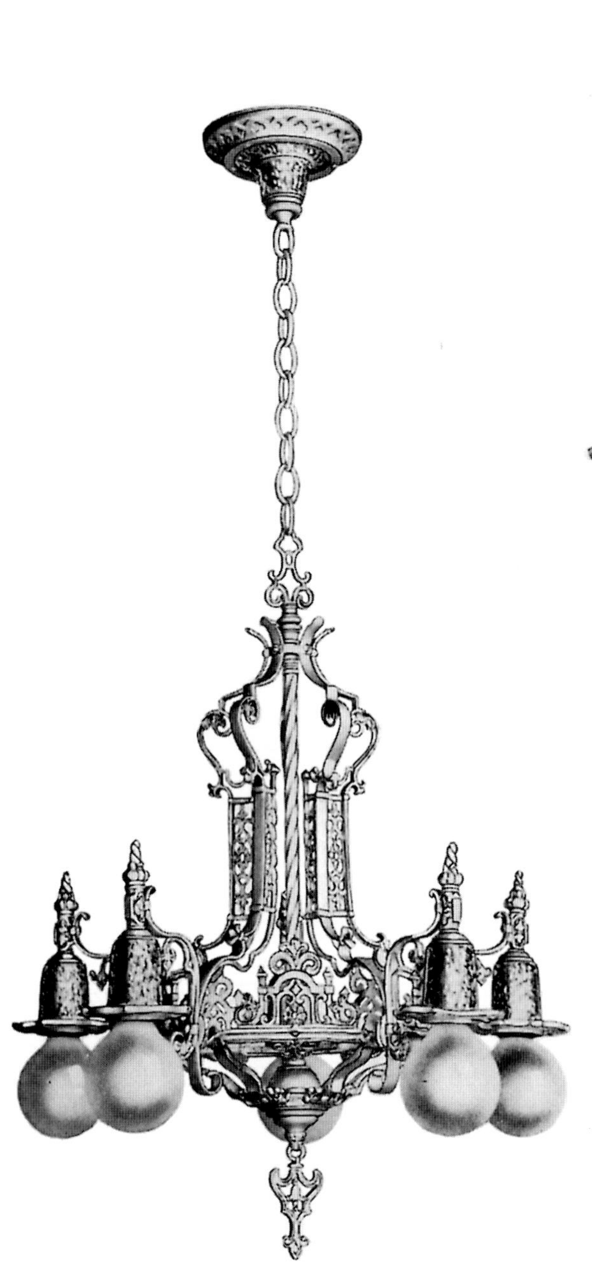

No. 1785

Made of Solid Bronze

Length over all 42″—Width over all 20″

Wired Keyless

Finish: Stained Bronze

Current value: $325.00 – 475.00

Note: Six light fixtures were unusual as not many companies made them.

No. 1795
Made of Solid Bronze
Diameter of plate 18″—Length over all 6½″
Wired Keyless
Finish: Stained Bronze
Current value: $250.00 – 300.00

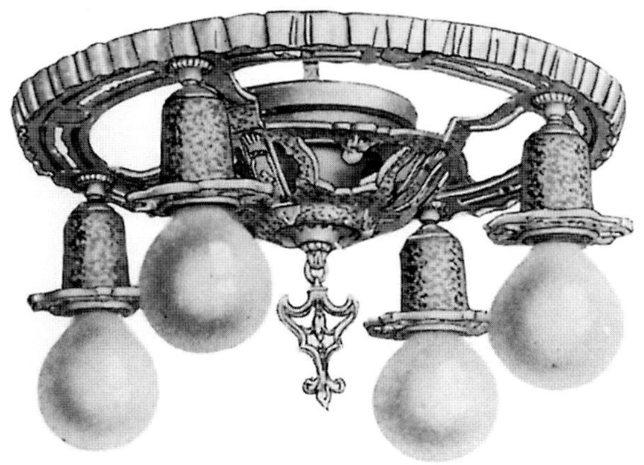

No. 1794
Made of Solid Bronze
Diameter of plate 15″—Length over all 6½″
Wired Keyless
Finish: Stained Bronze
Current value: $225.00 – 285.00

No. 1793
Made of Solid Bronze
Diameter of plate 13″—Length over all 6″
Wired Keyless
Finish: Stained Bronze
Current value: $200.00 – 245.00

No. 1051
Made of Solid Bronze
Spread 8½″
Length over all 6″
Wired Keyless
Finish: Stained Bronze
Current value: $35.00 – 45.00

No. 1753
Made of Solid Bronze
Length over all 36″—Width over all 8″
Wired Keyless
Finish: Stained Bronze
Current value: $200.00 – 250.00

No. 1762
Made of Solid Bronze
Length over all 28″—Width over all 10″
Wired Keyless
Finish: Stained Bronze
Current value: $215.00 – 265.00

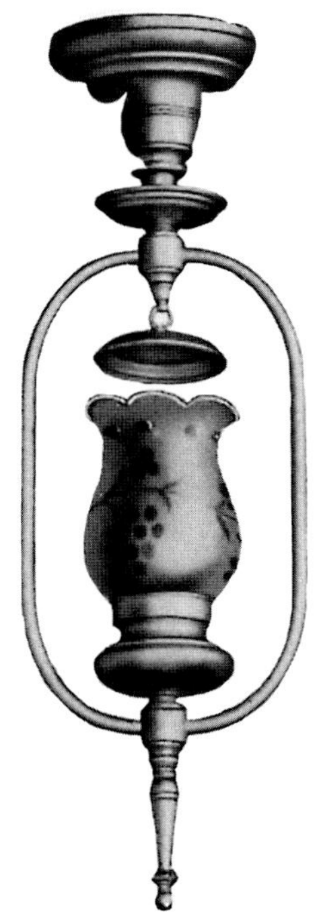

No. 1336

Equipped with hand cut Colonial shade

Length over all 20″—Width over all 7″

Wired Keyless

Finish: Colonial Brass
English Brass
Pewter

Current value: $125.00 – 150.00

No. 1322

Equipped with hand cut Colonial shades

Length over all 36″—Width over all 12¾″

Wired Keyless

Finish: Colonial Brass
English Brass
Pewter

Current value: $175.00 – 225.00

No. 1341
Equipped with hand cut Colonial shade
Plate 6"x4⅛"—Extension 6⅞"
Wired with Pin Switch
Finish: Colonial Brass
English Brass
Pewter

Current value: $75.00 – 100.00

No. 1332
Made of Cast Brass
Equipped with hand cut Colonial shades
Plate 10¼"x4½"—Extension 4¼"
Wired Pullchain
Finish: Colonial Brass
English Brass
Pewter

Current value: $130.00 – 150.00

No. 1337
Equipped with hand cut Colonial shades
Length over all 23"—Width over all 19"
Wired Keyless
Finish: Colonial Brass
English Brass
Pewter

Current value: $275.00 – 325.00

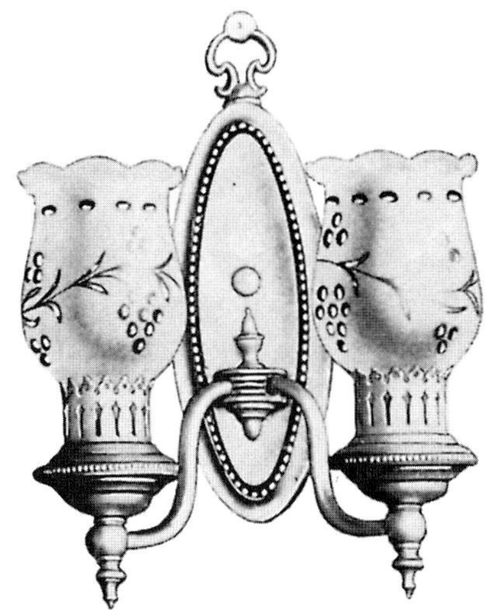

No. 1379
Made of Cast Brass
Equipped with rich Colonial hand cut shades
Will take a standard 25 watt bulb
Plate 10½"x3½"—Extension 6"
Wired with pin switch
Finish: English Brass, Colonial Brass and Black, Silver and Black
Current value: $150.00 – 200.00

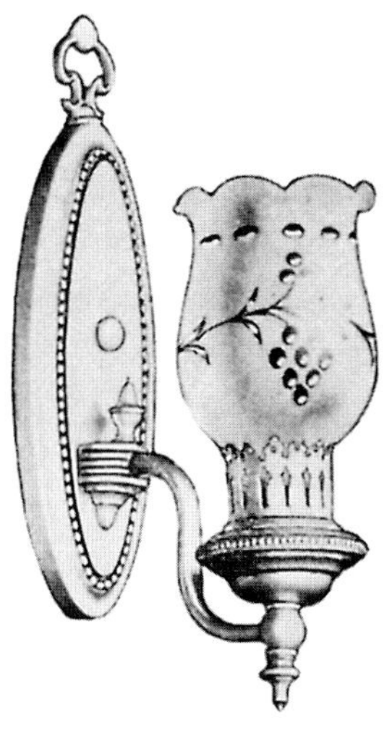

No. 1378
Made of Cast Brass
Equipped with rich Colonial hand cut shade
Will take a standard 25 watt bulb
Plate 10½"x3½"—Extension 6½"
Wired with pin switch
Finish: English Brass, Colonial Brass and Black, Silver and Black
Current value: $125.00 – 145.00

No. 1370
Equipped with rich Colonial hand cut shades
Will take a standard 25 watt bulb
Length over all 36"—Width over all 19½"
Wired Keyless
Finish: English Brass, Colonial Brass and Black, Silver and Black
Current value: $285.00 – 335.00

No. 1105

Equipped with rich Colonial
hand cut dish
Plate 12"—Depth 7"—Fitter 10"
Wired Keyless

Finish: Colonial Brass, English Brass

Current value: $165.00 – 200.00

No. 1376

Equipped with rich Colonial
hand cut shade
Will take a standard 25 watt bulb
Plate 6"x3½"—Extension 6"
Wired with pin switch

Finish: English Brass, Colonial Brass and Black, Silver and Black

Current value: $75.00 – 95.00

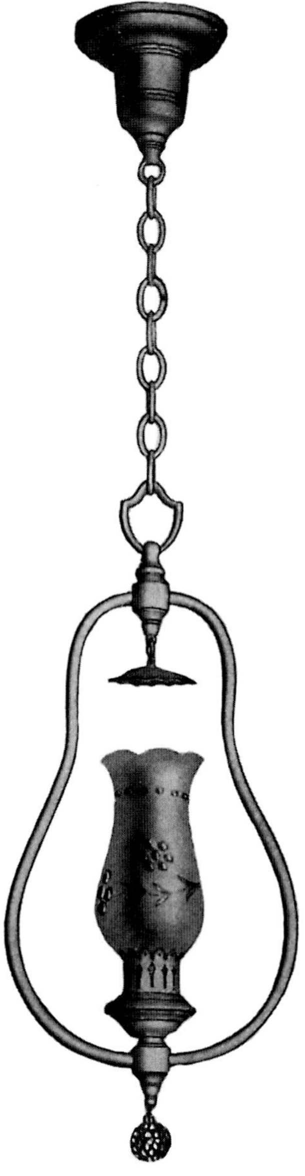

No. 1331

Equipped with rich Colonial
hand cut shade
Will take a standard 25 watt bulb
Length over all 36"—Width over all 9"
Wired Keyless

Finish: English Brass, Colonial Brass

Current value: $125.00 – 150.00

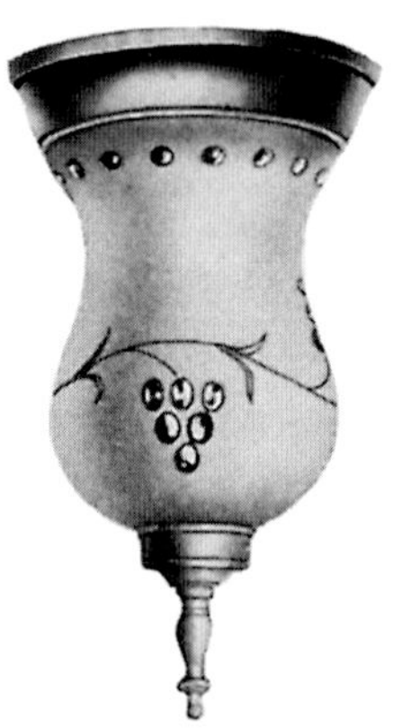

No. 1371

Equipped with rich Colonial
hand cut urn
Length over all 11½"—Fitter 4"
Wired Keyless

Finish: English Brass, Colonial Brass

Current value: $100.00 – 120.00

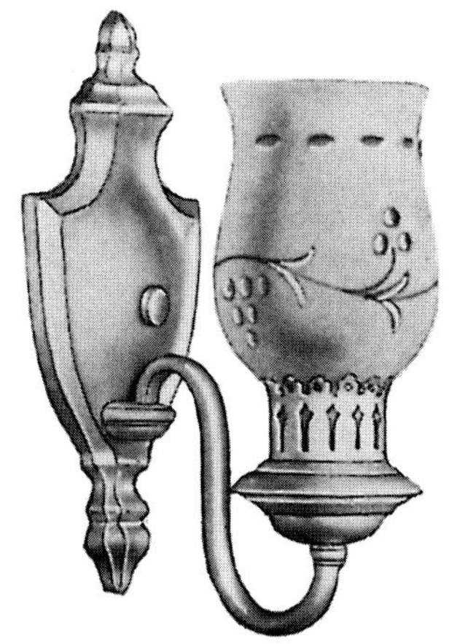

No. 1338

Made of Cast Brass
Equipped with rich Colonial hand cut shade
Will take a standard 25 watt bulb
Plate 8¾"x4½"—Extension 5¾"
Wired Pullchain

Finish: Colonial Brass, English Brass, Butler Silver

Current value: $100.00 – 125.00

No. 1339

Made of Cast Brass
Equipped with rich Colonial hand cut shades
Will take a standard 25 watt bulb
Plate 8¾"x4½"—Extension 4¾"
Wired Pullchain

Finish: Colonial Brass, English Brass, Butler Silver

Current value: $140.00 – 175.00

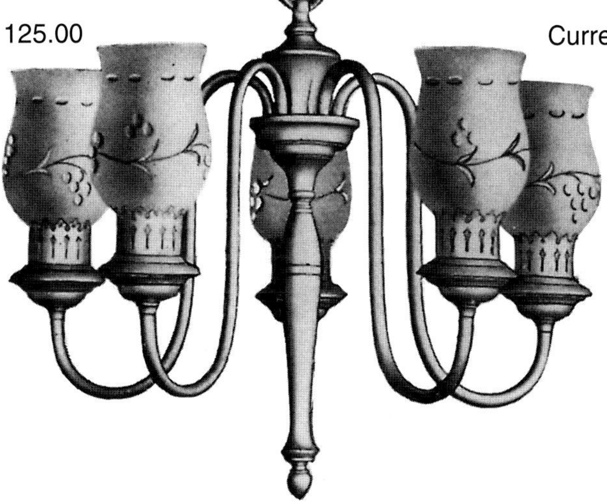

No. 1330

Spindle Made of Cast Brass
Equipped with rich Colonial hand cut shades
Will take a standard 25 watt bulb
Length over all 36"—Width over all 18½"

Finish: Colonial Brass, English Brass, Butler Silver

Current value: $250.00 – 285.00

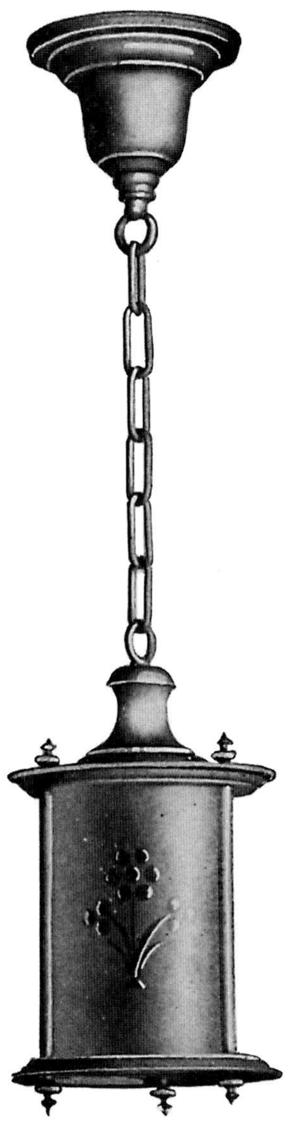

No. 686

Length over all 36″—Cylinder 4″x6″
Wired Keyless

Finish: Colonial Brass, English Brass

Current value: $150.00 – 200.00

No. 1197

Equipped with hand cut Colonial chimney

Length over all 36″—Width over all 7″
Wired Keyless

Finish: English Brass, Colonial Brass

Current value: $135.00 – 175.00

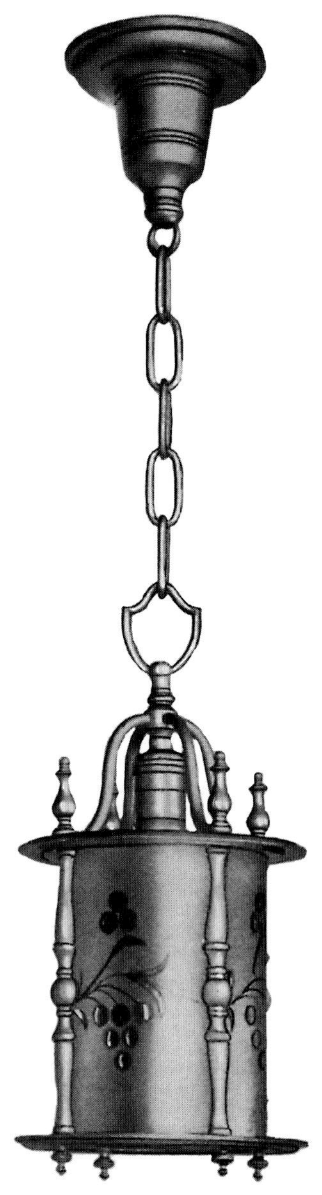

No. 1196

Equipped with 5″x6⅞″ hand cut cylinder

Length over all 36″—Cage 7⅛″x7″
Wired Keyless

Finish: English Brass, Colonial Brass

Current value: $175.00 – 225.00

HANDCRAFT HALCOLITES make it possible, for the first time, to equip the home with HAMMERED BRASS FIXTURES at a fairly moderate cost.

The hammered effect so tastefully carried out in designs and types of fixtures, which are recognized everywhere for their grace and beauty, makes these lighting fixtures particularly desirable for the builder of better homes.

HANDCRAFT HALCOLITES are made of brass and are finished either in Antique Hammered Brass or Oxidized Hammered Silver. Both finishes are guaranteed as to their durability. Their beauty and attractiveness are best appreciated when actually seen.

HANDCRAFT HALCOLITES are the exclusive creation of the Halcolite Company, Inc., and are covered by United States Design Patents and applications therefor.

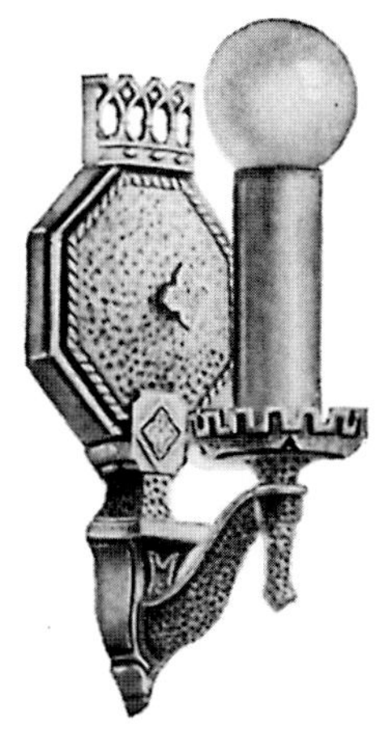

No. 418

Made of Cast Brass
Plate 9"x4"—Extension 3½"
Wired Pull Chain
Finish: Oxidized Silver
Antique Brass
Current value: $100.00 – 130.00

No. 419

Made of Cast Brass
Plate 9"x4"—Extension 2½"—Spread 6½"
Wired with Pin Switch
Finish: Oxidized Silver
Antique Brass
Current value: $140.00 – 185.00

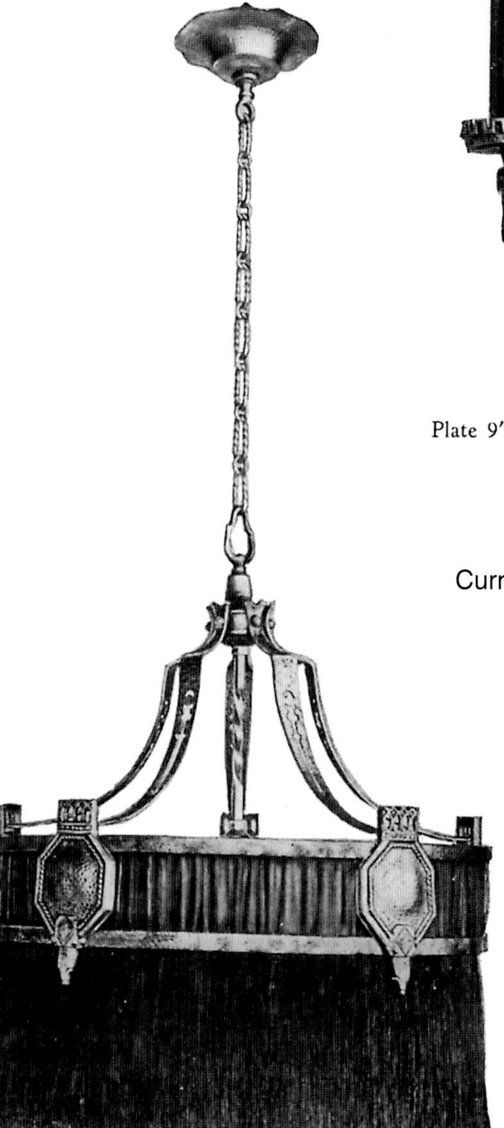

No. 400

Made of Cast Brass
Diameter 22"—Length over all 48"
Wired One-Light Pullchain
Equipped with Glass Reflector
Finish: Oxidized Silver with Blue Shade and Rose Lining; Antique Brass with Gold Shade and Rose Lining
Current value: $300.00 – 425.00

No. 449

Made of Cast Brass

Length over all 7"—Width over all 18½"

Wired Keyless

Finish: Oxidized Silver; Antique Brass

Current value: $150.00 – 200.00

No. 455

Made of Cast Brass

Length over all 42"—Width over all 18"

Wired Keyless

Finish: Oxidized Silver; Antique Brass

Current value: $250.00 – 300.00

No. 456

Made of Cast Brass

Length over all 36"—Width over all 18"

Wired Keyless

Finish: Oxidized Silver; Antique Brass

Current value: $250.00 – 300.00

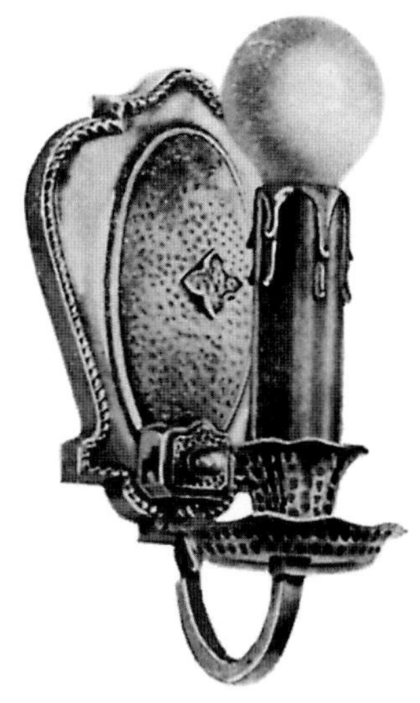

No. 478

Plate 6¾"x4¾"—Extension 4½"
Wired with Pin Switch
Finish: Oxidized Silver; Antique Brass
Current value: $100.00 – 120.00

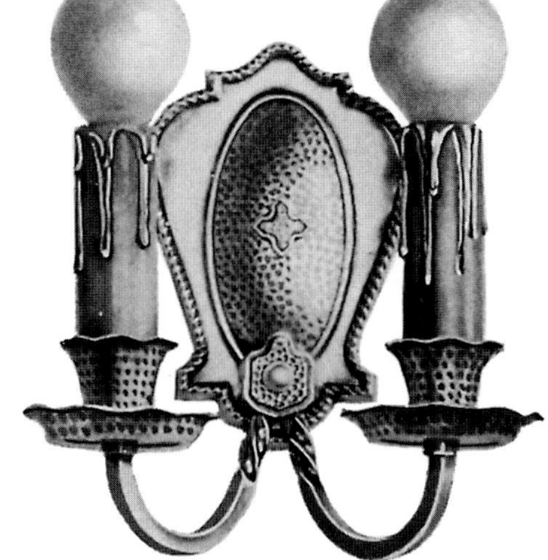

No. 479

Plate 6¾"x4¾"—Extension 4½"—Spread 6"
Wired with Pin Switch
Finish: Oxidized Silver; Antique Brass
Current value: $130.00 – 150.00

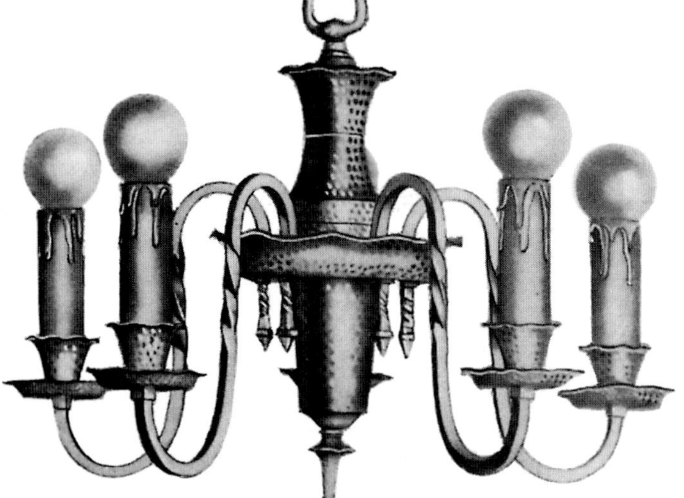

No. 405

Length over all 42"—Width over all 21"
Wired Keyless
Finish: Oxidized Silver; Antique Brass
Current value: $225.00 – 300.00

No. 410

Length over all 13"—Width over all 21"

Wired Keyless

Finish: Oxidized Silver; Antique Brass

Current value: $225.00 – 275.00

No. 406

Length over all 36"—Width over all 21"

Wired Keyless

Finish: Oxidized Silver; Antique Brass

Current value: $225.00 – 300.00

No. 474

Diameter of Top 7"

Depth over all 6"

Wired Keyless

Finish: Oxidized Silver

Antique Brass

Current value: $35.00 – 45.00

No. 435

Plate 15¾"—Depth 7"

Wired Keyless

Finish: Oxidized Silver; Antique Brass

Current value: $165.00 – 195.00

No. 420

Length over all 36"

Cage 7"

Wired Keyless

Finish: Oxidized Silver

Antique Brass

Current value: $100.00 – 135.00

No. 453

Plate 13½"—Depth 7"

Wired Keyless

Finish: Oxidized Silver; Antique Brass

Current value: $125.00 – 165.00

No. 433

Length over all 36"

Cage 8"

Wired Keyless

Finish: Oxidized Silver

Antique Brass

Current value: $150.00 – 185.00

San Remo Line

Grace and distinction are the chief characteristics which set this line aside from anything similar that has ever been offered in the field before.

Being made of cast bronze, it enables us to put on a stained bronze finish which is a polished finish with just a slight relief of color.

San Remo Halcolites come wired with approved wiring devices, completely assembled and ready to install, packed one to a carton.

SAN REMO HALCOLITES are the exclusive creation of the Halcolite Company, Inc., and are covered by United States Design Patents and applications therefor.

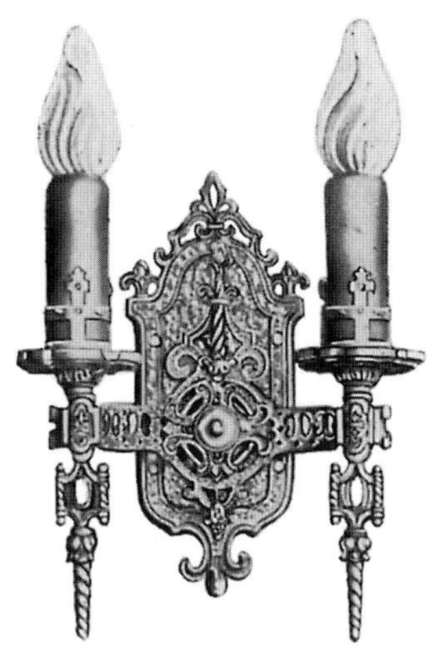

No. 1759

Made of Solid Bronze

Plate 9½"x4½"—Extension 3¾"

Wired with Pin Switch

Finish: Stained Bronze

Current value: $225.00 – 260.00

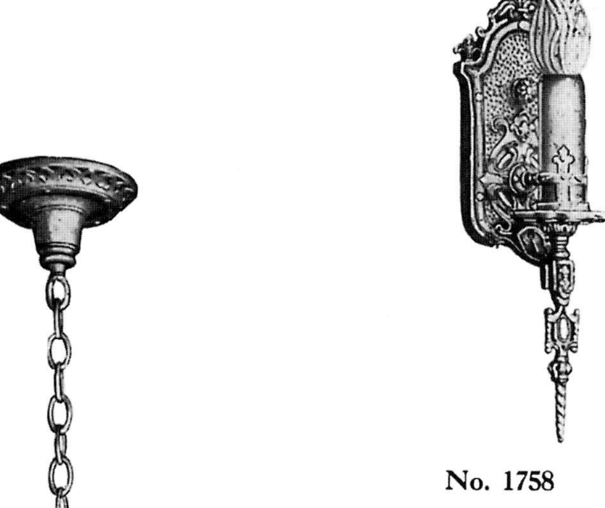

No. 1758

Made of Solid Bronze

Plate 8"x4½"—Extension 4"

Wired with Pin Switch

Finish: Stained Bronze

Current value: $200.00 – 235.00

No. 1750

Made of Solid Bronze

Length over all 42"—Width over all 21"

Wired Keyless

Finish: Stained Bronze

Current value: $325.00 – 475.00

No. 1757

Made of Solid Bronze

Length over all 22"—Width over all 21"

Wired Keyless

Finish: Stained Bronze

Current value: $300.00 – 400.00

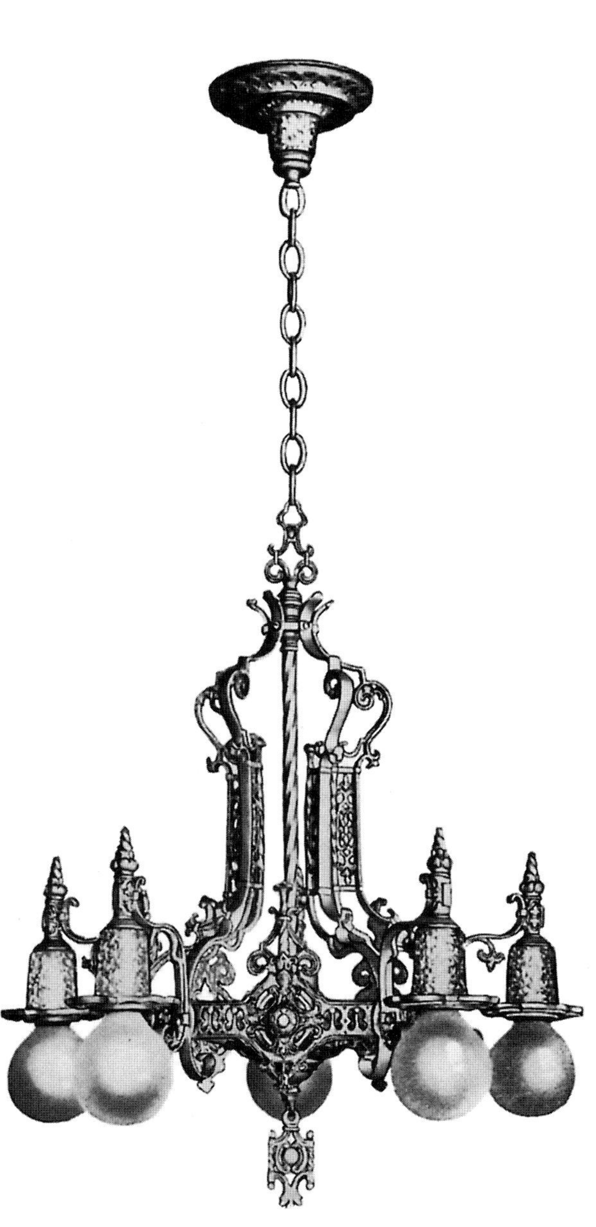

No. 1755

Made of Solid Bronze

Length over all 42"—Width over all 21"

Wired Keyless

Finish: Stained Bronze

Current value: $325.00 – 475.00

No. 1051
Made of Solid Bronze
Spread 8½"
Length over all 6"
Wired Keyless
Finish: Stained Bronze
Current value: $45.00 – 75.00

No. 1753
Made of Solid Bronze
Length over all 36"—Width over all 8"
Wired Keyless
Finish: Stained Bronze
Current value: $200.00 – 250.00

No. 1751
Made of Solid Bronze
Length over all 36"—Width over all 7⅜"
Wired Keyless
Finish: Stained Bronze
Current value: $150.00 – 185.00

Brewster Line

The graceful designs presented on BREWSTER HALCOLITES will interest the fixture buyer both from a standpoint of novelty and attractiveness.

Being made of cast brass with oval arms of deeply etched tubing, it enables us to apply a finish particularly flattering to a fixture of this type, and also conceal the wiring.

BREWSTER HALCOLITES come wired with approved wiring devices, completely assembled ready to install, and packed one to a carton.

Finish Lustrogold—A bright gold with a slight touch of coloring.

BREWSTER HALCOLITES are the exclusive creation of the Halcolite Company, Inc., and are covered by United States Design Patents and applications therefor.

No. 1727

Made of Cast Brass

Length over all 24½"—Width over all 19"

Wired Keyless

Finish: Lustrogold

Current value: $215.00 – 250.00

No. 1726

Made of Cast Brass

Length over all 36"—Width over all 19"

Wired with Key Sockets

Finish: Lustrogold

Current value: $235.00 – 275.00

No. 1721

Diameter of Plate 7¾"
Length over all 11"
Wired Keyless
Finish: Lustrogold
Current value: $100.00 – 125.00

Note: Six light fixtures were unusual as not many companies made them.

No. 1716

SIX LIGHT FIXTURE
Made of Cast Brass
Length over all 40"—Width over all 20"
Wired Keyless
Finish: Lustrogold
Current value: $300.00 – 325.00

No. 1733

Made of Cast Brass
Length over all 36"
Cage 6½"x13"
Wired Keyless
Finish: Lustrogold
Current value: $135.00 – 185.00

Winton Halcolites

A solid brass line of unusual merit. Notice that the wires are completely concealed. Arms are of oval tubing with etching tastefully applied.

Made in two finishes:

Silver and Black—A plated Silver finish with Black relief.

Dutch Gold — A soft gold background with rich coloring applied.

WINTON HALCOLITES are the exclusive creation of the Halcolite Co., Inc., and are covered by United States Design Patents and applications therefor.

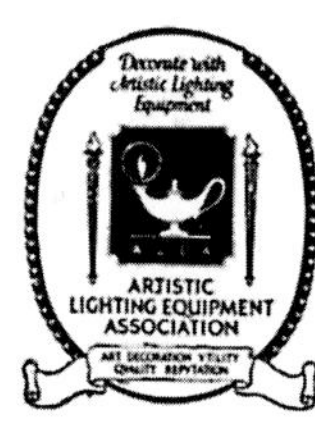

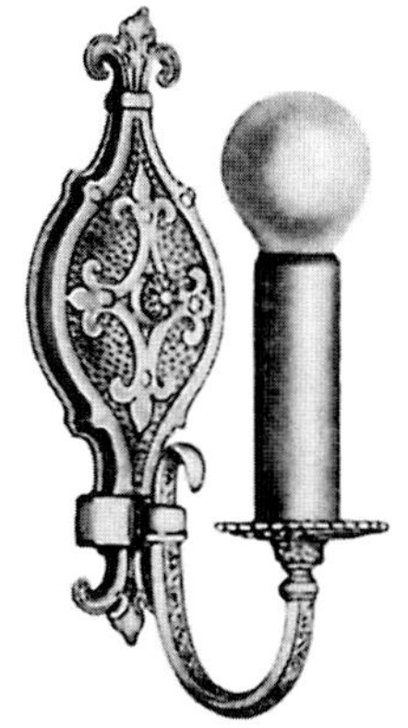

No. 1578

Made of Cast Brass

Plate 9½"x4"—Extension 5½"

Wired Pin Switch

Finish: Dutch Gold, Silver and Black

Current value: $100.00 – 125.00

No. 1579

Made of Cast Brass

Plate 9½"x4"—Spread 8½"

Wired Pin Switch

Finish: Dutch Gold, Silver and Black

Current value: $135.00 – 175.00

No. 1570

Made of Cast Brass

Length over all 36"—Width over all 18"

Wired Keyless

Finish: Dutch Gold, Silver and Black

Current value: $225.00 – 285.00

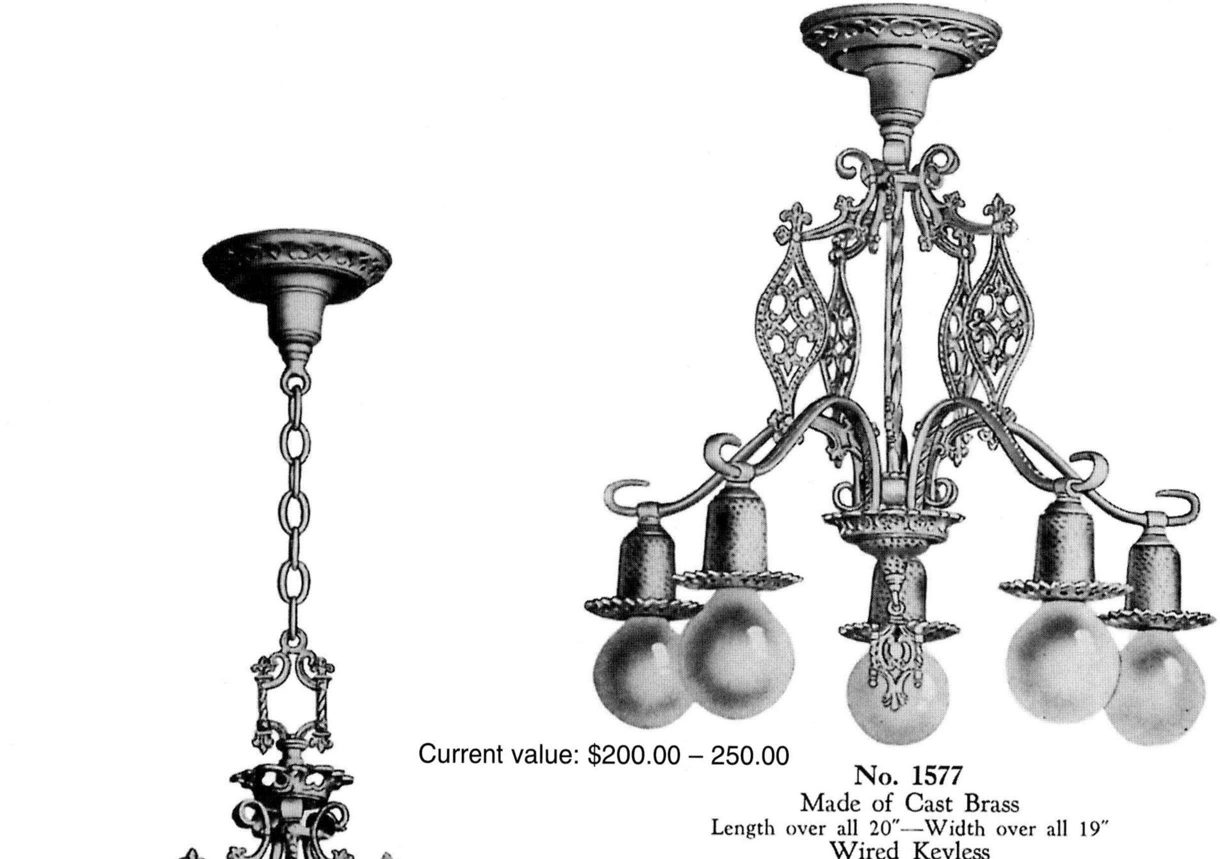

Current value: $200.00 – 250.00

No. 1577
Made of Cast Brass
Length over all 20″—Width over all 19″
Wired Keyless
Finish: Dutch Gold, Silver and Black

No. 1575
Made of Cast Brass
Length over all 36″—Width over all 19″
Wired Key Sockets
Finish: Dutch Gold, Silver and Black

Current value: $225.00 – 285.00

No. 1571
Made of Cast Brass
Length over all 13″—Dia. of plate 7″
Wired Keyless
Finish: Dutch Gold, Silver and Black

Current value: $120.00 – 145.00

No. 1583
Made of Cast Brass
Length over all 32″
Width over all 8″
Wired Keyless
Finish: Dutch Gold,
Silver and Black
Current value: $150.00 – 185.00

No. 1573
Made of Cast Brass
Length over all 36″—Width over all 17″
Wired Key Sockets
Finish: Dutch Gold, Maple Ivory,
Green and Gold
Current value: $185.00 – 225.00

No. 1572
Made of Cast Brass
Length over all 26″
Width over all 8″
Wired Keyless
Finish: Dutch Gold,
Silver and Black
Current value: $135.00 – 165.00

HAMILTON LINE

We present herewith a line of Halcolites suitable for those modern homes which still prefer to be classed as conservative.

HAMILTON HALCOLITES are made of brass with reeded tube arms, and offset with just enough castings to give the required decorative touch.

HAMILTON HALCOLITES are wired with approved wiring devices, packed one to a carton, unassembled.

Made in two finishes:—

TAUPE & GOLD—A beautiful taupe finish with the cast parts relieved in Gold.

SILVER & BLACK—A plated Silver finish with a slight relief of Black.

No. 329
Made of Cast Brass
Plate 9″ x 4¾″—Extension 4″
Wired with Pin Switch
Finish: Taupe and Gold
Silver and Black
Current value: $130.00 – 165.00

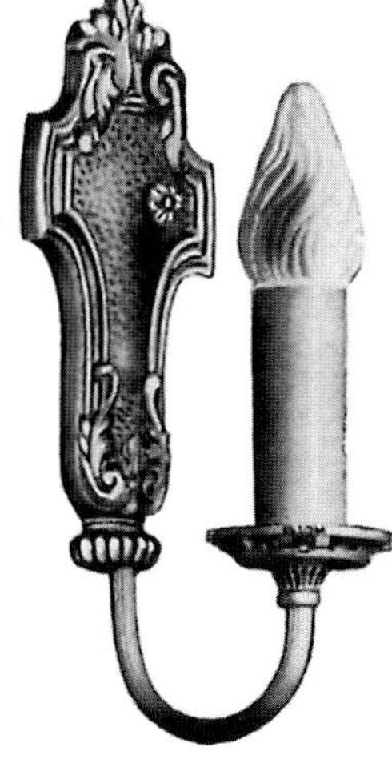

No. 328
Made of Cast Brass
Plate 9″ x 4¾″—Extension 5¼″
Wired with Pin Switch
Finish: Taupe and Gold
Silver and Black
Current value: $100.00 – 125.00

No. 310
Made of Brass with Cast Brass Ornamentations
Length over all 36″—Width over all 20½″
Wired Keyless
Finish: Taupe and Gold
Silver and Black
Current value: $225.00 – 265.00

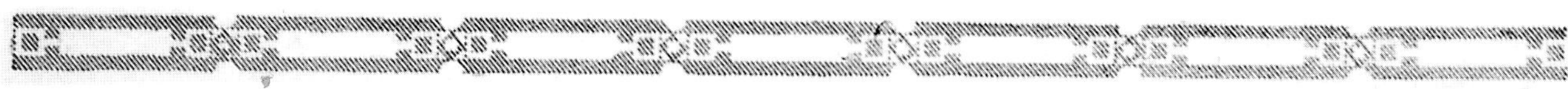

No. 317

Made of Brass with Cast Brass Ornamentations

Length over all 17"—Width over all 17"

Wired Keyless

Finish: Taupe and Gold

Silver and Black

Current value: $200.00 – 230.00

No. 315

Made of Brass with Cast Brass Ornamentations

Length over all 36"—Width over all 17"

Wired Keyless

Finish: Taupe and Gold

Silver and Black

Current value: $225.00 – 265.00

Aluminart Line

Herewith is presented a line of Halcolites made of cast aluminum.

In producing this line, we have brought the price down to a very low and attractive level.

Aluminart Halcolites are completely wired with approved wiring devices, and packed one to a carton.

Made in two finishes.

Silvertone—A blended coloring of sprayed silver with a slight relief of polychrome.

Goldentone—A soft gold finish relieved with a little coloring of polychrome.

ALUMINART HALCOLITES are the exclusive creation of the Halcolite Company, Inc., and are covered by United States Design Patents and applications therefor.

No. 1968

Plate 11¼"x4⅝"—Extension 4¼"
Wired Pullchain

Finish: Silvertone; Goldentone

Current value: $45.00 – 60.00

No. 1969

Plate 11¼"x4⅝"—Extension 4½"
Wired with Pin Switch

Finish: Silvertone; Goldentone

Current value: $65.00 – 100.00

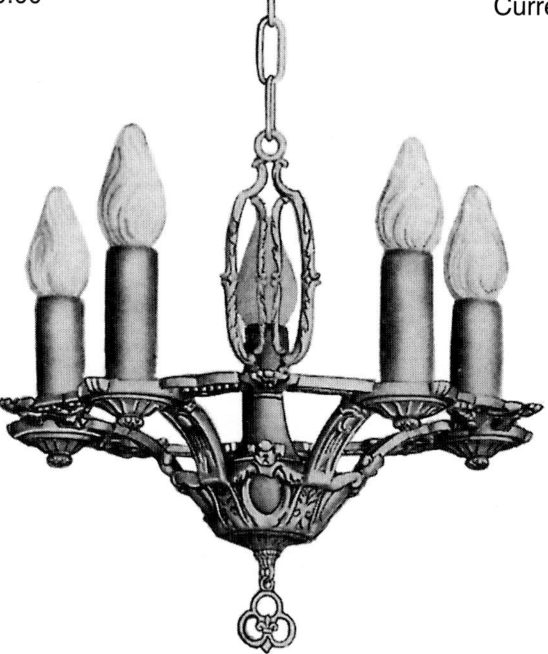

No. 1960

Length over all 36"—Width over all 16"
Wired Keyless

Finish: Silvertone; Goldentone

Current value: $125.00 – 175.00

No. 1951

Depth over all 6″—Diameter of Top 5¾″

Wired Keyless

Finish: Silvertone; Goldentone

Current value: $20.00 – 30.00

No. 1955

Length over all 10″—Width over all 16″

Wired Keyless

Finish: Silvertone; Goldentone

Current value: $100.00 – 140.00

No. 1965

Length over all 36″—Width over all 16″

Wired Keyless

Finish: Silvertone; Goldentone

Current value: $125.00 – 175.00

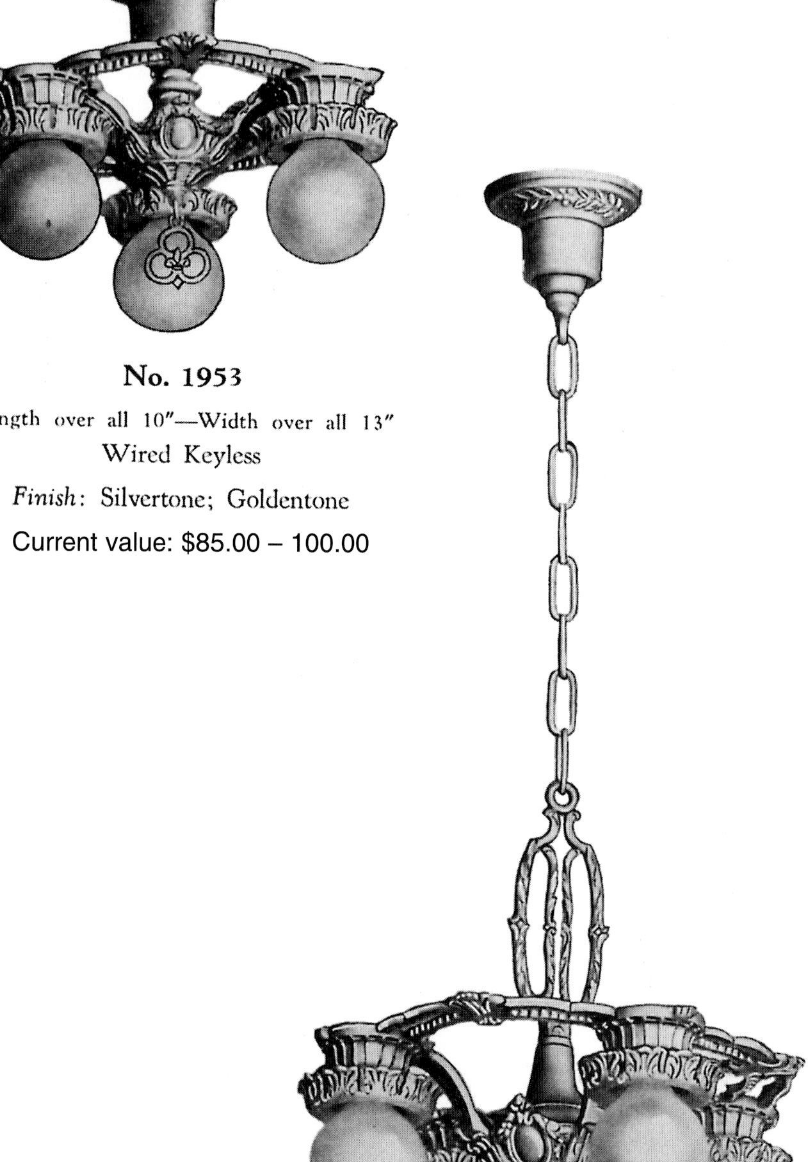

No. 1953

Length over all 10"—Width over all 13"

Wired Keyless

Finish: Silvertone; Goldentone

Current value: $85.00 – 100.00

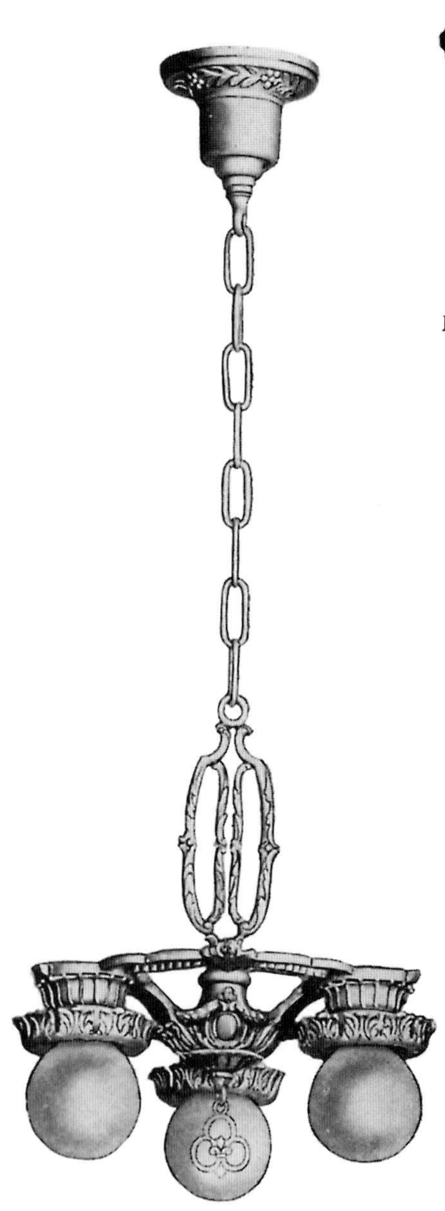

No. 1950

Length over all 36"—Width over all 13"

Wired Keyless

Finish: Silvertone; Goldentone

Current value: $95.00 – 120.00

No. 1974

Length over all 36"—Width over all 14"

Wired Keyless

Finish: Silvertone; Goldentone

Current value: $125.00 – 175.00

HALCOLITES
for the
BREAKFAST ROOM and SUN PORCH

We have given careful attention to the Breakfast room and Sun Porch. These spots call for bright and cheerful colors.

On the following pages you will find a selection of Halcolites that should please the most fastidious taste.

These Halcolites come to you wired complete ready to hang.

No. 542

Equipped with clear prismatic sunburst.
Width over all 10″—Length over all 8″

Wired Keyless

Finish: Antique Ivory
Antique Gold
Antique Green

Current value: $95.00 – 115.00

No. 543

Equipped with clear prismatic sunburst.
Width over all 12″—Length over all 8″

Wired Keyless

Finish: Antique Ivory
Antique Gold
Antique Green

Current value: $115.00 – 135.00

No. 522

Equipped with 10″ x 8″ beautiful hand decorated globe on an ivory background.

Holder Made of Cast Metal

Length over all 36″

Wired Keyless

Finish: Maple Ivory
Green Polychrome
Antique Gold

Current value: $165.00 – 200.00

No. 523

Equipped with beautiful hand decorated dish on an ivory background.
Diameter of dish 12″—Length over all 5½″

Wired Keyless

Finish: Tassel in Antique Ivory
Antique Gold
Antique Green

Current value: $125.00 – 150.00

No. 520

Equipped with Satin Finish Cased Glass Dish with Tan Etching
Diameter of Top 12″—Fitter 10″—Depth 7″

Wired Keyless

Finish: Colonial Brass
Ivory

Current value: $100.00 – 130.00

542
543
522
523
520

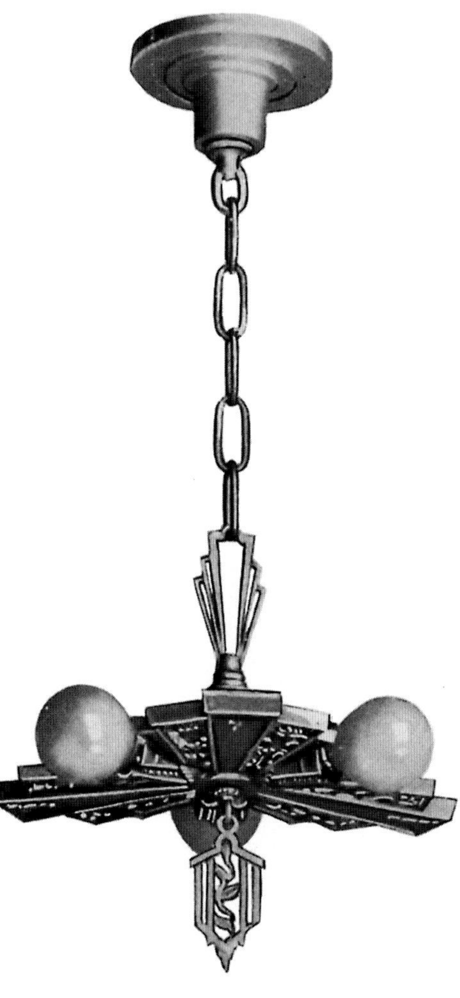

No. 1874
Made of Cast Metal
Length over all 36"—Width over all 10½"
Wired Keyless
Finish: Ivory Polychrome and Gold
Green Polychrome and Gold
Orchid Polychrome and Gold
Current value: $180.00 – 225.00

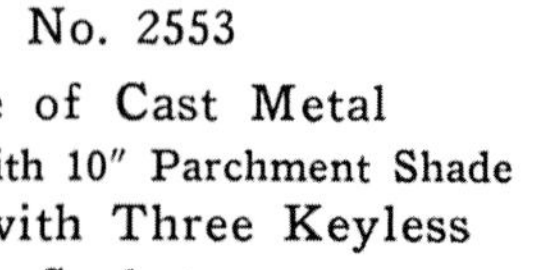

No. 2553
Made of Cast Metal
Equipped with 10" Parchment Shade
Wired with Three Keyless Sockets
Finish: Green Polychrome
Maple Ivory
Current value: $300.00 – 350.00

No. 1863
Made of Cast Metal
Equipped with hand painted mica shade
Length over all 36"—Width over all 11"
Wired Keyless
Finish: Green Polychrome
Maple Ivory
Current value: $350.00 – 400.00

No. 1842
Made of Cast Metal
Wired Keyless
Equipped with 5″ x 7″ hand decorated Amber cylinder.
Length over all 27″
Width over all 7½″
Finish: Maple Ivory
Green Polychrome
Current value: $225.00 – 275.00

No. 551
Equipped with 10″ x 10″ frosted globe with black lines.
Fitter 4″
Wired Keyless
Finish: Antique Ivory
Antique Gold
Antique Green
Current value: $135.00 – 165.00

No. 1862
Made of Cast Metal
Plate 10½″x8″—Length over all 36″
Wired Keyless
Finish: Maple Ivory
Green Polychrome
Current value: $150.00 – 185.00

No. 1833
Length over all 13½"—Width over all 11½"
Wired Keyless
Finish: Ivory Polychrome
Green Polychrome
Current value: $175.00 – 200.00

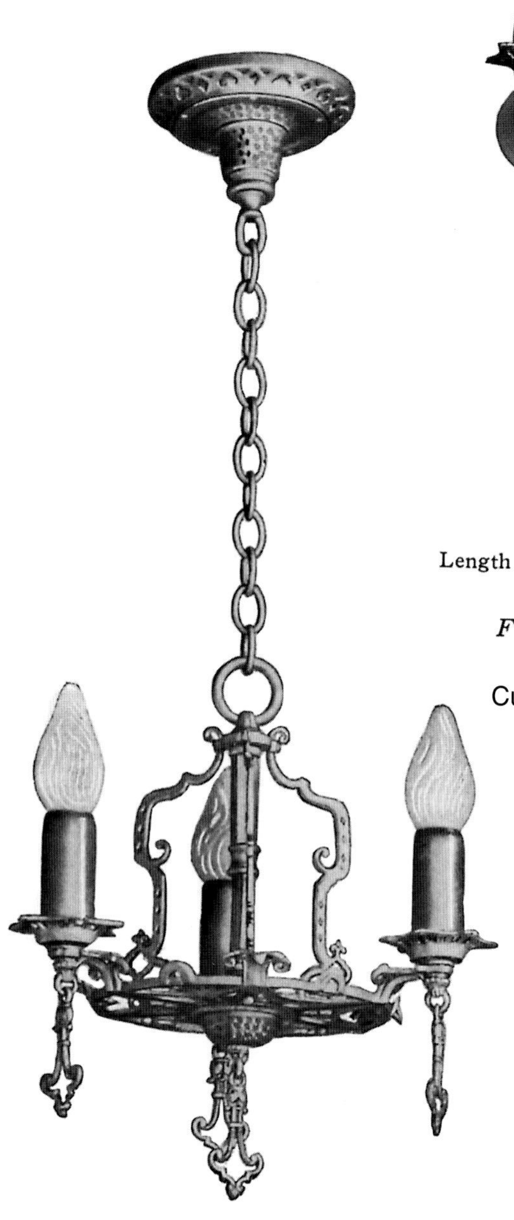

No. 1844
Made of Cast Metal
Length over all 36"—Width over all 14½"
Wired Keyless
Finish: Ivory Polychrome
Green Polychrome
Current value: $150.00 – 185.00

No. 1821
Length over all 13½"
Width over all 8"
Wired Keyless
Finish: Ivory Polychrome
Green Polychrome
Current value: $130.00 – 150.00

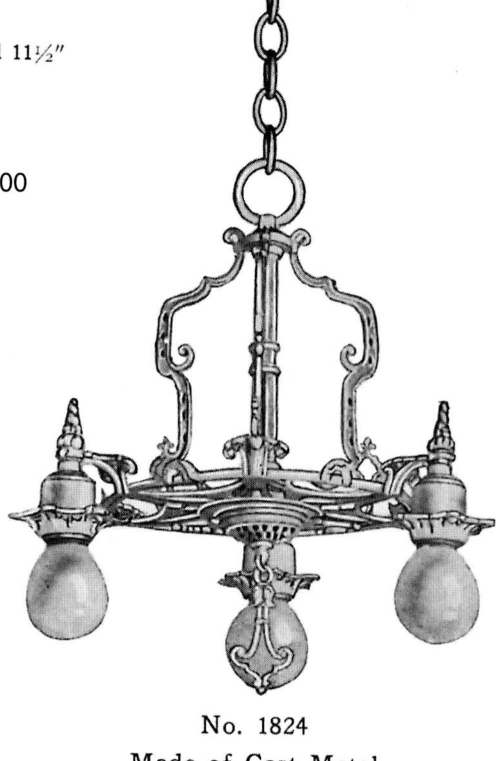

No. 1824
Made of Cast Metal
Length over all 36"—Width over all 14½"
Wired Keyless
Finish: Ivory Polychrome
Green Polychrome
Current value: $150.00 – 185.00

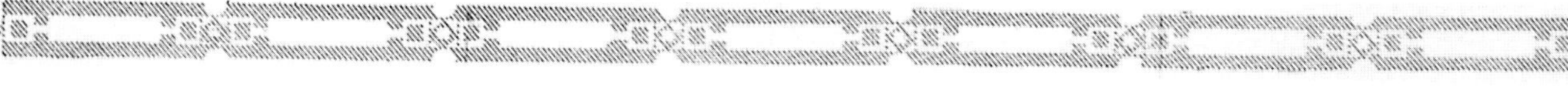

Odroom Halcolites

For the room that is hard to suit, for nooks and corners that are hard to furnish, to assist in solving a lighting problem and making a complete fixture job, we present ODROOM HALCOLITES.

ODROOM HALCOLITES come wired with approved wiring devices and packed one to a carton.

ODROOM HALCOLITES are the exclusive creation of the Halcolite Company, Inc., and are covered by United States Design Patents and applications therefor.

No. 802
Made of Cast Metal
Plate 11½"x6"—Length over all 6"
Wired Keyless
Finish:
Ivory, Ivory Polychrome
Green Polychrome
Current value: $50.00 – 65.00

No. 808
Made of Cast Metal
Plate 10½"x4¼"—Extension 4½"
Wired with Pin Switch
Finish:
Ivory, Ivory Polychrome
Green Polychrome
Current value: $45.00 – 55.00

No. 809
Made of Cast Metal
Plate 10½"x4¼"—Extension 4¼"
Wired with Pin Switch
Finish:
Ivory, Ivory Polychrome
Green Polychrome
Current value: $60.00 – 85.00

No. 800
Made of Cast Metal
Diameter of Plate 6¼"
Length over all 6'
Wired Keyless
Finish:
Ivory, Ivory Polychrome
Green Polychrome
Current value: $15.00 – 85.00

No. 803
Made of Cast Metal
Diameter of Plate 11½"—Length over all 6"
Wired Keyless
Finish:
Ivory, Ivory Polychrome
Green Polychrome
Current value: $65.00 – 85.00

No. 804
Made of Cast Metal
Length over all 36"—Width over all 11½"
Wired Keyless
Finish:
Ivory, Ivory and Polychrome
Green Polychrome
Current value: $80.00 – 95.00

No. 807
Made of Cast Metal
Length over all 36"—Width over all 11½"
Wired Keyless
Finish:
Ivory, Ivory and Polychrome
Green Polychrome
Current value: $65.00 – 80.00

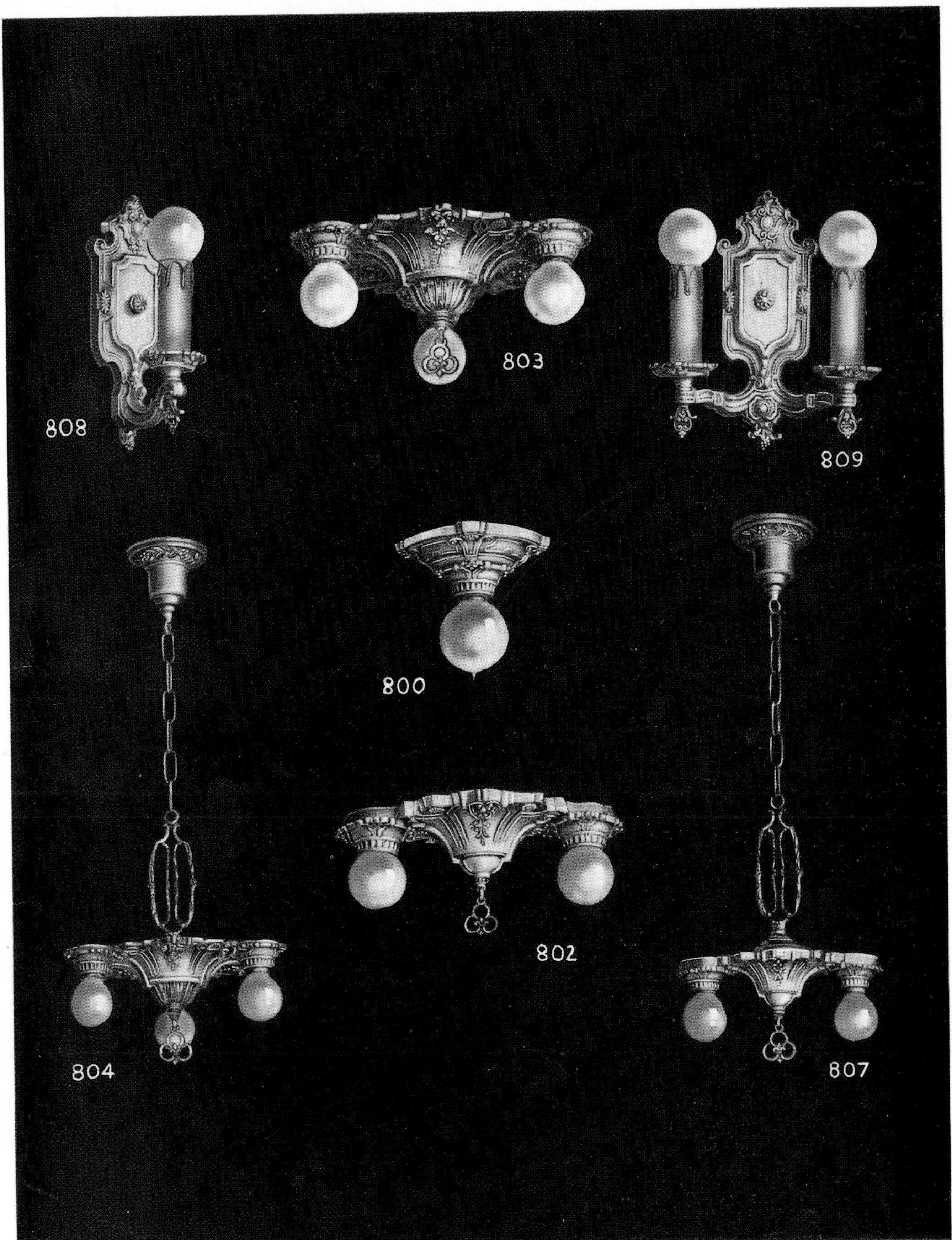
808
803
809
800
802
804
807

No. 828
Length over all 12"—Plate 6"x3½"
Wired Pullchain
Finish:
Ivory and Gold,
Green and Gold
Current value: $50.00 – 65.00

No. 818
Plate 6"x3½"—Extension 5½"
Wired Pullchain
Finish:
Ivory and Gold,
Green and Gold
Current value: $40.00 – 50.00

No. 812
Length over all 5½"—Plate 11"x4¼"
Wired Keyless
Finish:
Ivory and Gold,
Green and Gold
Current value: $55.00 – 65.00

No. 813
Length over all 6½"
Diameter of Plate 11"
Wired Keyless
Finish:
Ivory and Gold,
Green and Gold
Current value: $85.00 – 115.00

No. 822
Length over all 6½"—Plate 8¾"x4"
Wired Keyless
Finish:
Ivory and Gold,
Green and Gold
Current value: $45.00 – 65.00

No. 821
Length over all 9½"
Diameter of Top 6¼"
Wired Keyless
Finish:
Ivory and Gold,
Green and Gold
Current value: $20.00 – 35.00

No. 831
Length over all 12"—Width over all 5"
Wired Keyless
Finish:
Ivory and Gold,
Green and Gold
Current value: $50.00 – 75.00

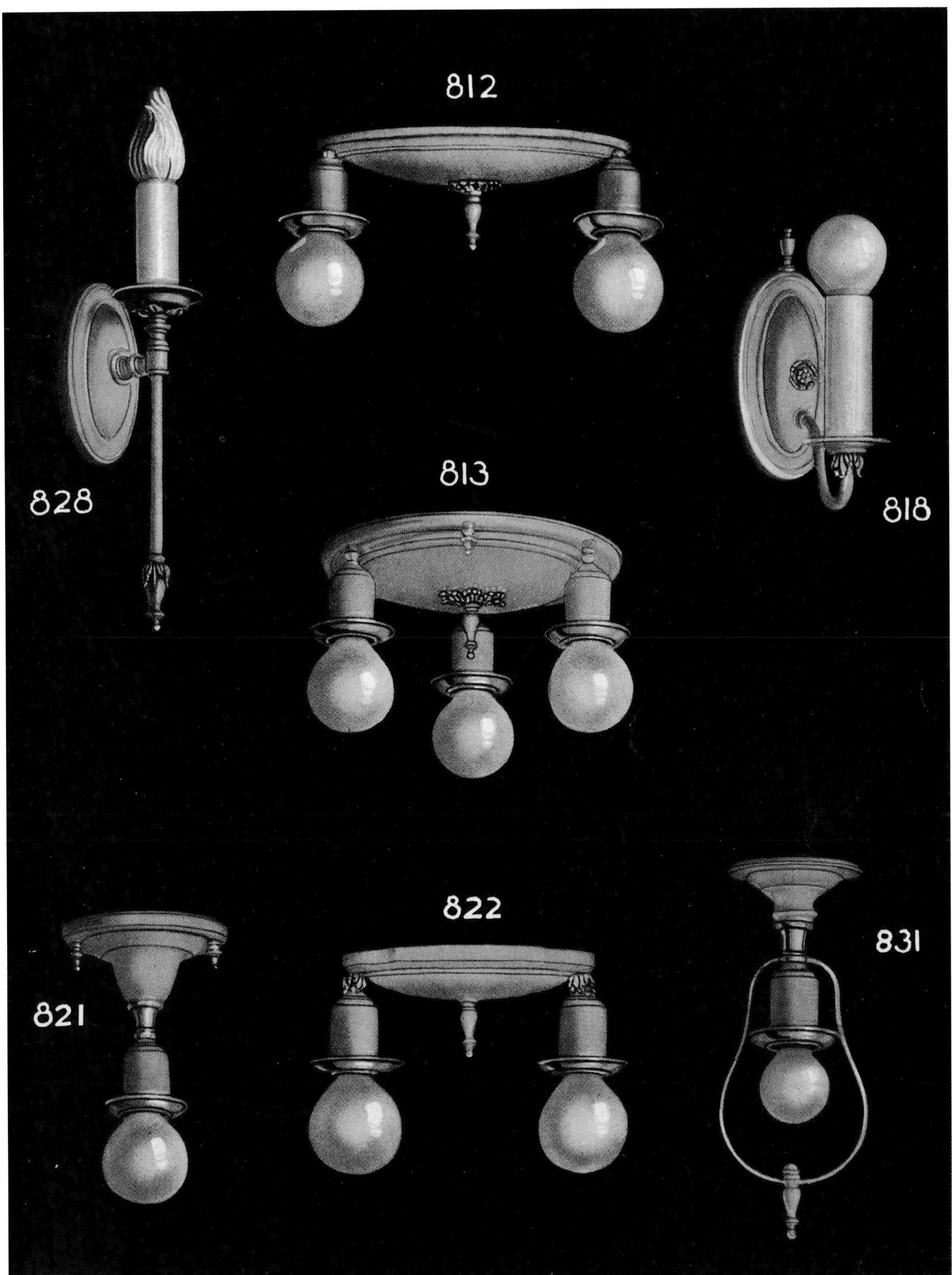
812
828
818
813
822
821
831

No. 1879
Made of Cast Metal
Plate 4½"x7¾"—Extension 3¾"
Wired with Pin Switch
Finish:
Ivory Polychrome and Gold
Green Polychrome and Gold
Orchid Polychrome and Gold
Current value: $150.00 – 200.00

No. 1878
Made of Cast Metal
Plate 4½"x7¾"—Extension 4½"
Wired with Pin Switch
Finish:
Ivory Polychrome and Gold
Green Polychrome and Gold
Orchid Polychrome and Gold
Current value: $120.00 – 150.00

No. 1873
Made of Cast Metal
Width over all 10½"—Depth over all 6½"
Wired Keyless
Finish:
Ivory Polychrome and Gold
Green Polychrome and Gold
Orchid Polychrome and Gold
Current value: $200.00 – 250.00

No. 1871
Made of Cast Metal
Width over all 9"—Depth over all 6"
Wired Keyless
Finish:
Ivory Polychrome and Gold
Green Polychrome and Gold
Orchid Polychrome and Gold
Current value: $75.00 – 100.00

No. 1872
Made of Cast Metal
Plate 11½"x6"—Depth over all 7¾"
Wired Keyless
Finish:
Ivory Polychrome and Gold
Green Polychrome and Gold
Orchid Polychrome and Gold
Current value: $165.00 – 195.00

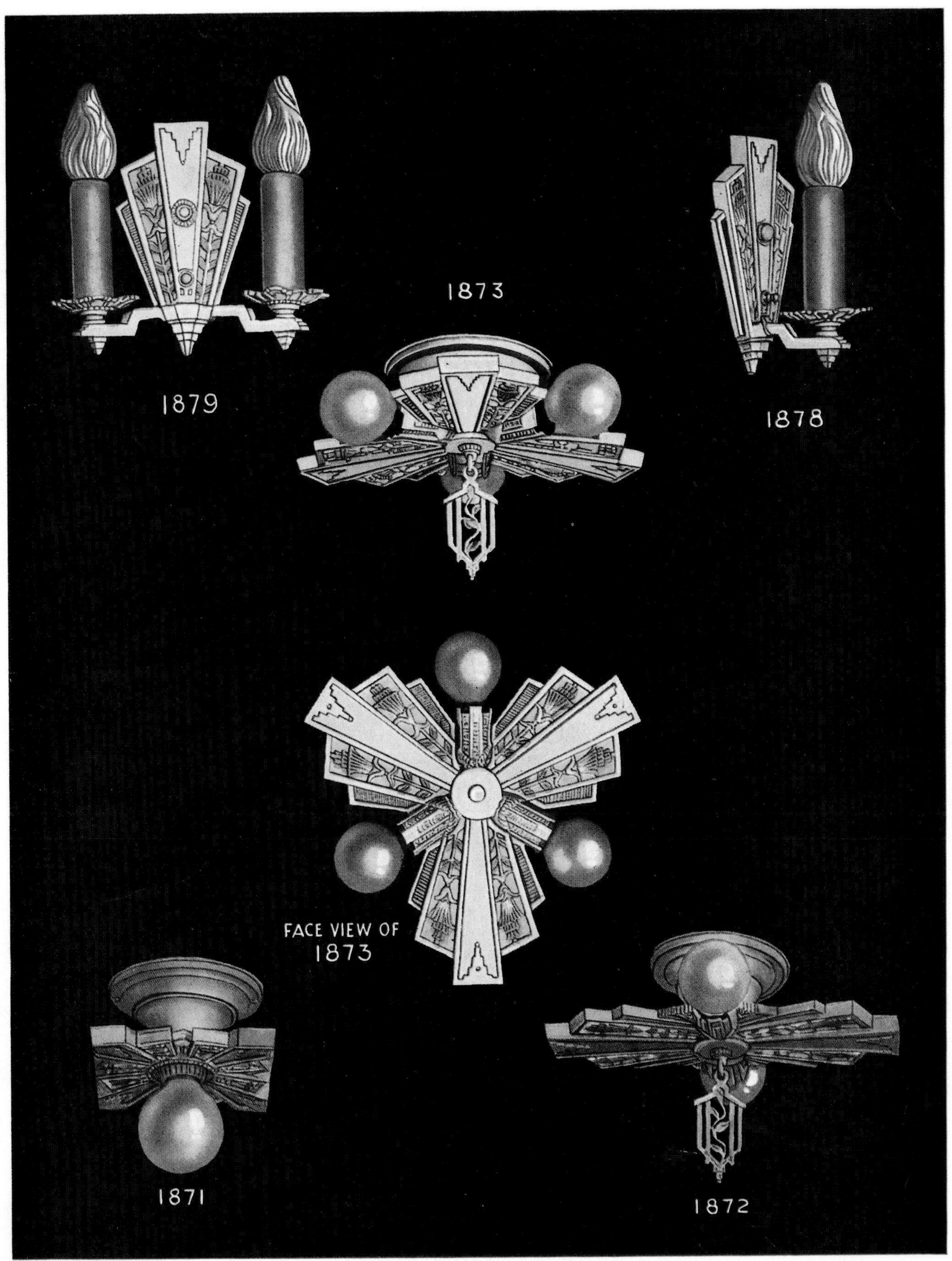

The Fixtures shown on this page are covered by United States Design Patents Nos. 77798-77799.

No. 1921

Made of Cast Metal

Plate 8¼"x4¼"—Extension 4"

Wired with Turn Candle Socket

Finish: Ivory, Ivory Polychrome, Green Polychrome

Current value: $50.00 – 85.00

No. 1931

Made of Cast Metal

Plate 9"x4¼"—Extension 4"

Wired with Turn Candle Socket and Convenience Outlet

Finish: Ivory, Ivory Polychrome, Green Polychrome

Current value: $50.00 – 85.00

No. 1933

Diameter of Plate 12"—Depth 5"

Wired Keyless

Finish: Ivory, Ivory Polychrome, Green Polychrome

Current value: $100.00 – 125.00

No. 1922

Plate 13"x6½"—Length 8½"

Wired Keyless

Finish: Ivory, Ivory Polychrome, Green Polychrome

Current value: $85.00 – 100.00

No. 1943

Diameter of Plate 12"—Length 12"

Wired Keyless

Finish: Ivory, Ivory Polychrome, Green Polychrome

Current value: $100.00 – 125.00

No. 1927

Diameter of Top 7¼"—Depth 6"

Wired Keyless

Finish: Ivory, Ivory Polychrome, Green Polychrome

Current value: $25.00 – 35.00

No. 1912

Plate 13"x6½"—Depth 5"

Wired Keyless

Finish: Ivory, Ivory Polychrome, Green Polychrome

Current value: $65.00 – 85.00

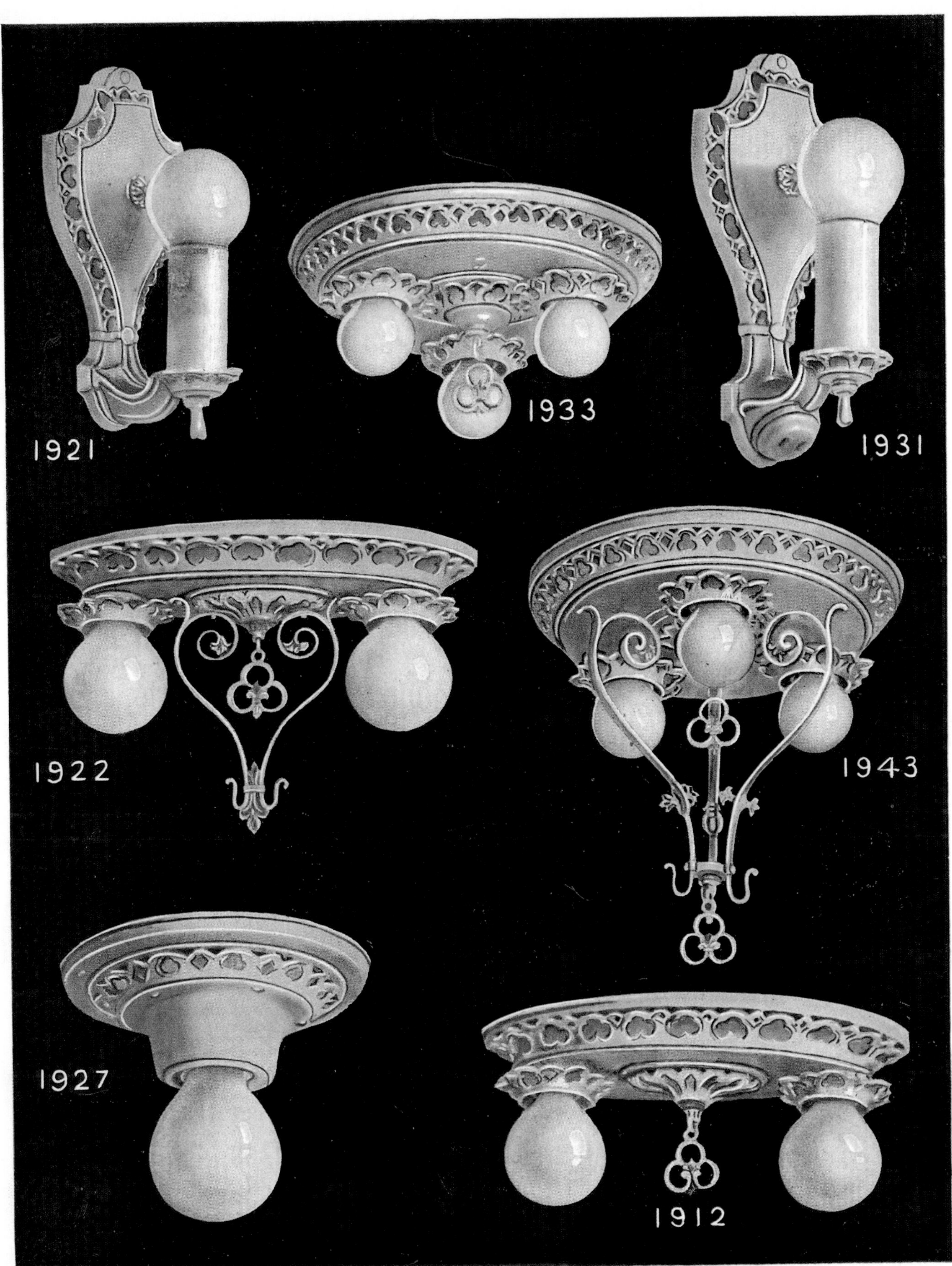
1921
1933
1931
1922
1943
1927
1912

No. 843

Length over all 7¾"—Width over all 12½"

Wired Keyless

Finish: Ivory and Gold
Green and Gold
Orchid and Gold

Current value: $55.00 – 75.00

No. 842

Length over all 7¾"—Width over all 11"

Wired Keyless

Finish: Ivory and Gold
Green and Gold
Orchid and Gold

Current value: $40.00 – 60.00

No. 848

Diameter of plate 4¾"—Extension 5½"

Wired Pull Chain

Finish: Ivory and Gold
Green and Gold
Orchid and Gold

Current value: $35.00 – 50.00

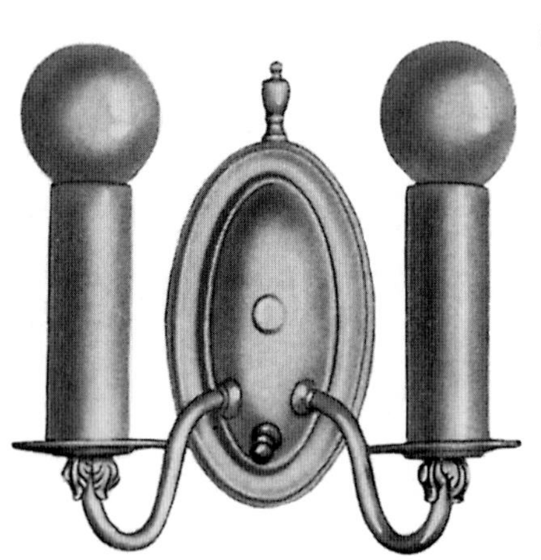

No. 819

Plate 6" x 3½"—Extension 4¼"

Wired with Pin Switch

Finish: Ivory and Gold
Green and Gold

Current value: $75.00 – 95.00

No. 801

Length over all 5¼"—Diameter of top 4¾"

Wired Keyless

Finish: Ivory and Gold
Green and Gold

Current value: $15.00 – 25.00

No. 801½

Same as above.

Wired Pullchain

Current value: $15.00 – 25.00

PORCELAIN LINE

Here is a line of fixtures ideal for the modern kitchen or bathroom.

Being made of the highest quality of porcelain, it is absolutely guaranteed to retain its natural white china finish.

All Porcelain Halcolites come to you wired complete, ready to install.

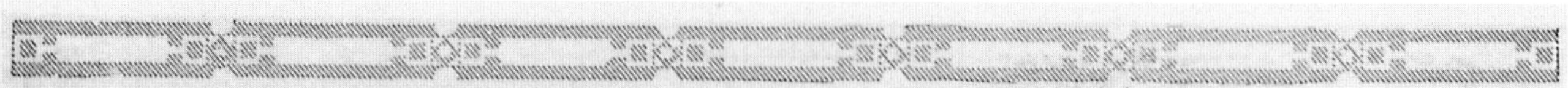

No. 121
Made of porcelain
Wired with levolier toggle switch
Plate 4¾"x7"—Extension 4"
Finish: White
White with black line
Solid Green
Solid Blue

Current value:
White, White with black line:
$30.00 – 45.00
Solid Green, Solid Blue
$60.00 – 85.00

No. 122
Made of porcelain
Wired with levolier toggle switch
Equipped with convenience outlet
Plate 4¾"x7"—Extension 4"
Finish: White
White with black line
Solid Green
Solid Blue

Current value:
White, White with black line:
$30.00 – 45.00
Solid Green, Solid Blue
$60.00 – 85.00

No. 101
Made of porcelain
Equipped with 8½"x4" glass unit
Wired Keyless
Finish: White
White with black line
Current value: $50.00 – 85.00

No. 101½
Same as above
Wired with pullchain socket

Current value: $50.00 – 85.00

No. 128
Made of porcelain
Length over all 6½"—Diameter of top 6½"
Wired Keyless
Finish: White
White with black line
Current value: $25.00 – 35.00

No. 128½
Same as above
Wired with pullchain socket

Current value: $25.00 – 35.00

No. 109
Made of porcelain
Back 5"x4"—Extension 8"
Equipped with white shade as shown
Wired pullchain
Finish: White
White with black line
Current value: $100.00 – 125.00

No. 109½
Same as above
Equipped with convenience outlet

Current value: $100.00 – 125.00

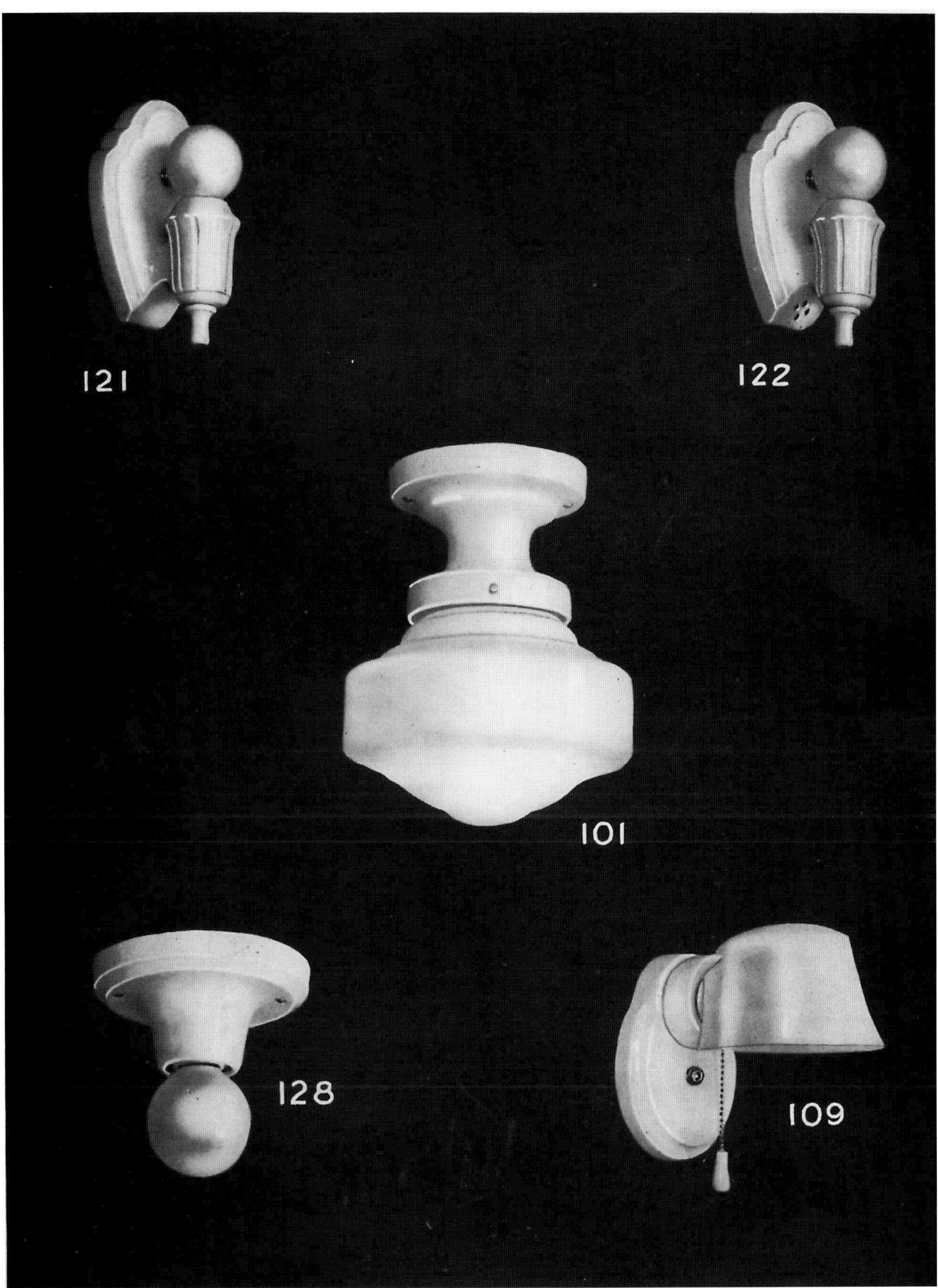
121
122
101
128
109

Gill Glass and Fixture Company

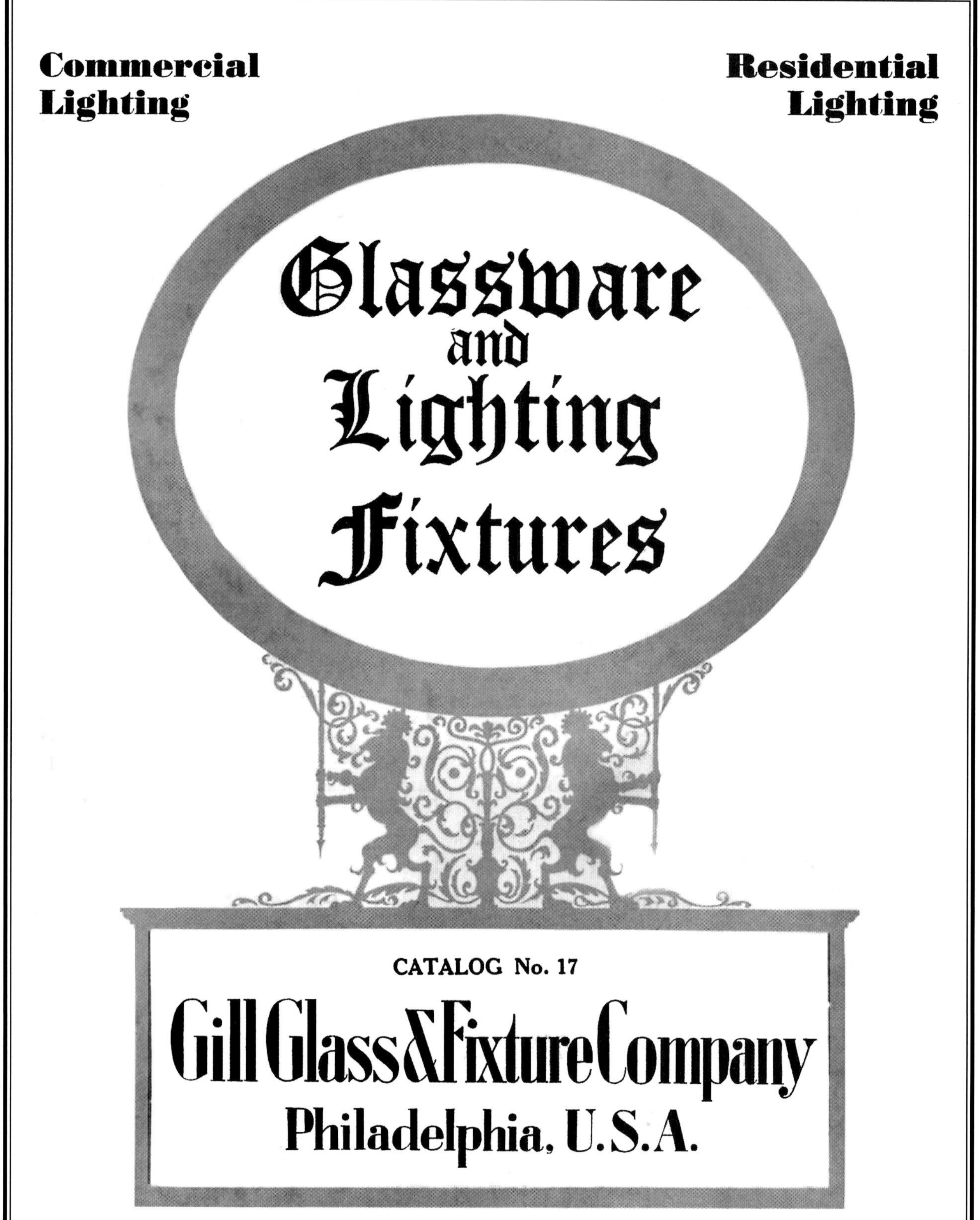

Ornamental Commercial Fixtures

(Hyperion Glass)

Finish:
Bank
Bronze

Note:
Eight
lights
outside

These fixtures will only be furnished "Bare" and "Knocked Down"—no sockets or wire will be supplied. (Assembly very simple—high packing cost eliminated).

Glassware and fixture parts packed together in individual cartons.

Number	Hyperion		Dimensions of Glass			Dimensions of Fixtures	
Fixture Compete	Etched Updated Value	Plain Updated Value	Length	Width	Fitter	Length Overall	Width Overall
3718-E	$850.00+	$825.00+	11⅞"	18"	8"	24"	24"
3716-E	$825.00+	$800.00+	11⅜"	16"	6"	23"	22"

Please specify whether Etched or Plain Glassware is desired.

Ornamental Commercial Fixtures

(Hyperion Glass)

Finish:
Bank
Bronze

Note:
Eight
lights
outside

These fixtures will only be furnished "Bare" and "Knocked Down"—no sockets or wire will be supplied. (Assembly very simple—high packing cost eliminated).

Glassware and fixture parts packed together in individual cartons.

Number	Hyperion		Dimensions of Glass			Dimensions of Fixtures	
Fixture Compete	Etched Updated Value	Plain Updated Value	Length	Width	Fitter	Length Overall	Width Overall
3618-E	$900.00+	$850.00+	11⅞"	18"	8"	48"	24"
3616-E	$875.00+	$825.00+	11⅜"	16"	6"	48"	22"

Please specify whether Etched or Plain Glassware is desired.

Ornamental Commercial Fixtures

(Hyperion Glass)

Finish:
Bank
Bronze

Glassware:
Etched
or
Plain

These fixtures will only be furnished "Bare" and "Knocked Down"—no sockets or wire will be supplied. (Assembly very simple—high packing cost eliminated).

Glassware and fixture parts packed together in individual cartons.

Number	Hyperion		Dimensions of Glass			Dimensions of Fixtures	
Fixture Compete	Etched Updated Value	Plain Updated Value	Length	Width	Fitter	Length Overall	Width Overall
3218-E	$850.00+	$825.00+	11⅞"	18"	8"	24"	24"
3216-E	$750.00+	$700.00+	11⅜"	16"	6"	23"	22"
3214-E	$650.00+	$600.00+	11⅜"	14"	6"	23"	20"
3212-E	$550.00+	$500.00+	11¼"	12"	6"	23"	18"
3209-E	$450.00+	$400.00+	9⅞"	9"	4"	18"	14"

Please specify whether Etched or Plain Glassware is desired.

Ornamental Commercial Fixtures

(Hyperion Glass)

Glassware: Etched or Plain

No. 3909E

Finish: Bank Bronze

No. 3809E

These fixtures will only be furnished "Bare" and "Knocked Down"—no sockets or wire will be supplied.

Glassware and fixture parts packed together in individual cartons.

Number	Hyperion		Dimensions of Glass			Dimensions of Fixtures	
Fixture Compete	Etched Updated Value	Plain Update Value	Length	Width	Fitter	Length Overall	Width Overall
3809-E	\$350.00–400.00	\$325.00–375.00	9⅞"	9"	4"	25"	12½"
3909-E	\$250.00–285.00	\$225.00–250.00	9⅞"	9"	4"	15"	10½"

Please specify whether Etched or Plain Glassware is desired.

Ornamental Commercial Fixtures

Finish:

Bank Bronze

(Hyperion Glass)

Glassware:

Etched or Plain

Prices will vary depending on shade sizes.

These fixtures will only be furnished "Bare" and "Knocked Down"—no sockets or wire will be supplied. (Assembly very simple—high packing cost eliminated.)

Glassware and fixture parts packed together in individual cartons.

Number	Hyperion		Dimensions of Glass			Dimensions of Fixtures	
Fixture Compete	Etched Updated Value	Plain Updated Value	Length	Width	Fitter	Length Overall	Width Overall
3018-E	$900.00+	$850.00+	11⅞"	18"	8"	48"	24"
3016-E	$800.00+	$750.00+	11⅜"	16"	6"	48"	22"
3014-E	$700.00+	$650.00+	11⅜"	14"	6"	48"	20"
3012-E	$600.00+	$550.00+	11¼"	12"	6"	48"	18"
3009-E	$500.00+	$450.00+	9⅞"	9"	4"	48"	14"

No. 3318E

Prices will vary depending on shade sizes.

Ornamental Commercial Fixtures

(Hyperion Glass)

No. 3418E

Finish: Bank Bronze

Glassware: Etched or Plain

These fixtures will only be furnished "Bare" and "Knocked Down"—no sockets or wire will be supplied. (Assembly very simple—high packing cost eliminated.)

Glassware and fixture parts packed together in individual cartons.

Number	Hyperion		Dimensions of Glass			Dimensions of Fixtures	
Fixture Compete	Etched Updated Value	Plain Updated Value	Length	Width	Fitter	Length Overall	Width Overall
3418-E	$350.00	$265.00	11⅞"	18"	8"	24"	18"
3416-E	$335.00	$240.00	11⅜"	16"	6"	23"	16"
3414-E	$315.00	$215.00	11⅜"	14"	6"	23"	14"
3412-E	$300.00	$200.00	11¼"	12"	6"	23"	12"
3318-E	$385.00	$275.00	11⅞"	18"	8"	48"	18"
3316-E	$375.00	$255.00	11⅜"	16"	6"	48"	16"
3314-E	$365.00	$235.00	11⅜"	14"	6"	48"	14"
3312-E	$350.00	$215.00	11¼"	12"	6"	48"	12"

Ornamental Commercial Fixtures

(Hyperion Glass)

No. 3309E

No. 3409E

Finish: Bank Bronze

Glassware: Etched or Plain

These fixtures will only be furnished "Bare" and "Knocked Down"—no sockets or wire will be supplied.

Glassware and fixture parts packed together in individual cartons.

Number	Hyperion		Dimensions of Glass			Dimensions of Fixtures	
Fixture Compete	Etched Updated Value	Plain Updated Value	Length	Width	Fitter	Length Overall	Width Overall
3309-E	$300.00–325.00	$200.00–235.00	9⅞"	9"	4"	48"	9"
3409-E	$265.00–285.00	$185.00–210.00	9⅞"	9"	4"	18"	9"

Decorative Ornamental Commercial Units

This hanger is unsurpassed in design and beauty, and quality of material and workmanship are of the best. A decorative type of commercial luminaire for the most fastidious requirements, combined with the best in lighting efficiency—"Hyperion."

Finish

Bronze and Gold.

Specifications

Special screw collar ceiling attachment. Heavy cast ornamental ring on holder.

No. 44 hanger wired with No. 16 slow burning wire and Edison base porcelain socket.

No. 45 hanger wired with No. 14 slow burning wire and mogul base porcelain socket.

Glassware when ordered separately will be furnished with holes, unless otherwise specified.

Values will vary depending on shade size.

Numbers		Values	Standard Package	Dimensions of Glass	Weights		
Fixture Complete	Glass Only	Each Fixture Complete Current Values	Glass Only	Length Width Fitter	Fixture Complete	Standard Package Glass Only	Recommended Wattage
44/8612G	8612G	$250.00–300.00	4	12 x 8 x 6	9 lbs.	18 lbs.	100–150
44/8614G	8614G	$250.00–300.00	2	14 x 9⅝ x 6	11 lbs.	14 lbs.	150–200
44/8616G	8616G	$250.00–300.00	1	12 x 11½ x 6	12 lbs.	10 lbs.	200–300
45/8616G	8616G	$250.00–300.00	1	12 x 11½ x 6	12 lbs.	10 lbs.	200–300

Note—Each complete fixture is a Standard Package.

Decorative Ornamental Commercial Units

HYPERION UNITS

Nos. 754-756 and 757—Suspension Type Hanger
Length of Hanger only, 30″

No. 786—Ceiling Type Holder

Finish

Statuary Bronze.
Loop and Crown Antique Gold.

Wiring Specifications

No. 786 furnished with slow burning wire, two lugs and one set screw, wired complete with Pigtail Receptacle. Deep Flanged Canopy, 7¼″ diam. with offset strap, lugs, and screws.

No. 754 and 756 furnished slow burning wire, two lugs and one set screw, wired complete with medium socket, deep flanged canopy with slip ring and ⅜″ female stem.

No. 757 same as 756 but equipped with mogul socket.

Glassware if ordered separately will be furnished without holes unless otherwise specified.

Numbers		Values	Dimensions of Glass		
Fixture Complete	Glass Only	Each Fixture Complete Current Values	Width	Length	Fitter
754/642G	642G	$250.00–300.00	10 x	7¼ x	4
754/643G	643G	$250.00–300.00	12 x	8½ x	4
755/643G	643G	$250.00–300.00	12 x	8½ x	6
756/644G	644G	$250.00–300.00	14 x	9½ x	6
756/645G	645G	$250.00–300.00	16 x	10¾ x	6
757/645G	645G	$250.00–300.00	16 x	10¾ x	6
784/642G	642G	$225.00–275.00	10 x	7¼ x	4
786/643G	643G	$225.00–275.00	12 x	8½ x	6
786/644G	644G	$225.00–275.00	14 x	9½ x	6
786/645G	645G	$225.00–275.00	16 x	10¾ x	6

Prices will vary depending on shade sizes.

Decorative Ornamental Commercial Units

HYPERION UNITS

Nos. 754-756 and 757—Suspension Type Hanger
Length of Hanger only, 30″

No. 786—Ceiling Type Holder

Finish

Statuary Bronze.
Loop and Crown Antique Gold.

Wiring Specifications

No. 786 furnished with slow burning wire, two lugs and one set screw, wired complete with Pigtail Receptacle. Deep Flanged Canopy, 7¼″ diam. with offset strap, lugs, and screws.

No. 754 and 756 furnished slow burning wire, two lugs and one set screw, wired complete with medium socket, deep flanged canopy with slip ring and ⅜″ female stem.

No. 757 same as 756 but equipped with mogul socket.

Glassware when ordered separately will be furnished without holes unless otherwise specified.

Prices will vary depending on shade sizes.

Numbers	Values	Dimensions of Glass		
Fixture Complete	Each Fixture Complete Current Values	Width	Length	Fitter
756/401H	$250.00–300.00	10 x	12 x	6
756/402H	$250.00–300.00	12 x	14 x	6
757/402H	$250.00–300.00	12 x	14 x	6
786/401H	$225.00–275.00	10 x	12 x	6
786/402H	$225.00–275.00	12 x	14 x	6

Lamps

Designed to conform with the German Modernistic Styles,
suitable for
End Table—Console—Radio—Mantel—Reception Hall and Boudoir

When ordering—kindly mention number and finish required.

Made of Solid Brass.
Finished in GOLD or SILVER.

Furnished with glass shades, made of genuine "IVORY" glass with Decalcomania decorations applied and fired in, and finished with an overlay of Lustrous Iridescence.

Wired complete with cord and plug including control switch in base of lamp.

L G. 2.——(2 Lights)

Shade: 8¾ inches wide—5¼ inches high
Stand: 18½ inches high overall

Price, wired complete............$19.50 List
[Packed 1 to a Standard Carton]

Current value: $1,750.00+

Note: These lamps are very rare.

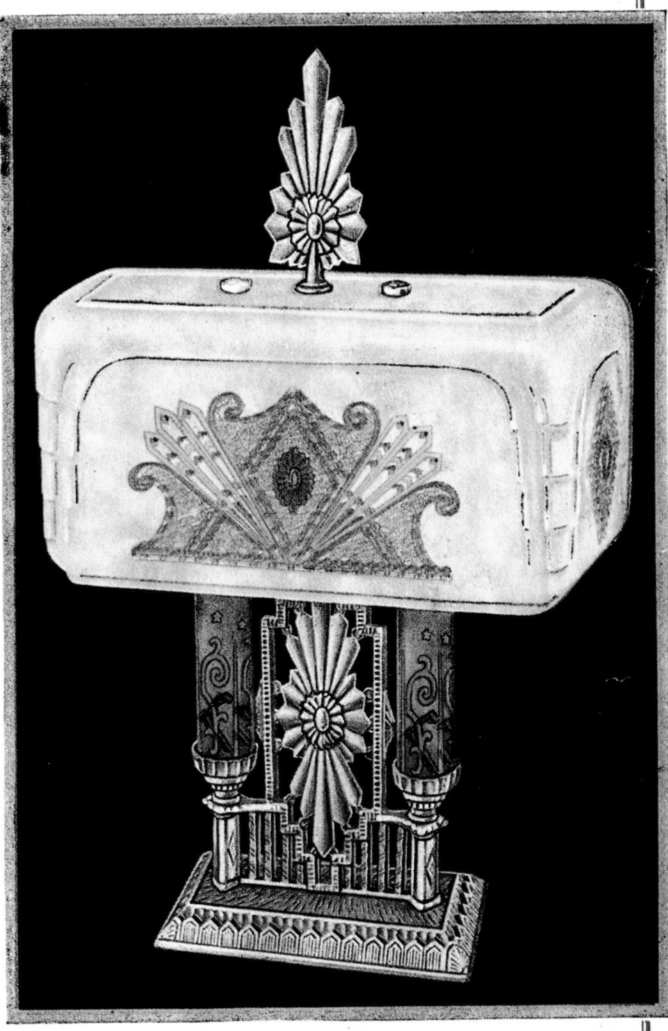

L G. 1.——(2 Lights)

Shade: 11¾ inches wide—6 inches high
Stand: 19½ inches high overall

Price, wired complete............$21.00 List
[Packed 1 to a Standard Carton]

Current value: $2,000.00+

Lamps

Designed to conform with the French Modernistic Styles,
suitable for
End Table—Console—Radio—Mantel—Reception Hall and Boudoir

When ordering—kindly mention number and finish required.

Made of Solid Brass.
Finished in GOLD or SILVER.

Furnished with glass shades, made of genuine "IVORY" glass with Decalcomania decorations applied and fired in, and finished with an overlay of Lustrous Iridescence.

Wired complete with cord and plug including control switch in base of lamp.

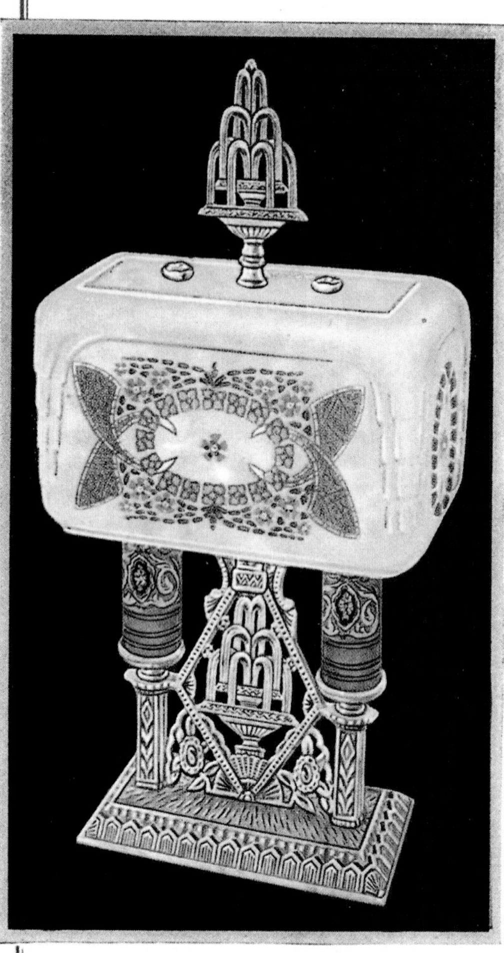

L F. 2.——(2 Lights)

Shade: 8¾ inches wide—5¼ inches high
Stand: 18½ inches high overall

Price, wired complete............$19.50 List
[Packed 1 to a Standard Carton]

Current value: $1,750.00+

Note: These lamps are very rare.

L F. 1.——(2 Lights)

Shade: 11¾ inches wide—6 inches high
Stand: 19½ inches high overall

Price, wired complete............$21.00 List

Current value: $2,000.00+

For the Dining Room Breakfast Room and Sun Parlor

No. 204G
16" Diameter—4 Lights
No. 203G
9" Diameter—3 Lights

No. 201G

All fixture parts are made of solid brass.

Fixtures complete with glassware are furnished wired complete in specially constructed cartons.

Note: Very rare and exquisite fixtures.

Number Fixture	Current Value Each, Wired	Length Overall	Number of Lights	Finish
204G	$1,200.00+	42 inches	4 lights	Gold and Poly.
203G	$800.00+	42 inches	3 lights	Gold and Poly.
201G	$400.00+	11¼ inches	1 light	Gold and Poly.

For the Dining Room, Breakfast Room and Sun Parlor

No. 224G

No. 223G

All fixture parts are made of solid brass.

Fixtures are furnished wired complete and packed with glassware in specially constructed cartons.

Note: Very rare and exquisite fixtures.

Number Fixture	Current Value Each, Wired	Length Overall	Number of Lights	Finish
224G	$1,200.00+	25 inches	4 lights	Gold and Poly.
223G	$800.00+	22 inches	3 lights	Gold and Poly.

For the Dining Room
Breakfast Room
and
Sun Parlor

No. 204S
16" Diameter—4 Lights

No. 203S
9" Diameter—3 Lights

No. 201S

All fixture parts are made of solid brass.

Fixtures complete with glassware are furnished wired complete in specially constructed cartons.

Note: Very rare fixtures, beautiful colors and detail. The grape pattern was very popular during this time period.

Number Fixture	Current Value Each, Wired	Length Overall	Number of Lights	Finish
204S	$1,500.00+	42 inches	4 lights	Silver and Poly.
203S	$900.00+	42 inches	3 lights	Silver and Poly.
201S	$500.00+	11¼ inches	1 light	Silver and Poly.

For the Dining Room, Breakfast Room and Sun Parlor

No. 224S

No. 223S

All fixture parts are made of solid brass.

Fixtures are furnished wired complete and packed with glassware in specially constructed cartons.

Note: Very rare fixtures, beautiful colors and detail. The grape pattern was very popular during this time period.

Number Fixture	Current Value Each, Wired	Length Overall	Spread Overall	Number Of Lights	Finish
224S	$1,500.00+	25 inches	16 inches	4 lights	Silver and Poly.
223S	$900.00+	22 inches	9 inches	3 lights	Silver and Poly.

For the Dining Room Breakfast Room and Sun Parlor

No. 204B
16" Diameter—4 Lights

No. 203B
9" Diameter—3 Lights

No. 201B

All fixture parts are made of solid brass.

Fixtures complete with glassware are furnished wired complete in specially constructed cartons.

Note: Very rare, excellent detail and colors.

Number Fixture	Current Value Each, Wired	Standard Package	Length Overall	Number Of Lights	Finish
204B	$1,000.00+	1	42 inches	4 lights	Bronze and Poly.
203B	$800.00+	1	42 inches	3 lights	Bronze and Poly.
201B	$400.00+	4	11¼ inches	1 light	Bronze and Poly.

For the Dining Room, Breakfast Room and Sun Parlor

No. 224B

No. 223B

All fixture parts are made of solid brass.

Fixtures are furnished wired complete and packed with glassware in specially constructed cartons.

Note: Very rare, excellent detail and colors.

Number Fixture	Current Value Each, Wired	Standard Package	Length Overall	Number Of Lights	Finish
224B	$1,000.00+	1	25 inches	4 lights	Bronze and Poly.
223B	$800.00+	1	22 inches	3 lights	Bronze and Poly.

"Dinerlites"

For Dining Room, Breakfast Room or Sun Parlor

The "Dinerlites" illustrated are, without doubt, the most honest-to-goodness Dollar-for-Dollar values ever offered in better grade Lighting Fixture and Glassware combinations.

"Dinerlites" are beautiful in appearance—well constructed—modern in design and above all very low in price and will be a source of complete satisfaction to the average home owner.

Finish:—

Poly—Gold

Note: Description does not show these fixtures as being made of cast brass.

No. 404

Length 48 inches—Spread 16 inches
Packed 1 to a Standard Carton

Price: Wired, $28.50 List

Current price: $750.00+

No. 401 (1 Light)

Length 11¼ in.—Width 7 in.
Packed 2 to a Standard Carton

Price: Wired, $8.55 List

Current price: $285.00

All "Dinerlites" are furnished completely wired, polarized and ready to install.

Approved wiring material is used throughout and "Dinerlites" are inspected and tested before being packed. Packing of "Dinerlites"—complete with glassware, is done in individual and specially constructed cartons with illustrated labels affixed.

"Dinerlites"

For Dining Room, Breakfast Room or Sun Parlor

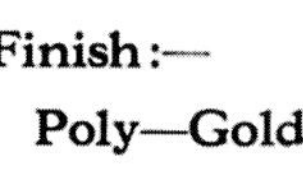

Finish:—
Poly—Gold

Note: Description does not show these fixtures as being made of cast brass.

No. 423
Length 23 inches—Spread 9 inches
Packed 1 to a Standard Carton
Price: Wired, $15.45 List

Current price: $400.00+

No. 403

Length 48 inches—Spread 9 inches
Packed 1 to a Standard Carton
Price: Wired, $17.25 List

Current price: $485.00+

No. 424
Length 26 inches—Spread 16 inches
Packed 1 to a Standard Carton
Price: Wired, $26.85 List

Current price: $700.00+

All "Dinerlites" are furnished completely wired, polarized and ready to install.

Approved wiring material is used throughout and "Dinerlites" are inspected and tested before being packed. Packing of "Dinerlites"—complete with glassware, is done in individual and specially constructed cartons with illustrated labels affixed.

Decorated Pendant

304/4010/S84 Green
Sun Parlor Luminaire

304/4010/S83 Canary
Sun Parlor Luminaire

Equipped with Keyless Socket. Finish: Ivory Pastelle.

Numbers		Prices	Dimensions of Glass		
Fixture Complete	Glass Only	Each Fixture Complete Current Prices	Width	Length	Fitter
304/4010/S84	4010/S84	$300.00–385.00	10 x	9 x	4
304/4010/S83	4010/S83	$275.00–325.00	10 x	9 x	4

Note: Prisms are glass in colors to complement or match the decoration on the shades.

If glass alone is ordered units will be furnished without holes unless otherwise specified.

Decorated Pendant

Note: Prisms are glass in colors to complement or match the decoration on the shades.

304/57/103 Amber
Sun Parlor Luminaire

Equipped with Keyless Socket. Finish: Ivory Pastelle.

Numbers		Prices	Dimensions of Glass
Fixture Complete	Glass Only	Each Fixture Complete Current Prices	Width Length Fitter
304/57/103	57/103	$350.00–400.00	10 x 10 x 4

If glass alone is ordered, item will be furnished without hole unless otherwise specified.

Decorated Pendants

304/641½/S87

216/641½/S87

Note: Prisms are glass in colors to complement or match the decoration on the shades.

Wired complete with Keyless Sockets.

Finish: Ivory Pastelle.

Numbers		Prices	Dimensions of Glass		
Fixture Complete	Glass Only	Each Fixture Complete Current Prices	Width	Length	Fitter
304/641½/S87	641½/S87	$150.00–200.00	9 x	6¾ x	4
216/641½/S87	641½/S87	$150.00–200.00	9 x	6¾ x	4

If glass alone is ordered units will be furnished without holes unless otherwise specified.

Decorated Pendants

20/453/8116 Key Socket
25/453/8116 Pull Socket

20/502/S77 Key Socket
25/502/S77 Pull Socket

20/453D Key Socket
25/453D Pull Socket

Please specify whether Ivory and Blue or Ivory and Pink finish is desired.

Numbers		Prices	Dimensions of Glass		
Fixture Complete	Glass Only	Each Fixture Complete Current Prices	Width	Length	Fitter
20/453/8116	453/8116	$100.00–125.00	7¾ x	5 x	2¼
25/453/8116	453/8116	$100.00–125.00	7¾ x	5 x	2¼
20/453/D	453D	$100.00–125.00	7¾ x	5 x	2¼
20/453/D	453D	$100.00–125.00	7¾ x	5 x	2¼
20/502/S77	502/S77	$100.00–125.00	7 x	5 x	2¼
25/502/S77	502/S77	$100.00–125.00	7 x	5 x	2¼

Decorated Pendants

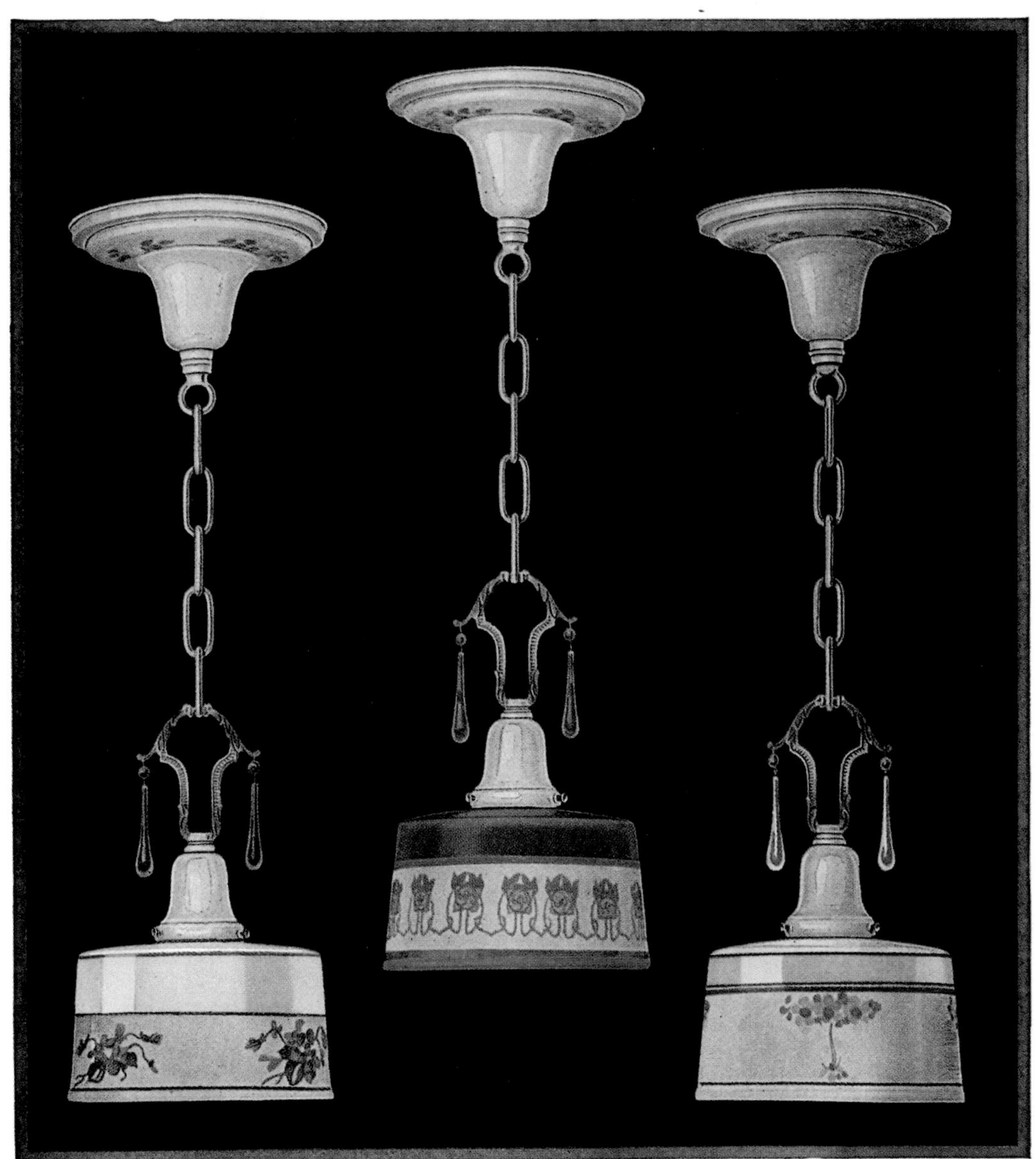

226/502/S75 Key Socket | 226/502/S76 Key Socket | 226/502/8128 Key Socket

Finish: Ivory Pastelle.

Numbers		Prices	Dimensions of Glass		
Fixture Complete	Glass Only	Each Fixture Complete Current Prices	Width	Length	Fitter
226/502/S75	502/S75	$135.00–165.00	7 x	5 x	2¼
226/502/S76	502/S76	$135.00–165.00	7 x	5 x	2¼
226/502/8128	502/8128	$135.00–165.00	7 x	5 x	2¼

Note: Lovely tear drop prisms in colors to match or complement color of decorations on shades.

Note—One fixture complete with Glass is a Standard Package.

Decorated Bedroom Units

304/641½/S79

216/641½/79

Note: Very deco designs on these shades. Notice the prisms used on bottom of the shades. Prisms are amethyst color.

Equipped with Keyless Sockets. Finish: Ivory Pastelle.

Numbers		Prices	Dimensions of Glass		
Fixture Complete	Glass Only	Each Fixture Complete Current Prices	Width	Length	Fitter
304/641½/S79	641½/S79	$185.00–235.00	9 x	6¾ x	4
216/641½/S79	641½/S79	$185.00–235.00	9 x	6¾ x	4

If glass alone is ordered units will be furnished without holes unless otherwise specified.

Decorated Bedroom Units

216/641½/78

Note: Prisms are glass in colors to complement or match the decoration on the shades.

304/641½/S78

Equipped with Keyless Socket. Finish: Ivory Pastelle.

Numbers		Prices	Dimensions of Glass		
Fixture Complete	Glass Only	Each Fixture Complete Current Prices	Width	Length	Fitter
304/641½/S78	641½/S78	$165.00–200.00	9 x	6¾ x	4
216/641½/S78	641½/S78	$165.00–200.00	9 x	6¾ x	4

If glass alone is ordered units will be furnished without holes unless otherwise specified.

Decorated Bedroom Units

304/4709/S88

216/4709/S88

Note: Prisms are glass in colors to complement or match the decoration on the shades.

Wired complete with Keyless Sockets.
Finish: Ivory Pastelle.

Numbers		Prices	Dimensions of Glass
Fixture Complete	Glass Only	Each Fixture Complete Current Prices	Width Length Fitter
304/4709/S88	4709/S88	\$195.00–225.00	9 x 6¾ x 4
216/4709/S88	4709/S88	\$195.00–225.00	9 x 6¾ x 4

If glass alone is ordered units will be furnished without holes unless otherwise specified.

Bedroom and Sun Parlor

Finish: Ivory Pastelle

No. 931

No. 921

Wired complete with keyless sockets.

Fixtures are packed complete with glassware in specially constructed cartons.

Note: Prisms are glass in colors to complement or match the decoration on the shades.

Number Fixture Complete	Current Value Each, Wired	Length Overall	Spread Overall
931	$225.00–250.00	36 inches	13½ inches
921	$225.00–250.00	13½ inches	13½ inches

Bedroom and Sun Parlor

Finish: Ivory Pastelle

No. 831

No. 821

Wired complete with keyless sockets.

Fixtures are packed complete with glassware in specially constructed cartons.

Note: Prisms are glass in colors to complement or match the decoration on the shades.

Number Fixture Complete	Current Value Each, Wired	Length Overall	Spread Overall
831	$225.00–250.00	36 inches	13 inches
821	$225.00–250.00	13½ inches	13 inches

BEDROOM AND SUN PARLOR FIXTURES

With "IVORY" Decorated Glassware

No. 8523D (3 Lights)

Length 13 inches—Spread 16 inches
Packed 4 to a Standard Carton

Price:
Wired........................$15.15 List

Current value: $250.00 – 300.00

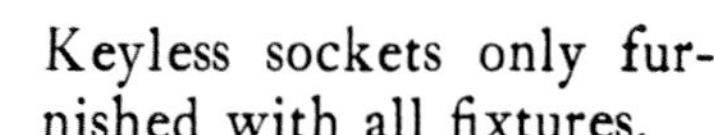

Keyless sockets only furnished with all fixtures.

Fixtures are all packed complete with glassware in individual cartons with illustrated labels affixed to denote the contents.

No. 8522D (2 Lights)

Length—13 inches—Spread 16 inches
Packed 4 to a Standard Carton

Price:
Wired........................$11.10 List

Current value: $200.00 – 250.00

WHEN ORDERING:
Kindly mention number and Finish desired.

No. 8501D (1 Light)

Length 11 inches—Extension 6 inches
Packed 4 to a Standard Carton

Price:
Wired (with Canopy Switch)...$7.80 List

Current value: $150.00 – 185.00

Fixtures are all wired with approved wiring material and are polarized and tested before being packed.

FINISH

Ivory Pastelle

BEDROOM AND SUN PARLOR FIXTURES

With "IVORY" Decorated Glassware

No. 1541D (1 Light)
Length 10½ in.—Spread 9¾ in.
Packed 4 to a Standard Carton
Price: Wired........... $7.80 List
Current value: $235.00 – 265.00

Keyless sockets only furnished with all fixtures.

Fixtures are all packed complete with glassware in individual cartons with illustrated labels affixed to denote the contents.

No. 8541D (2 Lights)
Length 13 in.—Spread 10½ in.
Packed 1 to a Standard Carton
Price: Wired..... $9.60 List
Current value: $150.00 – 175.00

No. 1551D (1 Light)
Length 36 inches—Spread 9¾ inches
Packed 4 to a Standard Carton
Price: Wired......... $10.80 List
Current value: $250.00 – 285.00

FINISH

Ivory Pastelle

Fixtures are all wired with approved wiring material and are polarized and tested before being packed.

WHEN ORDERING:

Kindly mention number and Finish desired.

No. 8551D (2 Lights)
Length 36 in.—Spread 10½ in.
Packed 1 to a Standard Carton
Price: Wired.... $11.85 List
Current value: $200.00 – 225.00

"ROSEMONT" LINE

Design by AGLOW

Illustrated in this folder is a line of "Shaded Light" fixtures which is not only "Moderne" and original—but is entirely different from any Lighting fixtures ever produced. The "Rosemont" fixtures are made of Solid Brass finished in a beautiful Old Gold with highlights in relief. With the addition of touches of subdued tints, here and there a rich conservative finish has been attained.

The special shaped glass shades are made of "Ivory" glass, with a rich mottled iridescent finish and a beautiful "Moderne" floral decoration is applied to the protruding panels of the glass, which is both charming and appealing. The complete combination gives the impression of "Shaded Light" in a most artistic and refined form.

No. 7535 (5 lights)
Length 36 inches—Spread 18 inches
Packed 1 to a Standard Carton
Price, Wired, $40.50 List

Current value: $1,000.00+

When Ordering
Please specify number desired.

No. 7501 (1 light)
Length 10½ inches
Extension 4 inches
Packed 2 to a Standard Carton
Price, Wired, $10.50 List
[With Canopy Switch]

Current value: $500.00+

"Rosemont" Line

Fixtures are all packed, complete with glassware, in individual and specially constructed cartons—with illustrated labels affixed to denote the contents.

Fixtures are all wired with approved wiring material and are Polarized and tested before being packed.

Keyless sockets used throughout.

No. 7545 (5 lights)
Length 13 inches—Spread 18 inches
Packed 1 to a Standard Carton
Price, Wired, $25.50 List
Current value: $800.00+

Note: Solid brass fixtures.

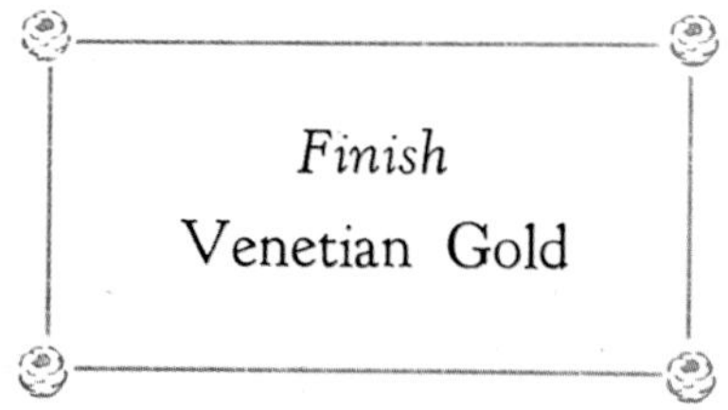

No. 7533 (3 lights)
ngth 36 inches—Spread 15 inches
acked 1 to a Standard Carton
Price, Wired, $25.50 List
Current value: $750.00+

No. 7522 (2 lights)
Length 20 inches—Spread 15 inches
Packed 1 to a Standard Carton
Price, Wired, $19.50 List
Current value: $600.00+

"Rosemont" Line

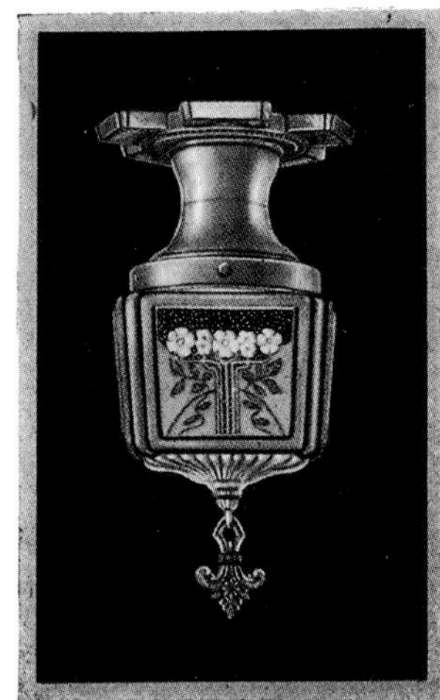

No. 7531 (1 light)
Length 10 inches—Glassware 5 x 5 inches
Packed 4 to a Standard Carton
Price, Wired, $6.75 List
Current value: $135.00 – 185.00

No. 7551 (1 light)
Length 36 inches—Spread 9 inches
Packed 1 to a Standard Carton
Price, Wired, $12.75 List
Current value: $200.00 – 250.00

No. 7525 (5 lights)
Length 20 inches—Spread 18 inches
Packed 1 to a Standard Carton
Price, Wired, $39.00 List
Current value: $900.00+

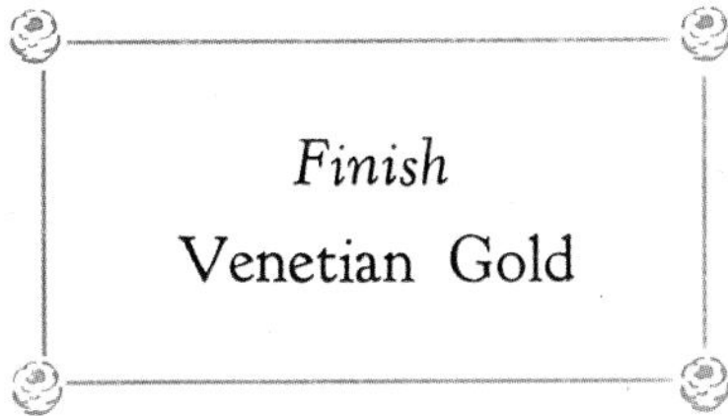

Note: Solid brass fixtures.

No. 7543 (3 lights)
Length 12 inches—Spread 15 inches
Packed 2 to a Standard Carton
Price, Wired, $16.50 List
Current value: $450.00+

"Rosemont" Line

No. 7541 (1 light)
Length 12 inches—Spread 9 inches
Packed 1 to a Standard Carton
Price, Wired, $11.25 List
Current value: $200.00 – 235.00

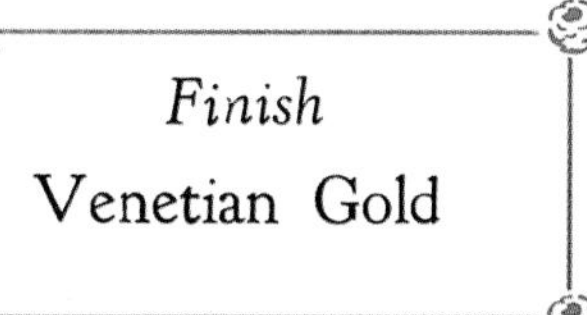

Note: Solid brass fixtures.

7523 (3 lights)
Length 12 inches—Spread 15 inches
Packed 1 to a Standard Carton
Price, Wired, $ 4.00 List
Current value: $700.00+

No. 7542 (2 lights)
Length 12 inches—Spread 15 inches
Packed 2 to a Standard Carton
Price, Wired, $13.50 List
Current value: $400.00+

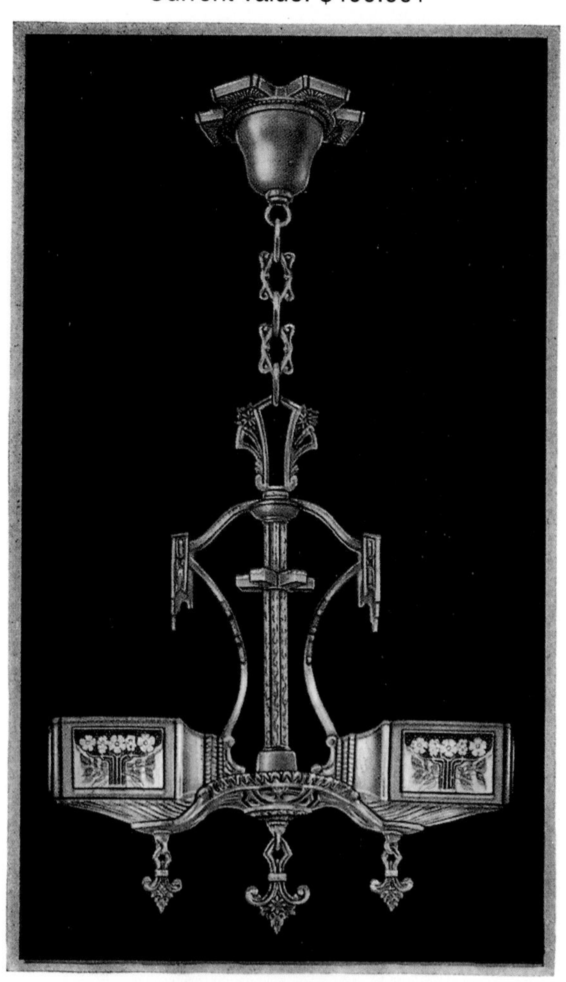

No. 7532 (2 lights)
Length 36 inches—Spread 15 inches
Packed 1 to a Standard Carton
Price, Wired, $21.00 List
Current value: $775.00+

DU BARRY LINE

Design by AGLOW

DURING the reign of Louis XVI of France when Madame Du Barry was mistress at the beautiful Palace of Versailles, the decorative schemes which were carried out throughout the country, were of a very ornate and elaborate character.

The Du Barry line of Lighting Fixtures has been designed to conform with the decorative motifs of that period, and with the addition of "Feather Etched" glass shades the ornamentation has been sustained.

The illustrations shown on the following pages are good examples of this charming combination.

The "Du Barry" Line
Pastelle Gold

No. 3535
Length 36 inches
Spread 18 inches
Packed 1 to a Standard Carton
Price, Wired, $20.25 List

Current value: $550.00 – 650.00

Note: Description does not list these fixtures as being made of cast or solid brass.

No. 3535 is a 5 light.

Fixtures are wired with approved wiring material and are polarized and tested before leaving the factory.

Fixtures are packed complete with Glassware in individual cartons with illustrated labels affixed.

All fixtures are wired with keyless sockets—Brackets are supplied with canopy switch.

No. 3522

Length 10½ inches
Spread 14 inches
Packed 4 to a Standard Carton
Price, Wired, $9.00 List

2 Light
Current value: $250.00 – 300.00

Note: Description does not list these fixtures as being made of cast or solid brass.

No. 3533

Length 36 inches
Spread 13½ inches
Packed 4 to a Standard Carton
Price, Wired, $12.75 List

3 Light
Current value: $350.00+

No. 3511

Extension 6¾ inches
Packed 4 to a Standard Carton
Price, Wired, $6.75 List

Current value: $200.00 – 235.00

WHEN ORDERING

Specify number and finish required.

Note: Description does not list these fixtures as being made of cast or solid brass.

No. 3525
Length 12 inches
Spread 18 inches
Packed 1 to a Standard Carton
Price, Wired, $18.75 List
5 Light
Current value: $550.00+

No. 3523
Length 10½ inches
Spread 13½ inches
Packed 4 to a Standard Carton
Price, Wired, $12.00 List
3 Light
Current value: $450.00+

No. 3532. Length 36 inches
Spread 14 inches
Packed 4 to a Standard Carton
Price, Wired, $10.50 List
2 Light
Current value: $300.00+

Finish:- Pastelle Gold

CASCADE LINE

Design by Aglow

THE "CASCADE" LINE of fixtures illustrated in this folder do not require any special sales effort—they sell themselves.

Great pains was taken to design and produce a line of "Shaded Light" fixtures which would instantly appeal to the home-owner.

The effect obtained by the reflection of light from the glass bowls upon the crystal spray-drips is both original and irresistible.

The bowls are made of "Ivory" glass, which has only been used in the more expensive lighting glassware, and the finish is a beautiful iridescent with mottled colors.

In addition the unique decoration adds a touch of the "Moderne" without any appearance of gaudiness.

The "Cascade" fixtures are made of solid brass and finished in Butler Silver which effectively harmonizes with the color scheme of the glass bowls, producing "Shaded Light" fixtures with charm and personality.

No. 9535 (5 lights)

Length 36 inches—Spread 20 inches
Packed 1 to a Standard Carton
Price, Wired, $45.00 List
Current value: $1,200.00+

When Ordering
Please specify number desired

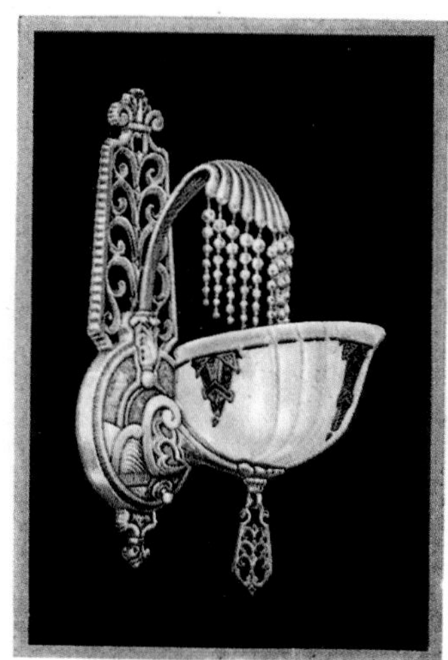

No. 9501 (1 light)

Length 12 inches
Extension 7½ inches
Packed 2 to a Standard Carton
Price, Wired, $12.00 List
(With Canopy Switch)
Current value: $400.00+

Note: The shades on this Cascade Line of fixtures appear to be "lite-o-lier" shades. If so, they are probably signed. They are really beautiful shades. They could also be interchanged with the shades on the Morrow Line fixtures.

"Cascade" Line

Fixtures are all packed, complete with glassware, in individual and specially constructed cartons—with illustrated labels affixed to denote the contents.

Fixtures are all wired with approved wiring material and are Polarized and tested before being packed.

Keyless sockets used throughout.

No. 9545 (5 lights)
Length 13 inches—Spread 20 inches
Packed 1 to a Standard Carton
Price, Wired, $24.00 List
Current value: $650.00+

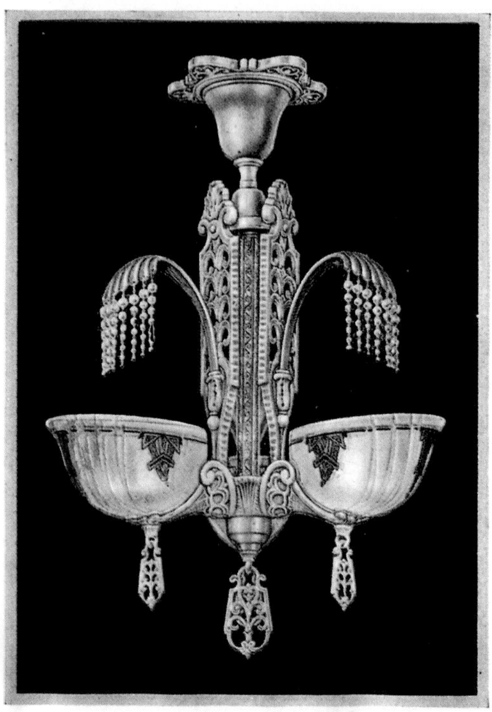

No. 9523 (3 lights)
Length 19 inches—Spread 15 inches
Packed 1 to a Standard Carton
Price, Wired, $28.50 List
Current value: $850.00+

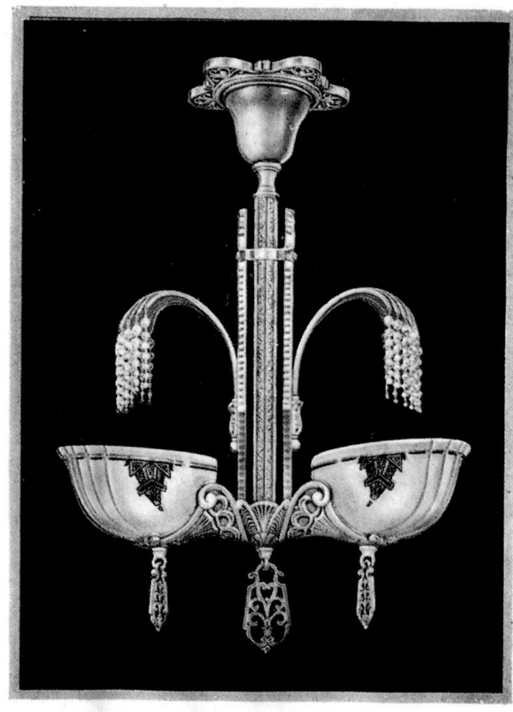

No. 9522 (2 lights)
Length 19 inches—Spread 15 inches
Packed 1 to a Standard Carton
Price, Wired, $21.00 List
Current value: $450.00+

"Cascade" Line

No. 9531 (1 light)
Diameter 6½ inches
Packed 4 to a Standard Carton
Price, Wired, $8.25 List
Current value: $100.00 – 150.00

No. 9525 (5 lights)
Length 21 inches—Spread 20 inches
Packed 1 to a Standard Carton
Price, Wired, $43.50 List
Current value: $900.00+

No. 9551 (1 light)
Length 36 inches
Spread 9 inches
Packed 1 to a Standard Carton
Price, Wired, $17.25 List
Current value: $200.00 – 250.00

No. 9543 (3 lights)
Length 12 inches—Spread 15 inches
Packed 1 to a Standard Carton
Price, Wired, $15.00 List
Current value: $400.00+

"Cascade" Line

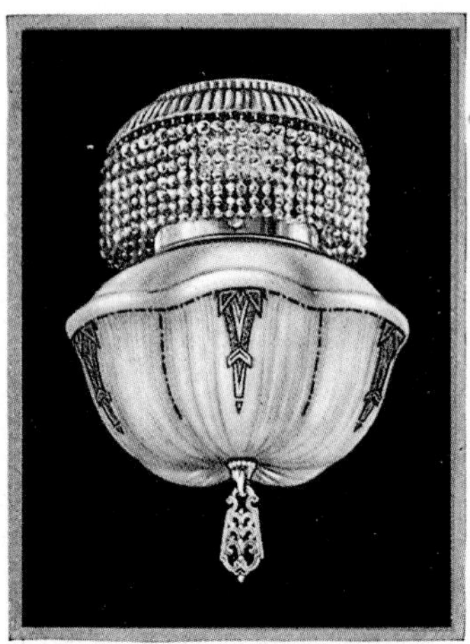

No. 9541 (1 light)
Length 15 inches—Spread 9 inches
Packed 1 to a Standard Carton
Price, Wired, $15.75 List
Current value: $175.00 – 225.00

No. 9542 (2 lights)
Length 12 inches—Spread 15 inches
Packed 1 to a Standard Carton
Price, Wired, $12.00 List
Current value: $350.00+

No. 9533 (3 lights)
Length 36 inches—Spread 15 inches
Packed 1 to a Standard Carton
Price, Wired, $30.00 List
Current value: $800.00+

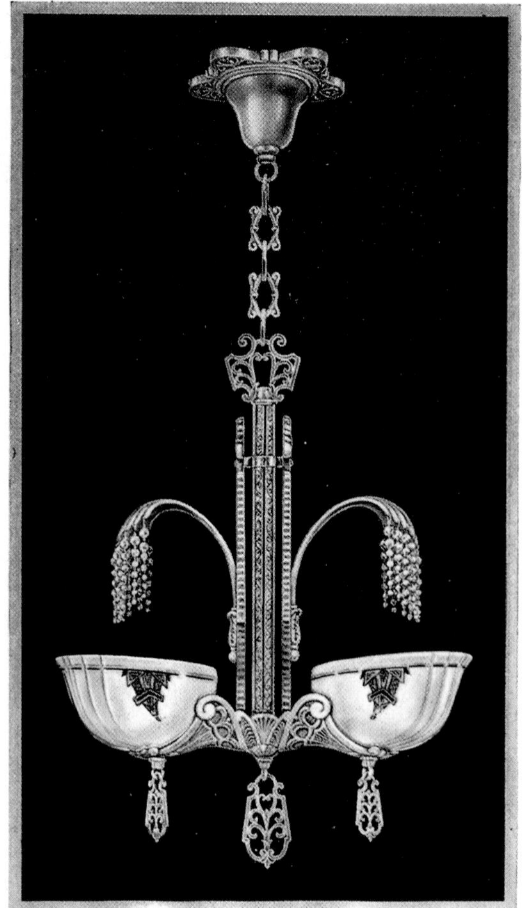

No. 9532 (2 lights)
Length 36 inches—Spread 15 inches
Packed 1 to a Standard Package
Price, Wired, $22.50 List
Current value: $425.00+

"Panelle" Line

Design by Aglow

The "Panelle" line illustrated in this folder, is the newest and most original idea in modern lighting fixtures.

The glass panels are made of "IVORY" glass and the beautiful colored decorations are applied by decalcomanias. Added to this, the "IVORY" glass is finished in a mottled iridescent color, producing a very charming effect. The metal work is of Solid Brass, finished in Butler-Silver, harmonizing perfectly with the colored panels, producing a very artistic and pleasing effect.

No. 5538—4 Lights

Length ....36 inches
Spread ....19½ inches
Packed 1 to a Standard Carton
Price, Wired.................$45.00 List

Current value: $1,200.00+

When Ordering:
Please specify number desired.

No. 5501—1 Light Bracket

Length ....12 inches
Spread .... 7 inches
Packed 2 to a Standard Carton
Price, Wired..................$9.75 List
(With Canopy Switch)

Current value: $400.00+

"Panelle" Line

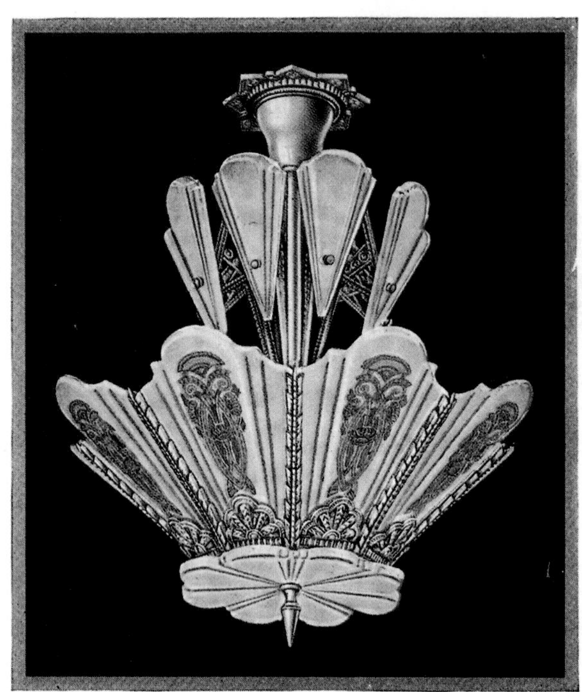

No. 5528—4 Lights

Length ....25 inches
Spread ....19½ inches
Packed 1 to a Standard Carton
Price, Wired.................$42.75 List

Current value: $900.00+

No. 5504—2 Lights

Length ....36 inches
Spread .... 9 inches
Packed 1 to a Standard Carton
Price, Wired.................$18.45 List

Current value: $500.00+

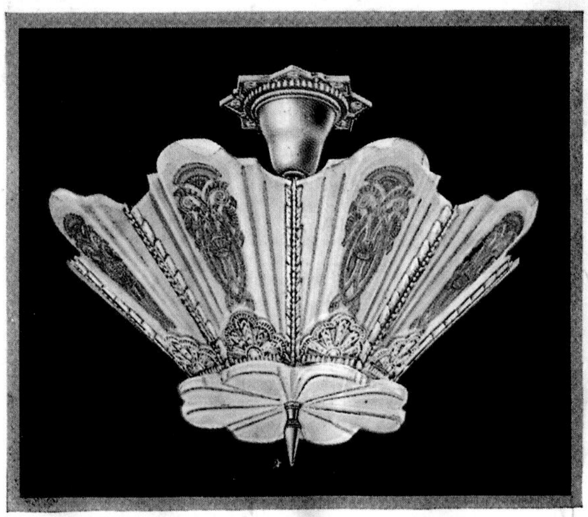

No. 5518—4 Lights

Length ....12 inches
Spread ....19½ inches
Packed 1 to a Standard Carton
Price, Wired.................$27.75 List

Current value: $700.00+

NOTE

All fixtures are wired complete and keyless sockets only are furnished.

Canopy Switch is furnished on Wall Brackets.

"Panelle" Line

All fixtures are wired with approved wiring material, and are polarized and tested. Careful inspection is made before fixtures are packed.

No. 5536—3 Lights

Length .... 36 inches
Spread .... 14 inches
Packed 1 to a Standard Carton
Price, Wired .... $34.50 List

Current value: $1,000.00+

All fixtures are packed complete with glass panels in individual and specially constructed cartons, with illustrated labels affixed to denote the contents.

No. 5506—3 Lights

Length .... 36 inches
Spread .... 14 inches
Packed 1 to a Standard Carton
Price, Wired .... $24.00 List

Current value: $775.00+

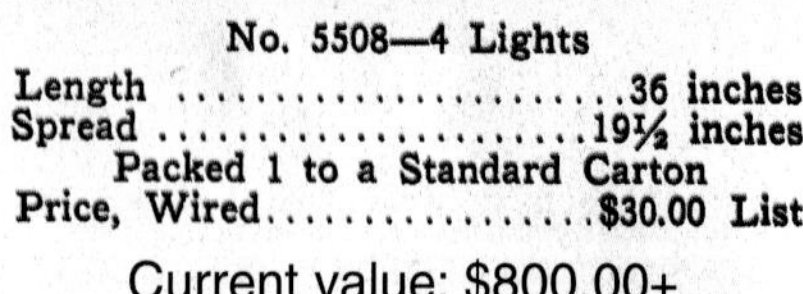

No. 5508—4 Lights

Length ....36 inches
Spread ....19½ inches
Packed 1 to a Standard Carton
Price, Wired.................$30.00 List

Current value: $800.00+

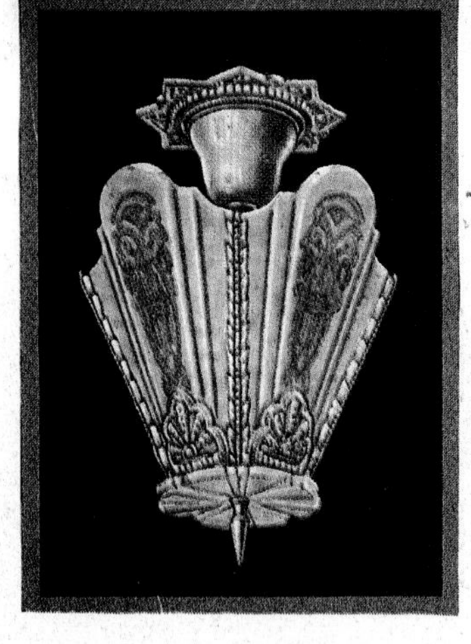

No. 5514—2 Lights

Length ....15 inches
Spread .... 9 inches
Packed 1 to a Standard Carton
Price, Wired.................$16.20 List

Current value: $350.00 – 450.00

No. 5516—3 Lights

Length ....14 inches
Spread ....14 inches
Packed 1 to a Standard Carton
Price, Wired.................$21.75 List

Current value: $575.00+

No. 5526—3 Lights

Length ....25 inches
Spread ....14 inches
Packed 1 to a Standard Carton
Price, Wired.................$32.25 List

Current value: $900.00+

"FOUNTAIN" LINE

Designed by AGLOW

THE "Fountain" line fixtures illustrated in this folder are, without doubt, the most beautiful and artistically designed lighting fixtures, of residential type ever produced at such moderate prices.

The charming effect obtained by the reflection of light upon the crystal spray-drips is a source of delight and satisfaction even to the most discriminating connoisseur.

In addition, the "feather-etched" glass bowls produce shaded light without glare and add materially to the wonderful effect which has been attained.

The "Fountain" line "Sells on Sight" and is a welcome addition to the decorative interior of practically every home.

"FOUNTAIN" Line

FINISHES:—GOLDTONE and SILVERTONE

(Please specify finish desired)

No. 6535

Length 36 inches—Spread 20 inches
Packed 1 to a Standard Carton
Price, Wired, $31.50 List

4 Light
Current value: $1,000.00+

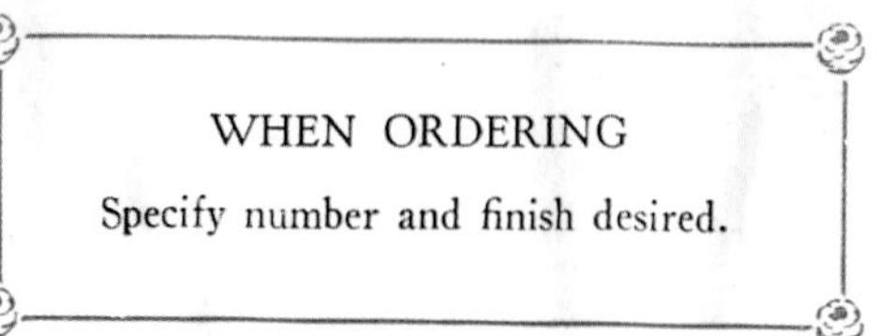

WHEN ORDERING

Specify number and finish desired.

Current value:
$350.00+

No. 6551

Length 36 inches—Spread 13 inches
Packed 1 to a Standard Carton
Price, Wired, $18.00 List

No. 6502—2 Light Wall Bracket

Length 14½ inches—Spread 11¼ inches
Packed 2 to a Standard Carton
Price, Wired, $10.50 List

Current value:
$250.00 – 350.00

FINISHES:—GOLDTONE and SILVERTONE
(Please specify finish desired)

No. 6533
Length 36 inches—Spread 16 inches
Packed 1 to a Standard Carton
Price, Wired, $22.50 List

3 Light
Current value: $550.00+

No. 6525

Length 22 inches—Spread 20 inches
Packed 1 to a Standard Carton
Price, Wired, $30.75 List

5 Light
Current value: $625.00+

No. 6522

Length 20 inches—Spread 16 inches
Packed 2 to a Standard Carton
Price, Wired, $18.00 List

2 Light
Current value: $350.00+

"FOUNTAIN" Line

Designed by AGLOW

FINISHES:—GOLDTONE and SILVERTONE

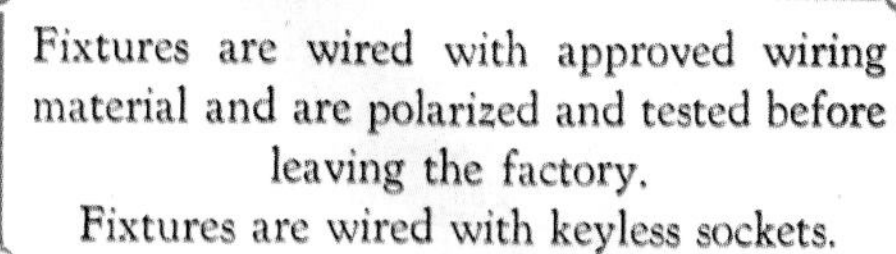
Fixtures are wired with approved wiring material and are polarized and tested before leaving the factory.
Fixtures are wired with keyless sockets.

No. 6523
Length 20 inches—Spread 16 inches
Packed 1 to a Standard Carton
Price, Wired, $21.75 List

3 Light
Current value:
$450.00+

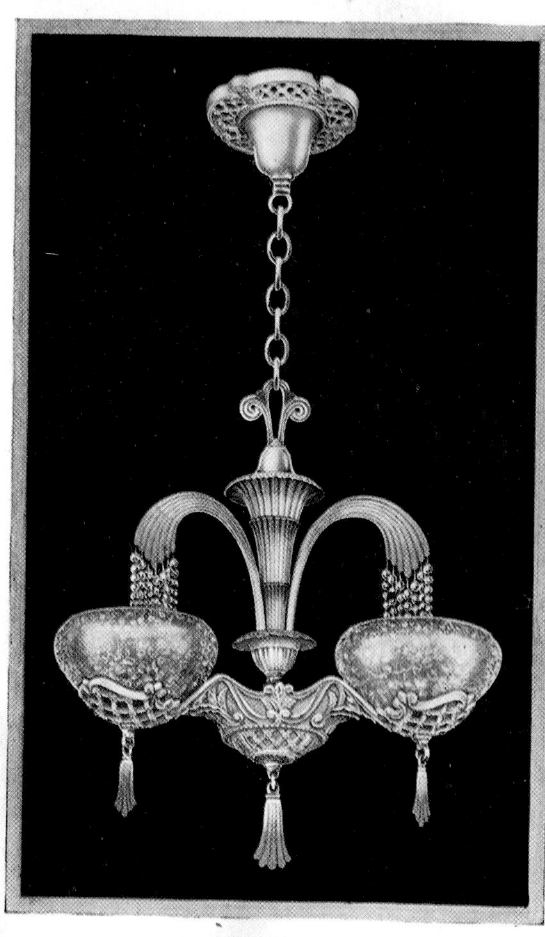

No. 6532
Length 36 inches—Spread 16 inches
Packed 1 to a Standard Carton
Price, Wired, $18.75 List

2 Light
Current value:
$400.00+

No. 6541
Length 20 inches—Spread 13 inches
Packed 1 to a Standard Carto
Price, Wired, $17.25 Lis

Current value:
$325.00+

Fixtures are packed complete with Glassware in individual cartons with illustrated labels affixed.

MODERNIQUE

Design by AGLOW

IN designing the MODERNIQUE LINE of Lighting Fixtures, illustrated on the following pages—utmost care was taken not to suggest the Ultra-modern which in most cases is freakish and far from pleasing to the eye.

The MODERNIQUE designs illustrate the artist's attempt to combine Modern Art with practicability and pleasing contour—producing a combination which is a change from styles of the past and those of Futuristic motif.

The beautiful effect of the "Feather Etched" glass shades, adds still more to the charming effect obtained by this combination.

THE "MODERNIQUE" LINE

Finish—Pastelle Gold

Current value:
$185.00 – 235.00

No. 2531

Length......13 inches
Spread...... 6 inches

Packed 4 to a Standard Carton.

Price, Wired, $4.50 List

No. 2501

Length......12¾ inches
Spread...... 6½ inches

Packed 4 to a Standard Carton.

Price, Wired, $7.50 List

Current value: $250.00+

No. 2535

Length......36 inches
Spread......18½ inches

Packed 1 to a Standard Carton.

Price, Wired, $24.00 List

5 Light
Current value: $750.00+

No. 2522

Length..........10 inches
Spread..........15 inches
Packed 4 to a Standard Carton.
Price, Wired, $9.00 List
2 Light
Current value: $285.00+

No. 2541

Length..........12 inches
Spread..........10 inches
Packed 4 to a Standard Carton.
Price, Wired, $6.75 List
5 Light
Current value: $200.00+

WHEN ORDERING

Specify number and finish.

Fixtures are packed complete with Glassware in individual cartons with illustrated labels affixed.

No. 2545

Length........12 inches Spread........18½ inches
Packed 1 to a Standard Carton.
Price, Wired, $18.00 List
5 Light
Current value: $400.00+

No. 2525

Length..........18½ inches
Spread..........18½ inches
Packed 1 to a Standard Carton.
Price, Wired, $23.25 List
5 Light
Current value: $585.00+

No. 2551

Length..........36 inches
Spread..........10 inches
Packed 4 to a Standard Carton.
Price, Wired, $9.00 List
Current value: $275.00+

No. 2523

Length..........10 inches
Spread..........15 inches
Packed 4 to a Standard Carton
Price, Wired, $12.00 List
3 Light
Current value: $350.00+

Fixtures are wired with approved wiring material and are polarized and tested before leaving the factory.

Fixtures are wired with keyless sockets.

Brackets are supplied with canopy switch.

Bedroom Line

Finish:—IVORY PASTELLE

On the following pages are grouped an attractive selection of appropriate fixtures for Bedroom Lighting.

These are all finished in Ivory Pastelle which is a background of Rich Creamy Ivory with delicate subdued color shadings.

The lovely and pleasing effect obtained by this combination of delicate colors is particularly adaptable for Bedroom decoration and harmonizes with any artistic bedroom setting.

The glassware shown on the majority of these bedroom fixtures is made of "Ivory" glass with mottled iridescent finish, which has only been used in lighting glassware of the most expensive type.

Finish:—IVORY PASTELLE
[Please mention finish when ordering]

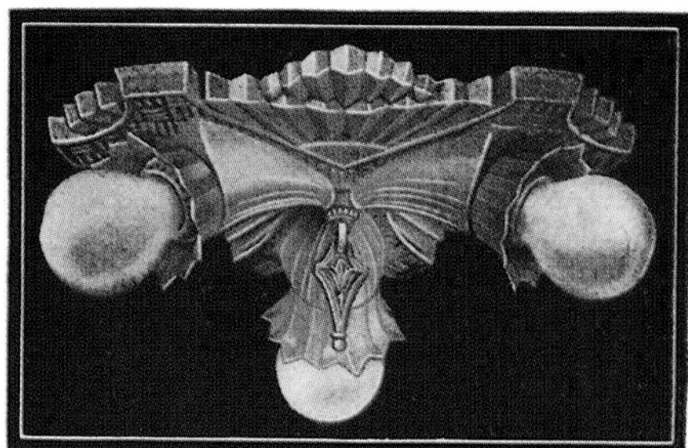

No. 553—3 Lights
Spread, 13 inches
Packed 4 to a Standard Carton
Price, Wired..................$4.95 List

Current value: $125.00 – 150.00

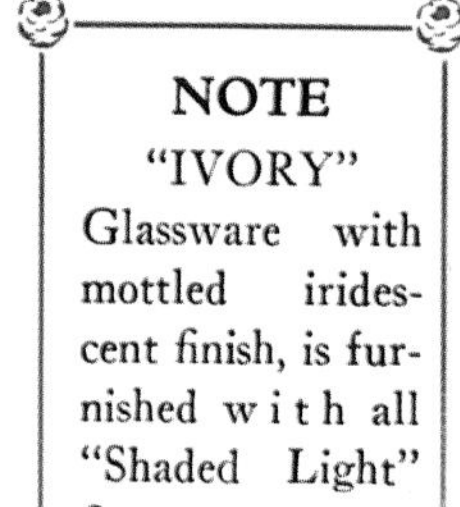

NOTE

"IVORY" Glassware with mottled iridescent finish, is furnished with all "Shaded Light" fixtures except No. 52, with which "IVORY" glassware only is furnished.

No. 3523-X—3 Lights
Length ....10½ inches
Spread ....13½ inches
Packed 4 to a Standard Carton
Price, Wired..................$12.00 List

Current value: $350.00+

When Ordering

Please specify *number* and *Finish:—Ivory Pastelle.*

No. 2551-X—1 Light
Length ....36 inches
Spread ....10 inches
Packed 4 to a Standard Carton
Price, Wired..................$9.00 List

Current value: $285.00+

Current value: $85.00 – 100.00

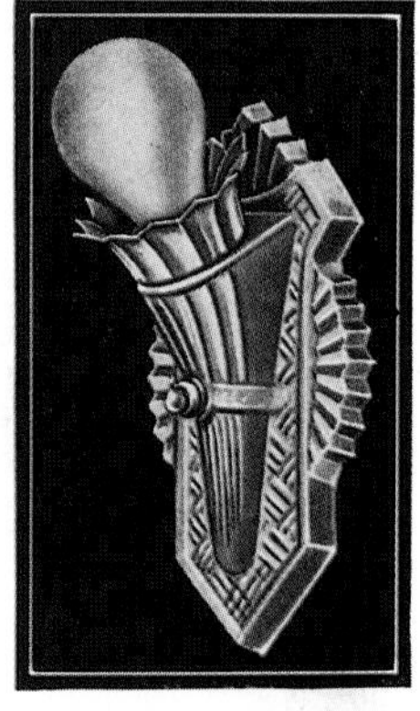

No. 551—1 Light
Wall Bracket
Packed 8 to a Standard Carton
Price, Wired, $3.45 List
(With Canopy Switch)

No. 2501-X—1 Light
Length ....12¾ inches
Spread ....6½ inches
Packed 4 to a Standard Carton
Price, Wired..................$7.50 List
(With Canopy Switch)

Current value: $250.00+

Finish:—IVORY PASTELLE

[Please mention finish when ordering]

No. 2522-X—2 Lights

Length ....10 inches
Spread ....15 inches
Packed 4 to a Standard Carton
Price, Wired..................$9.00 List

Current value: $285.00+

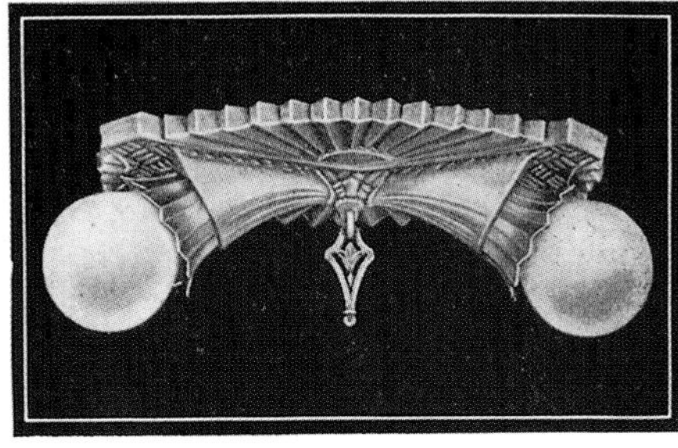

No. 552—2 Lights

Spread ....12 inches
Packed 8 to a Standard Carton
Price, Wired..................$3.00 Net

Current value: $100.00 – 125.00

NOTE

Keyless sockets only are furnished with all fixtures.

Current value: $200.00 – 235.00

No. 3511-X—1 Light

Length ....$11\frac{1}{2}$ inches
Extension .... $6\frac{3}{4}$ inches
Packed 4 to a Standard Carton
Price, Wired..................$6.75 List
(With Canopy Switch)

No. 2531-X—1 Light

Length ......13 inches
Spread ...... 6 inches
Packed 4 to a Standard Carton
Price, Wired, $4.50 List

Current value: $150.00+

Current value: $250.00 – 285.00

No. 1551-X

Length ....36 inches
Spread .... $9\frac{3}{4}$ inches
Packed 4 to a Standard Carton
Price, Wired..................$9.75 List

Finish:—IVORY PASTELLE
[Please mention finish when ordering]

No. 2541-X—1 Light
Length ....12 inches
Spread ....10 inches
Packed 4 to a Standard Carton
Price, Wired..................$6.75 List

Current value: $200.00+

No. 52-D—2 Lights
Spread ....15 inches
Packed 4 to a Standard Carton
Price, Wired..................$6.75 List
(With Decorated "Ivory" Glass)

Current value: $150.00 – 225.00

No. 52—2 Lights
Spread ....15 inches
Packed 4 to a Standard Carton
(Plain "Ivory" Glass)
Price, Wired.................. $6.15 List

Current value: $135.00 – 185.00

No. 3522-X—2 Lights
Length ....10½ inches
Spread ....14 inches
Packed 4 to a Standard Carton
Price, Wired..................$9.00 List

Current value: $250.00 – 300.00

No. 2523-X—3 Lights
Length ....10 inches
Spread ....15 inches
Packed 4 to a Standard Carton
Price, Wired..................$12.00 List

Current value: $350.00+

Fixtures are all wired with approved wiring material and are polarized and tested before being packed.

Fixtures are packed complete with glassware in individual cartons with illustrated labels affixed to denote the contents.

No. 1541-X—1 Light
Length ....10½ inches
Spread .... 9¾ inches
Packed 4 to a Standard Carton
Price, Wired..................$6.75 List

Current value: $185.00 – 225.00

"MORROW" LINE

Design by AGLOW

The year 1930 will see a radical change in lighting fixture styles — "Shaded Light" with glass will be the vogue.
Originated in Europe, "Shaded Light" has at last manifested itself to the extent that this year will see the real beginning of a new era of "Shaded Light."

The "MORROW" LINE illustrated is a good example of "Shaded Light," expensive in looks but reasonably priced. Made of cast aluminum and finished in a mellow gold, with subdued touches of color for contrast.

The glass shades are made of "Ivory" glass, decorated in two-tone design and finished a Mottled Iridescent—producing a most pleasing and beautiful effect.

Note: The shades on the Morrow Line appear to be "lite-o-lier" shades. If so, they are probably signed. They are really beautiful shades. They could be interchanged with the shades on the Cascade Line fixtures.

"MorroW" Line

No. 125 (5 lights)

Length 12 inches—Spread 20 inches
Packed 1 to a Standard Carton
Price, Wired, $20.25 List

Current value: $400.00+

NOTE

Fixtures are all wired with approved wiring material and are Polarized and tested before being packed.

NOTE

Fixtures are all packed, complete with Glassware, in individual and specially constructed cartons — with illustrated labels affixed to denote the contents.

No. 132 (2 lights)

Length 36 inches—Spread 15 inches
Packed 4 to a Standard Carton
Price, Wired, $14.25 List

Current value: $250.00+

"MorroW" Line

No. 135 (5 lights)

Length 36 inches—Spread 20 inches
Packed 1 to a Standard Carton

Price, Wired, $23.25 List

Current value: $475.00+

No. 101 (1 light)

Length 12 inches
Extension 7½ inches

Packed 4 to a Standard Carton

Price, Wired, $7.50 List

Current value: $100.00 – 200.00

"MorroW" Line

No. 123 (3 lights)
Length 10 inches—Spread 15 inches
Packed 4 to a Standard Carton
Price, Wired, $14.25 List
Current value: $300.00+

No. 122 (2 lights)
Length 10 inches—Spread 15 inches
Packed 4 to a Standard Carton
Price, Wired, $11.25 List
Current value: $225.00+

No. 133 (3 lights)
Length 36 inches—Spread 15 inches
Packed 4 to a Standard Carton
Price, Wired, $17.25 List
Current value: $350.00+

"VICTORIAN" Line

Design by Aglow

More and more, the demand for shaded light is becoming a great factor in the planning of Lighting Fixture installations for the home.

Combinations of Glassware and Fixtures, as illustrated in this folder, not only furnish shaded light, but add materially to the decorative interior of the home.

Moderately priced, yet artistically designed, and furnished with "Feather-Etched" glass shades—which produce soft, mellow and pleasing illumination.

"VICTORIAN" Line

Design by Aglow

Finish Poly—Gold

No. 8541 (2 lights)
Length 13 inches—Spread 10½ inches
Packed 4 to a Standard Carton
Price, Wired, $8.25 List
Current value: $200.00+

No. 8532 (2 lights)
Length 36 inches—Spread 16 inches
Packed 4 to a Standard Carton
Price, Wired, $11.25 List
Current value: $350.00+

No. 8525 (5 lights)
Length 15 inches—Spread 20 inches
Packed 1 to a Standard Carton
Price, Wired, $18.75 List
Current value: $500.00+

Fixtures are wired with approved wiring material and are polarized and tested before leaving the factory.

Fixtures are wired with keyless sockets.

"VICTORIAN" Line

Design by Aglow

Finish Poly—Gold

No. 8522 (2 lights)
Length 13 inches—Spread 16 inches
Packed 4 to a Standard Carton
Price, Wired, $9.00 List

Current value: $250.00+

No. 8551 (2 lights)
Length 36 inches—Spread 10½ inches
Packed 1 to a Standard Carton
Price, Wired, $10.50 List

Current value: $275.00 – 300.00

No. 8533 (3 lights)
Length 36 inches—Spread 16 inches
Packed 4 to a Standard Carton
Price: Wired, $14.25 List

Current value: $385.00+

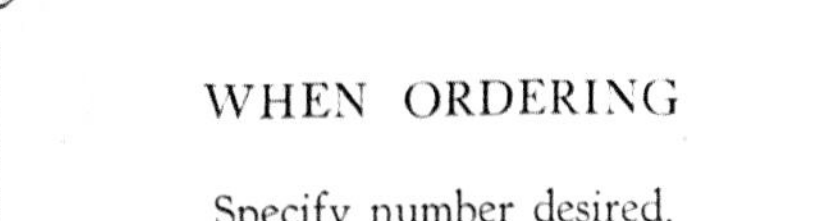

WHEN ORDERING

Specify number desired.

"VICTORIAN" Line

Design by Aglow

Finish Poly—Gold

No. 8501

Length 11 inches
Extension 6 inches
Packed 4 to a Standard Carton
Price, Wired, $6.75 List

Current value: $200.00+

No. 8535 (5 lights)

Length 36 inches—Spread 20 inches
Packed 1 to a Standard Carton
Price, Wired, $21.00 List

Current value: $575.00+

Fixtures are packed complete with Glassware in individual cartons with illustrated labels affixed.

No. 8523 (3 lights)

Length 13 inches—Spread 16 inches
Packed 4 to a Standard Carton
Price, Wired, $12.00 List

Current value: $325.00+

Marquette Line

Design by Aglow

WITH the advent of "Shaded Light" fixtures with glass, it became necessary to design a line of lighting fixtures which would carry out the principle of "Shaded Light" but be moderately priced, so as to be within the reach of the average home-owner, and in addition still retain the beautiful contour and charming effect.

The "MARQUETTE" LINE illustrated is without doubt the answer to this problem, and advanced sales have already proven that "Marquette" Shaded Light Fixtures will surpass in sales, any other "Shaded Light" fixtures on the market.

The castings of the "Marquette" line are sharp in detail and the complete fixtures are finished in a beautiful gold color with slight touches of polychrome here and there.

The glassware is made of "Ivory" glass, which heretofore has only been seen on more expensive fixtures and the decorations are applied with decalcomanias, which have only been used on higher-priced glass.

"Marquette"—a real "Shaded Light" fixture—at a price.

No. 535 (5 lights)

Length 36 inches—Spread 20 inches

Packed 1 to a Standard Carton

Price, Wired, $16.50 List

Current value: $600.00+

When Ordering

Please specify number desired.

Keyless sockets used throughout.

"Marquette" Line

When Ordering

Please specify number desired.

No. 522 (2 lights)
Length 9 inches—Spread 15 inches
Packed 4 to a Standard Carton
Price, Wired, $8.25 List

Current value: $250.00+

No. M-551 (1 Light)
Length 36 inches
Spread 6 inches
Amber-Glo
Decorated Art Lantern
Packed 1 to a Standard Carton
Price, Wired, $9.75 List

Current value: $225.00 – 250.00

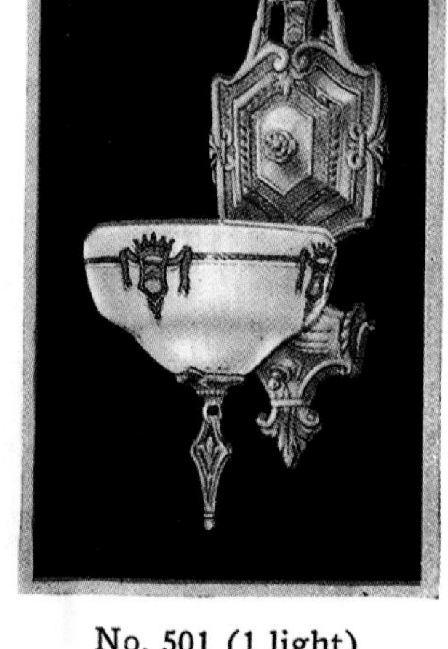

No. 501 (1 light)
Length 10½ inches
Extension 6½ inches
Packed 4 to a Standard Carton
Price, Wired, $5.25 List
(With Canopy Switch)

Current value: $235.00+

"Marquette" Line

No. 523 (3 lights)
Length 10 inches—Spread 15 inches
Packed 4 to a Standard Carton
Price, Wired, $11.25 List
Current value: $325.00+

When Ordering

Please specify number desired.

No. 541 (1 light)
Length 13 inches
Spread 6 inches
Packed 1 to a Standard Carton
Price, Wired, $8.25 List
With
Amber-Glo
Decorated Art Lantern
Current value: $135.00 – 165.00

No. 532 (2 lights)
Length 36 inches—Spread 15 inches
Packed 4 to a Standard Carton
Price, Wired, $9.00 List
Current value: $300.00+

"Marquette" Line

No. 525 (5 lights)
Length 11 inches—Spread 20 inches
Packed 1 to a Standard Carton
Price, Wired, $15.75 List

Current value:
$485.00+

NOTE

Fixtures are all wired with approved wiring material and are Polarized and tested before being packed.

NOTE

Fixtures are all packed complete with glassware, in individual and specially constructed cartons — with illustrated labels affixed to denote the contents.

No. 533 (3 lights)
Length 36 inches—Spread 15 inches
Packed 4 to a Standard Carton
Price, Wired, $12.00 List

Current value:
$350.00+

Moderne "Directo-Lite"

For special lighting installations where the principal rays of light are to be directed downward upon a working plane, the Moderne Directo-lite illustrated below is the utmost in efficiency. The Moderne Directo-lite is made of "Hyperion" glass with and without black line decoration, and with a polished Crystal Cut Reflector bowl inserted in the bottom.

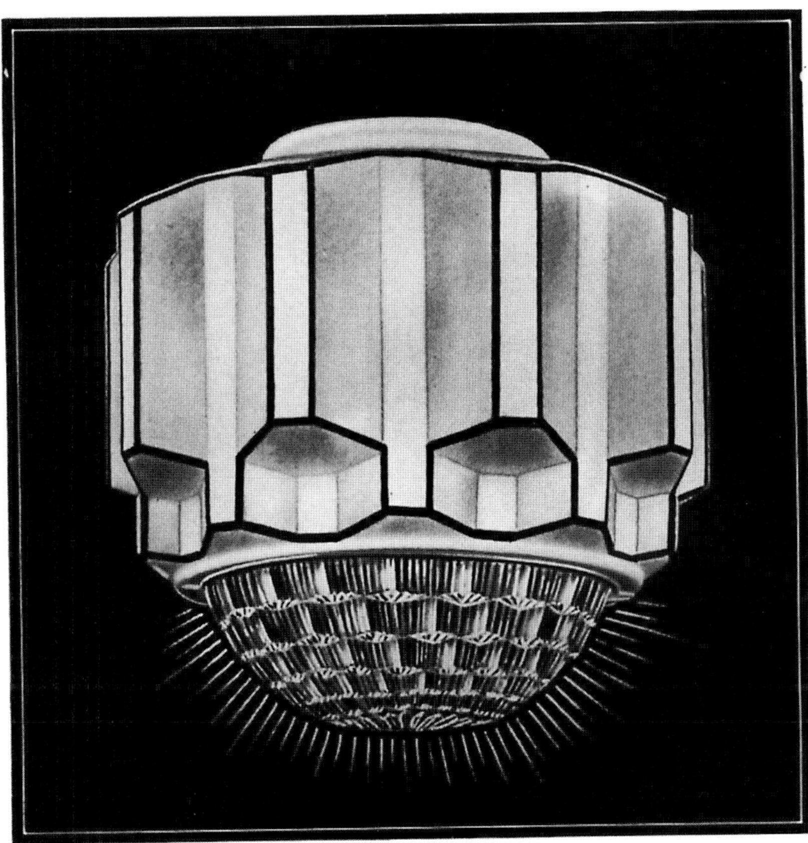

"Hyperion" Glass with Crystal Cut Bowl

Prices vary depending on size of shades.

NUMBERS FIXTURE COMPLETE	PRICES EACH FIXTURE COMPLETE CURRENT PRICES	DIMENSIONS OF GLASS WIDTH	 LENGTH	 FITTER	FINISH
465	$75.00 – 100.00	1?	x 11¼	x 6	plain white
465D	$75.00 – 100.00	1?	x 11¼	x 6	plain white
	$115.00 – 175.00	6	x 8	x 4	black lines
1464D	$115.00 – 175.00	6	x 8	x 4	black lines

Moderne Lighting Units

Made of "Hyperion" Glass

Illustrated on this page are new and original Moderne lighting units which have met with instant approval and for which the demand is constantly increasing.

Not only are they in keeping with the present trend of style and design, but are a means of real efficient and beautiful lighting.

These Moderne lighting units are made of "Hyperion" glass—the glass of highly efficient lighting qualities and with the addition of black line decoration the truly Modernistic effect is brought out very artistically.

No. 1458D—10¼ in. x 16¼ in. x 6 in. Fitter

No. 1457D—6 in. x 9 in. x 4 in. Fitter

Current value: $145.00 – 250.00

LIST PRICES

Modernistic Glassware

Number	Standard Package	Width	Length	Fitter	Finish	Price Each
1457	12	6"	9"	4"	Plain	$2.25
1457-D	12	6"	9"	4"	Black Line	3.75
1458	1	10¼"	16¼"	6"	Plain	6.75
1458-D	1	10¼"	16¼"	6"	Black Line	9.75
1459	8	9"	7½"	4"	Plain	2.25
1459-D	8	9"	7½"	4"	Black Line	3.75
1460	1	12½"	10¾"	6"	Plain	5.25
1460-D	1	12½"	10¾"	6"	Black Line	6.75

Note: Prices may vary depending on shade size.

No. 1460D—12½ in. x 10¾ in. x 6 in. Fitter

No. 1459D—9 in. x 7 in. x 4 in. Fitter

Current value: $100.00 – 200.00

Moderne Lighting Fixtures

Finishes:—Bank Bronze and Antique Silver

Illustrating Moderne Lighting fixtures in both hanging and semi-flush types which have been designed particularly to conform with the general contour of Moderne glass units.

These Lighting Fixtures are furnished "BARE" (no sockets or wire being supplied), eliminating the necessity of rewiring when special lengths and special sockets are required.

No. 146—6 in. Fitter
No. 144—4 in. Fitter

No. 196—6 in. Fitter
No. 194—4 in. Fitter

LIST PRICES

Number	Bank Bronze Each	Antique Silver Each
146	$85.00	$50.00
144	$85.00	$50.00
196	$50.00	$30.00
194	$50.00	$30.00

"MODERNLITES"

Made of "HYPERION" GLASS

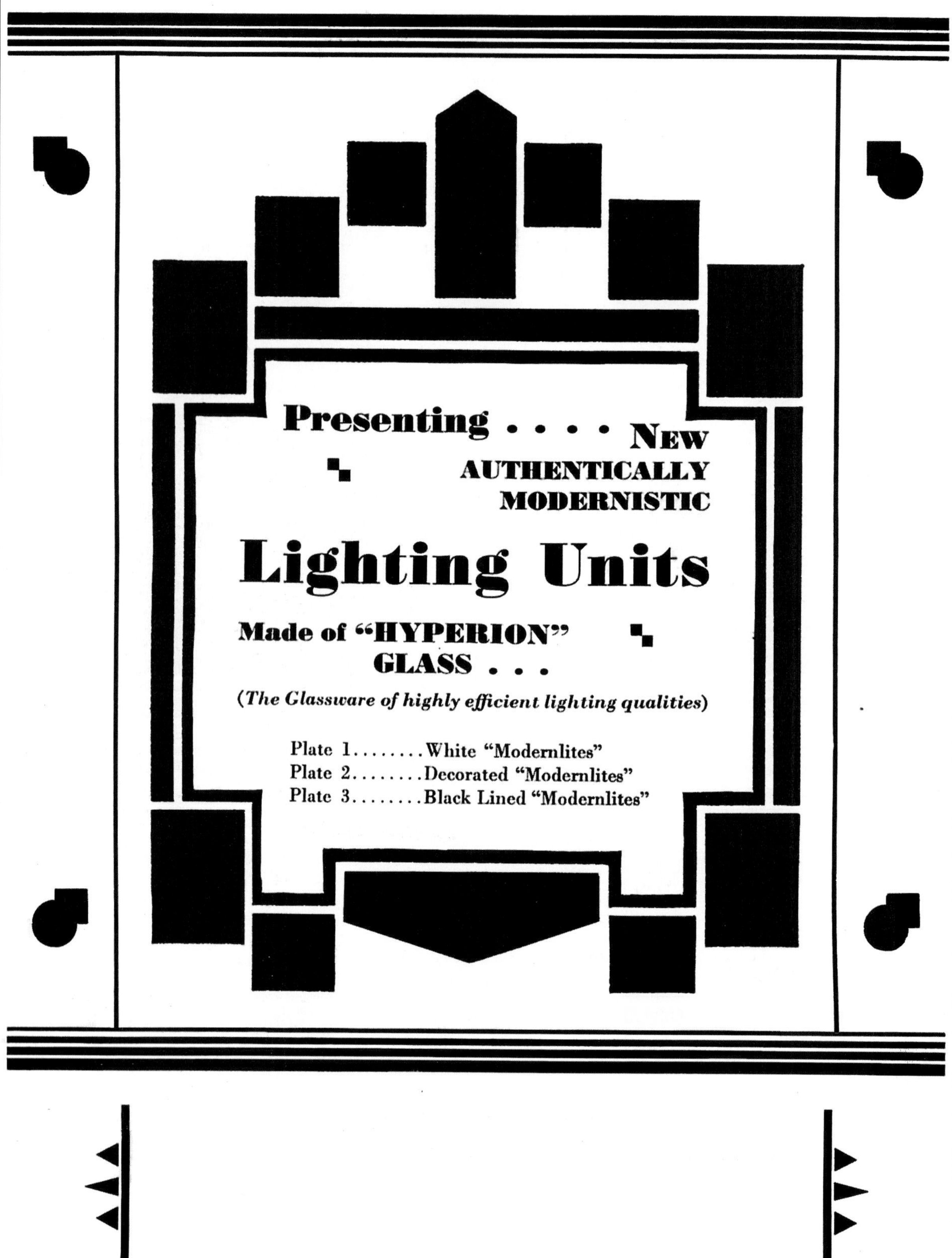

"MODERNLITES"

[PLAIN WHITE]

Made of **"HYPERION" GLASS**

Photometric tests of "Hyperion" glass show a lighting efficiency averaging 88%.

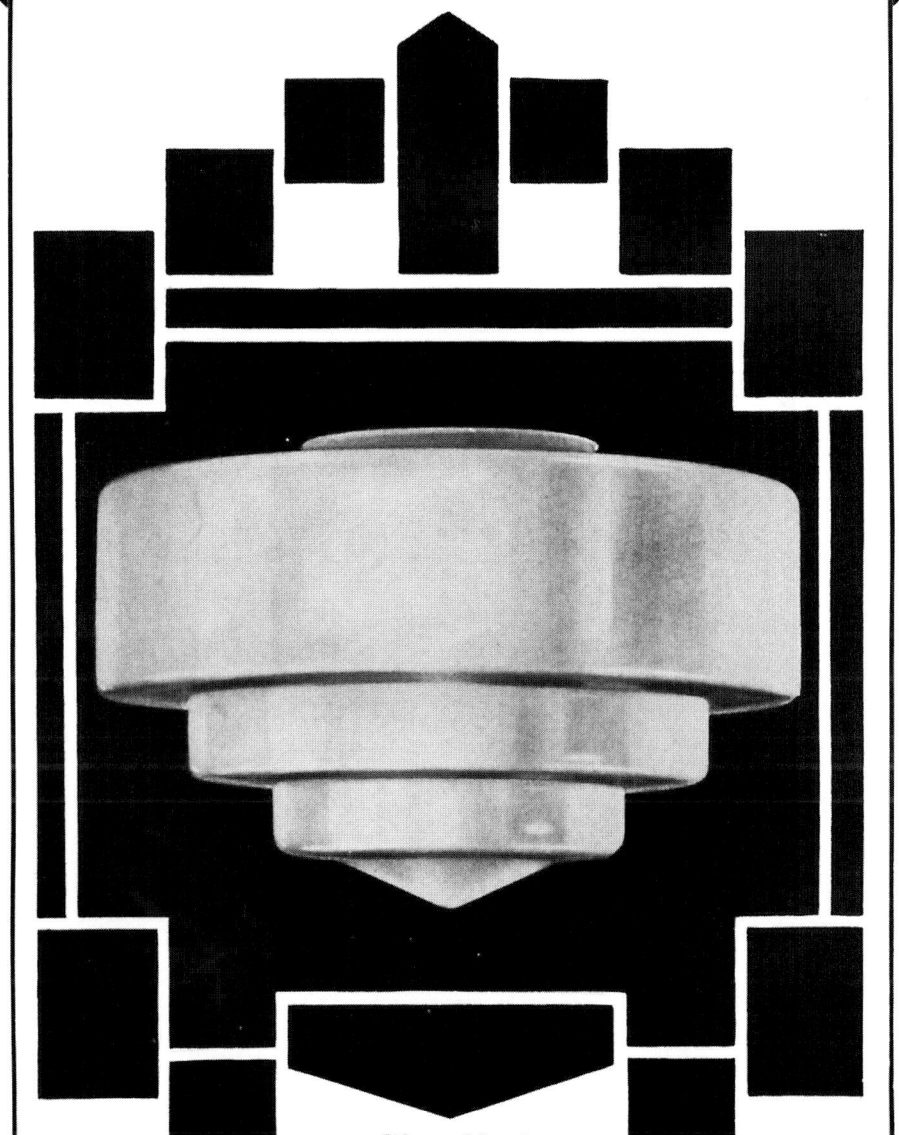

Plate No. 1

Number	Prices Each Fixture Complete Current Prices	Dimensions of Glass Width x Length x Fitter
1712	$25.00–35.00	12 x 8½ x 6
1714	$40.00–50.00	14 x 9¼ x 6
1716	$55.00–65.00	16 x 10 x 6

"MODERNLITES"

[DECORATED]

THE ADDITION of Etched modernistic decorations to the plain "Modernlite," makes the glassware even more attractive, and will appeal particularly, where installations require decorative Lighting.

Note: Prices vary depending on shade size.

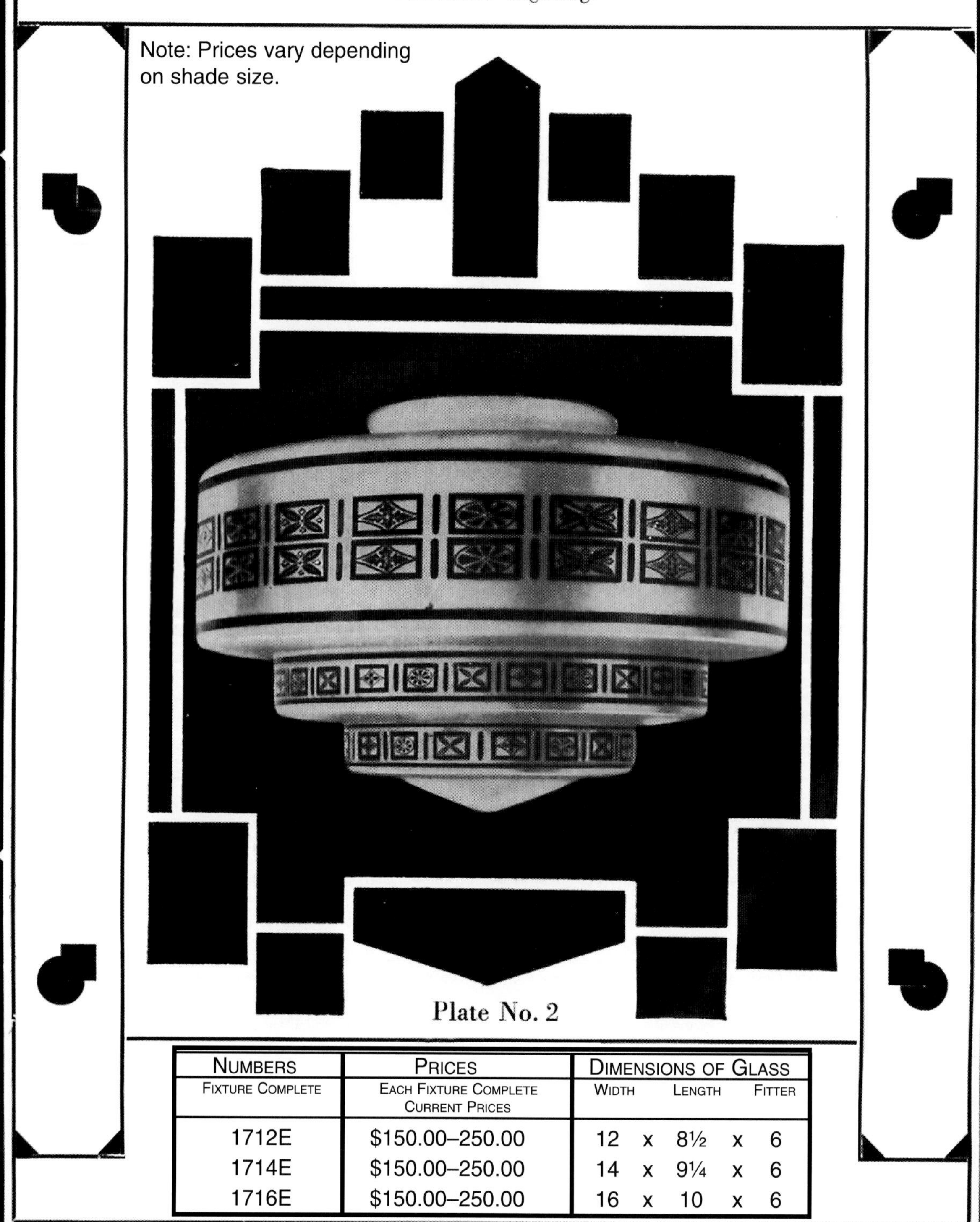

Plate No. 2

NUMBERS FIXTURE COMPLETE	PRICES EACH FIXTURE COMPLETE CURRENT PRICES	DIMENSIONS OF GLASS WIDTH LENGTH FITTER
1712E	$150.00–250.00	12 x 8½ x 6
1714E	$150.00–250.00	14 x 9¼ x 6
1716E	$150.00–250.00	16 x 10 x 6

"MODERNLITES"

[BLACK LINED]

For lighting installations where simplicity of decoration is the keynote, the Black Lined "Modernlite" is the ideal lighting unit.

Note: Prices vary depending on shade size.

Plate No. 3

Numbers Fixture Complete	Prices Each Fixture Complete Current Prices	Dimensions of Glass Width x Length x Fitter
1712D	$100.00–135.00	12 x 8½ x 6
1714D	$100.00–135.00	14 x 9¼ x 6
1716D	$100.00–135.00	16 x 10 x 6

Compact Units

"Compact" Ceiling Shade Type
Shown with
WHITE "HYPERION" GLASS

		List
C-15.	Keyless	$3.15
C-16.	Pull Chain	3.60

Packed 12 to a Master Carton.

Current values each: $35.00 – 50.00

"Compact" Wall Type
Shown with
WHITE "HYPERION" GLASS

		List
C-13.	Keyless	$2.85
C-14.	Pull Chain	3.30

12 Packed to a Master Carton.

Current values: $45.00 – 60.00 each

"COMPACT"

novel "one-piece"
lighting units

FOR BEDROOM—KITCHEN—BATH—
HALL—FOYER—OFFICE

in

"HYPERION" GLASS

"Compact" Ceiling Type
Shown with
WHITE "HYPERION" GLASS

		List
C-1.	Keyless—9" Diameter	$4.50
C-2.	Pull Chain—9" Diameter	6.00
C-3	Levolier—9" Diameter	6.75
C-4.	C. O. & Switch—9" Diameter	7.50

(Each packed in individual carton.)

Current values each: $85.00 – 125.00

Manufactured under License Patent Application No. 273324.

Compact Units

"Compact" Ceiling Type

Shown with Colored Band Designs—Blue, Black or Green

on

WHITE "HYPERION" GLASS

		List
D-5.	Keyless—9" Diameter	$6.00
D-6.	Pull Chain—9" Diameter	7.50
D-11.	Levolier—9" Diameter	8.25
D-12.	C. O. & Switch—9" Diameter	9.00

Each "Compact" Ceiling Type Unit is packed in an individual carton.

Current values each: $100.00 – 135.00

Specify colored band desired. Blue, Black or Green.

Manufactured under License Patent Application No. 273324.

"Compact" Ceiling Shade Type

Shown with Colored Band Designs—Blue, Black or Green on

WHITE "HYPERION" GLASS

		List
D-19.	Keyless	$3.90
D-20.	Pull Chain	4.35

Packed 12 to a Master Carton.

Current values each: $55.00 – 75.00

"Compact" Wall T pe

Shown with Colored Band Designs—Blue, Black or Green on

WHITE "HYPERION" GLASS

		List
D-27.	Keyless	$3.60
D-28.	Pull Chain	4.05

Packed 12 to a Master Carton.

Current values each: $75.00 – 90.00

Compacts

Solid Color Effects

For those requiring Wall Type and Ceiling Shade Type "*Compacts*" in Solid Translucent color effect, there is a choice of three colors:—

PALE BLUE, PINK or PALE GREEN

Ceiling Shade Type

	List
D-31. Keyless	$3.90
D-32. Pull Chain	4.35

Packed 12 to a Master Carton.

Current values each: $120.00 – 145.00

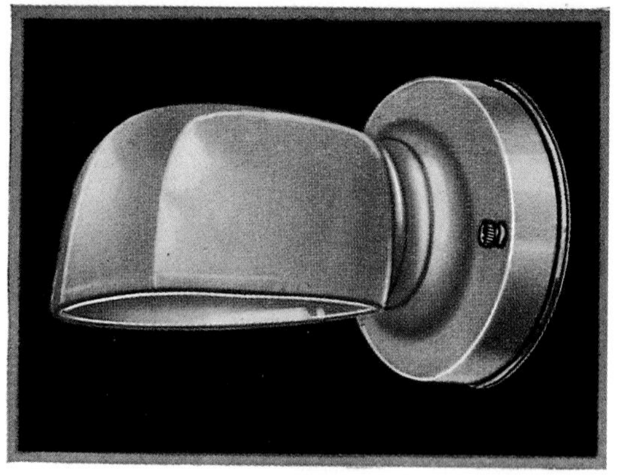

Wall Type

	List
D-29. Keyless	$3.60
D-30. Pull Chain	4.05

Packed 12 to a Master Carton.

Current values each: $125.00 – 195.00

Specify color desired.

Manufactured under License Patent Application No 273324.

White Enamel Kitchen and Bathroom Units

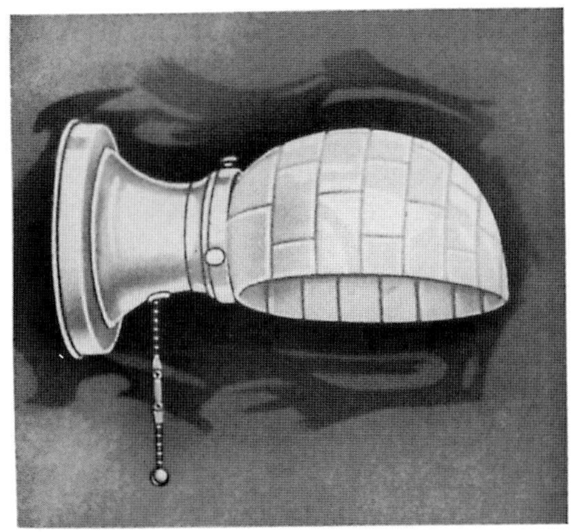

No. 11/302—Wired with Pull Chain Receptacle

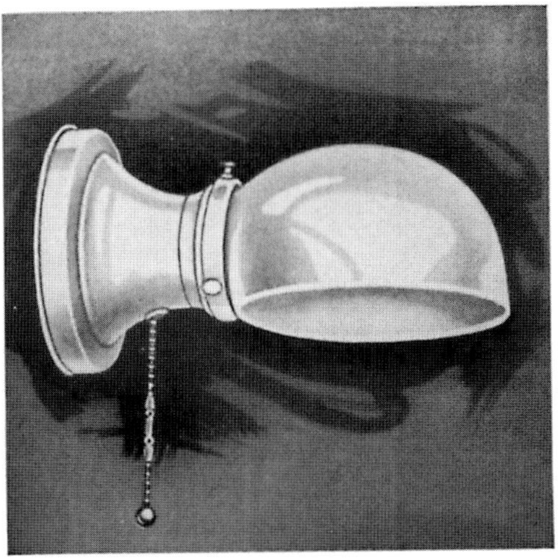

No. 11/499—Wired with Pull Chain Receptacle

No. 15/682—Keyless Bathroom Unit

Numbers	Prices	Dimensions of Glass		
Fixture Complete	Each Fixture Complete Current Prices	Width	Length	Fitter
15/682	$100.00–125.00	9 x	? x	?
11/499	$45.00–65.00	6 x	? x	?
11/302	$65.00–85.00	6 x	? x	?

Decorated Kitchen and Bathroom Units

Furnished Keyless only.
Please specify color of finish desired.

Numbers Fixture Complete	Prices Each Fixture Complete Current Prices	Dimensions of Glass Width Length Fitter
13/8608/71	$135.00–165.00	8½ x 7 x 4

Note—Each complete fixture is a Standard Package.

Decorated Kitchen and Bathroom Units

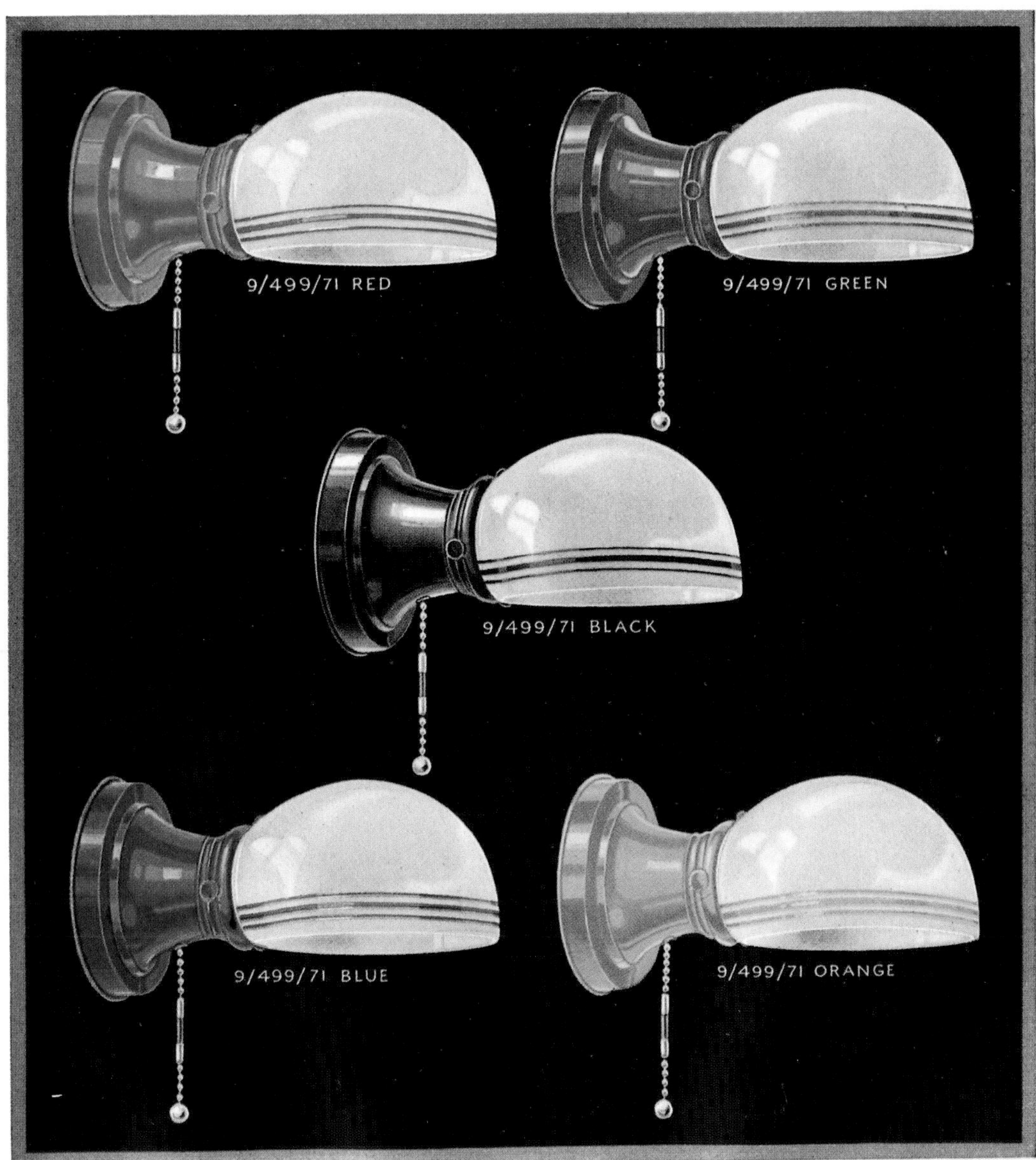

Please specify color of finish desired.

NUMBERS FIXTURE COMPLETE	PRICES EACH FIXTURE COMPLETE CURRENT PRICES	SIZE OF FITTER
9/499/71	$125.00–180.00	2¼ inches

Hyperion Units

With "Amco" Safety Screwless Holders

Note: Prices vary depending on shade size.

Nos. 54, 56 and 57—Suspension Type "Amco" Safety Screwless Hanger
Finish—Statuary Bronze.
Wiring Specifications—Length of Hanger only, 30".

Nos. 64 and 66—Ceiling Type "Amco" Safety Screwless Holder

"AMCO" Safety Screwless Holder

Close Lever to Lock.

No. 54 and 56 Hanger wired with No. 16 slow burning wire and special Edison base socket.

No. 57 Hanger wired with No. 14 slow burning wire and Mogul base porcelain socket.

No. 64 and 66 Holder equipped with Edison base porcelain receptacle.

All fixtures will be furnished wired complete.

Numbers Fixture Complete	Prices Each Fixture Complete Current Prices	Dimensions of Glass Width x Length x Fitter	Recommended Wattage
54/637	$75.00–125.00	10 x 6½ x 4	100
54/638	$75.00–125.00	12 x 6½ x 4	100–150
56/638	$75.00–125.00	12 x 6½ x 6	100–150
56/639	$75.00–125.00	14 x 7¾ x 6	150–200
56/640	$75.00–125.00	16 x 9¾ x 6	200–300
57/640	$75.00–125.00	16 x 9¾ x 6	200–300
64/637	$65.00–100.00	10 x 6½ x 4	100
64/638	$65.00–100.00	12 x 6½ x 4	100–150
66/638	$65.00–100.00	12 x 6½ x 6	100–150
66/639	$65.00–100.00	14 x 7¾ x 6	150–200
66/640	$65.00–100.00	16 x 9¾ x 6	200–300

Hyperion Units

Note: Prices vary depending on shade size.

With "Amco" Safety Screwless Holders

Nos. 54, 56 and 57—Suspension Type "Amco" Safety Screwless Hanger

Finish—Statuary Bronze.

Wiring Specifications—Length of Hanger only, 30".

Nos. 64 and 66—Ceiling Type "Amco" Safety Screwless Holder

"AMCO" Safety Screwless Holder

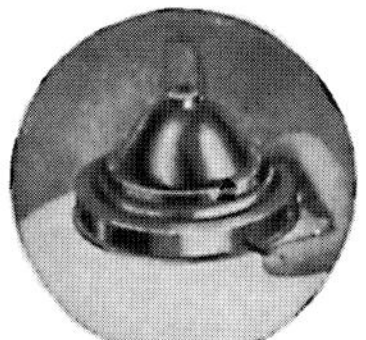

Close Lever to Lock.

No. 54 and 56 Hanger wired with No. 16 slow burning wire and special Edison base socket.

No. 57 Hanger wired with No. 14 slow burning wire and Mogul base porcelain socket.

No. 64 and 66 Holder equipped with Edison base porcelain receptacle.

All fixtures will be furnished wired complete.

No. 400, 401 and 402 are furnished without hole, unless contrary is specified.

Numbers	Prices	Dimensions of Glass			
Fixture Complete	Each Fixture Complete Current Prices	Width	Length	Fitter	Recommended Wattage
54/400	$100.00–135.00	8 x	9 x	4	100–150
56/401	$100.00–135.00	10 x	12 x	6	150–200
56/402	$100.00–135.00	12 x	14 x	6	200–300
57/402	$100.00–135.00	12 x	14 x	6	300–500
64/400	$65.00–100.00	8 x	9 x	4	100–150
66/401	$65.00–100.00	10 x	12 x	6	150–200
66/402	$65.00–100.00	12 x	14 x	6	300–500

Hyperion Units

Note: Prices vary depending on shade size.

Nos. 30, 31 and 32—Suspension Type Gillway Hanger

Nos. 15 and 33—Ceiling Type Gillway Holder

Finish

Statuary Bronze.

Wiring Specifications

Length of Hanger only, 30″.

No. 30 and No. 31 Hanger—Edison base, porcelain socket and No. 16 slow burning wire.

No. 32 Hanger—Mogul base, porcelain socket and No. 14 slow burning wire.

No. 15—4″ fitter Ceiling Ring—6″ diameter, 4½″ deep. Pigtail porcelain receptacle and crossbar.

No. 33—6″ fitter Ceiling Ring—8″ diameter, 5″ deep. Equipped with pigtail porcelain receptacle and crossbar.

Numbers	Prices	Dimensions of Glass			Recommended Wattage
Fixture Complete	Each Fixture Complete Current Prices	Width	Length	Fitter	
30/4110	$145.00–175.00	10 x	6½ x	4	100
31/4112	$145.00–175.00	12 x	6⅝ x	6	100–150
31/4114	$145.00–175.00	14 x	7⅞ x	6	150–200
31/4116	$145.00–175.00	16 x	8¾ x	6	200–300
32/4116	$145.00–175.00	16 x	8¾ x	6	200–300
15/4116	$100.00–135.00	10 x	6½ x	4	100
33/4112	$100.00–135.00	12 x	6⅝ x	6	100–150
33/4114	$100.00–135.00	14 x	7⅞ x	6	150–200
33/4116	$100.00–135.00	16 x	8¾ x	6	200–300

Hyperion Units

Note: Prices vary depending on shade size.

Nos. 15 and 33—Ceiling Type Gillway Holder

Finish

Statuary Bronze.

Wiring Specifications

Length of Hanger only, 30″.

No. 30 and No. 31 Hanger—Edison base, porcelain socket and No. 16 slow burning wire.

No. 32 Hanger—Mogul base, porcelain socket and No. 14 slow burning wire.

No. 15—4″ fitter Ceiling Ring—6″ diameter, 4¼″ deep. Pigtail porcelain receptacle and crossbar.

No. 33—6″ fitter Ceiling Ring—8″ diameter, 5″ deep. Equipped with pigtail porcelain receptacle and crossbar.

Nos. 30-31 and 32—Suspension Type Gillway Hanger

Numbers Fixture Complete	Prices Each Fixture Complete Current Prices	Dimensions of Glass Width x Length x Fitter	Recommended Wattage
30/4010	$95.00–120.00	10 x 8⅞ x 4	100
30/4012	$95.00–120.00	12 x 7⅝ x 4	100–150
31/4012	$95.00–120.00	12 x 7⅝ x 6	100–150
31/4014	$95.00–120.00	14 x 8¾ x 6	150–200
31/4016	$95.00–120.00	16 x 10⅜ x 6	200–300
32/4016	$95.00–120.00	16 x 10⅜ x 6	200–300
15/4010	$65.00–85.00	10 x 8⅞ x 4	100
15/4012	$65.00–85.00	12 x 7⅝ x 4	100–150
33/4012	$65.00–85.00	12 x 7⅝ x 6	100–150
33/4014	$65.00–85.00	14 x 8¾ x 6	150–200
33/4016	$65.00–85.00	16 x 10⅜ x 6	200–300

Una Glassware

Note: Prices vary depending on shade size.

1911—Electric

1938—Reflector

1914—Urn

1910—Bowl

Note: Prices vary depending on shade size.

Numbers Fixture Complete	Prices Each Fixture Complete Current Prices	Dimensions of Glass Width	Length	Fitter
1938	$20.00–30.00	7 x	4⅞ x	2¼
1911	$20.00–25.00	4½ x	5⅛ x	2¼
1914	$30.00–40.00	6 x	6 x	3¼
1914	$30.00–40.00	8 x	8 x	4
1910	$50.00–100.00	11 x	5 x	10
1910	$50.00–100.00	13 x	5¼ x	12
1910	$50.00–100.00	15 x	6 x	14

Black Lined Balls

Note: Prices vary depending on shade size.

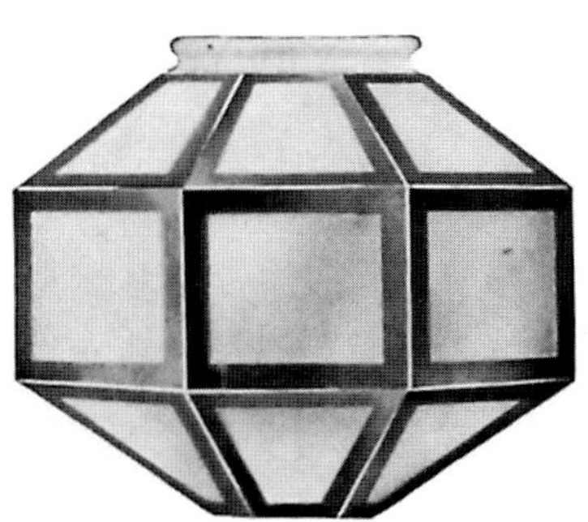

No. B-70—Black Line on White Glass

7 x 7 x 3¼

No. 1451—Black Line on White Glass

6 x 6 x 3¼
8 x 8 x 4

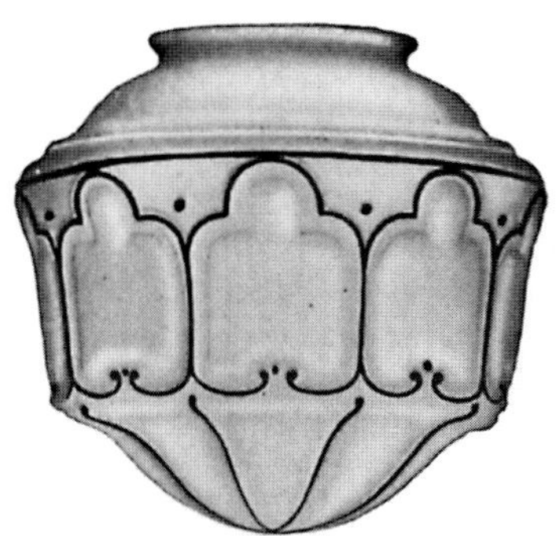

No. 1452—Black Line on White Glass

7½ x 6¾ x 4

Note: Prices vary depending on shade size.

Numbers	Prices	Dimensions of Glass					Glass
Fixture Complete	Current Prices	Width		Length		Fitter	
1451	$45.00–75.00	6	x	6	x	3¼	Black L.
1451	$45.00–75.00	8	x	8	x	4	Black L.
1452	$85.00–135.00	7½	x	6¾	x	4	Black L.
B-70	$40.00–65.00	7	x	7	x	3¼	Black L.